MASSACRES

Bioarchaeological Interpretations of the Human Past:
Local, Regional, and Global Perspectives

MASSACRES

BIOARCHAEOLOGY AND FORENSIC ANTHROPOLOGY APPROACHES

EDITED BY

Cheryl P. Anderson and Debra L. Martin

Foreword by Clark Spencer Larsen

University of Florida Press
Gainesville

This book may be available in an electronic edition.

23 22 21 20 19 18   6 5 4 3 2 1

Library of Congress Cataloging-in-Publication Data
Names: Anderson, Cheryl P., editor. | Martin, Debra L., editor. | Larsen,
   Clark Spencer, author of foreword.
Title: Massacres : bioarchaeology and forensic anthropology approaches /
   edited by Cheryl P. Anderson and Debra L. Martin ; foreword by Clark Spencer
   Larsen.
Other titles: Bioarchaeological interpretations of the human past.
Description: Gainesville : University of Florida Press, 2018. | Series:
   Bioarchaeological interpretations of the human past: local, regional, and
   global perspectives | Includes bibliographical references and index.
Identifiers: LCCN 2018003968 | ISBN 9781683400691 (cloth : alk. paper)
Subjects: LCSH: Massacres—History. | Mass murder—History. | Excavations
   (Archaeology)
Classification: LCC HV6505 .M385 2018 | DDC 363.32—dc23
LC record available at https://lccn.loc.gov/2018003968

UF PRESS

**UNIVERSITY
OF FLORIDA**

University of Florida Press
15 Northwest 15th Street
Gainesville, FL 32611-2079
http://upress.ufl.edu

CONTENTS

FIGURES

MAPS

TABLES

FOREWORD

Although a considerable volume of scholarship in the social and behavioral sciences has been devoted to the study of violent death in general and massacre settings in particular, only rarely has the science and scholarship of biological anthropologists been included. As the contributors to this important book point out, biological anthropologists engaged in the study of past and present societies have much to offer in addressing the key details of horrific mass deaths, especially the details of injury and death in human skeletal remains. In the last decade or so we have seen the publication of important bioarchaeological research that has been laying the groundwork for understanding the social and behavioral contexts of mass killings as documented in the archaeological record (e.g., Knüsel and Smith 2014; Redfern 2017; see also Martin and Anderson 2014). In this volume editors Cheryl Anderson and Debra Martin present recent bioarchaeological scholarship investigating the skeletal record of violence. In the following pages the editors and contributors make clear that anthropologists who study human remains from archaeological and forensic contexts do so not just with an eye toward the description of the remains of the victims of violence. Rather, biological anthropology in general and bioarchaeology in particular also seek to address the contexts and circumstances leading to violent acts.

Fundamental questions remain: Why does one group or society regard the death and extermination of the "enemy" as a goal? Why violence? Why is massacre a priority? Why should there be mutilation of the remains of the deceased? Isn't death enough? These are tough questions with no simple answers. But, as these investigations of massacre victims show, social and behavioral contexts involving multiple and complex circumstances are at play, often involving dehumanization of the victims both before and after death. That is, massive death circumstances are always highly culturally contextualized. The authors of the following chapters all recognize the central nature of context in the complex circumstances of massacre and mass death.

What impresses me most about the chapters presented in this thought-provoking book is the sheer complexity of violence, especially as it pertains to entire communities, from planning stages to the subsequent events. In the context of complexity and the range of social, cultural, and behavioral issues contributing to that complexity, it remains clear that there are no simple answers to the simple questions that we often read about in the popular and scholarly literature (for example, why are people violent?). Much more important to the broader discussion of violence and massacre is the growing understanding that humans exhibit some universal behaviors: a penchant for violence may be one of them. Importantly, as scientists, we demand answers to questions relating to violent acts, whatever the scale. Simply put, what factors motivate violence? That question and the development of informed answers will facilitate a more informed understanding of violence and its outcome. This is a challenge, but the research tools offered by the contributors to this book give us a way forward and a set of concepts for addressing fundamental questions about the dark side of human behavior.

The following pages provide a snapshot of various times in various places, representing archaeological and forensic contexts. As the investigations show, violent acts resulting in massacre are preserved in the bioarchaeological record. This preserved bioarchaeological record, in both the recent and the remote past, allows us to examine the end result of a social act. But the record also offers clues to the circumstances that led to the act. One clear priority going forward is the development of hypotheses regarding the rationale for the attack. Research in social psychology tells us that most victims are viewed as "other" by the perpetrators, likely in a dehumanized fashion. As the studies presented in this book demonstrate, it is not possible to provide simple reasons why a group of individuals died at the hands of another group. However, as anthropologists, we have the research tools and global perspective needed to address the tough questions that the authors of these chapters acknowledge and address. The continued development of these tools will facilitate the development of answers to the tough questions.

Clark Spencer Larsen
Series Editor

References

Knüsel, C., and M. Smith (editors). 2014. *The Routledge Handbook of the Bioarchaeology of Human Conflict*. New York: Routledge.

Martin, D. L., and C. P. Anderson (editors). 2014. *Bioarchaeological and Forensic Perspectives on Violence*. Cambridge: Cambridge University Press.

Redfern, R. C. 2017. *Injury and Trauma in Bioarchaeology: Interpreting Violence in Past Lives*. Cambridge: Cambridge University Press.

ACKNOWLEDGMENTS

The authors would like to thank the Graduate and Professional Student Association and the College of Liberal Arts at the University of Nevada, Las Vegas, for providing funding for this research.

1

Introduction

CHERYL P. ANDERSON AND DEBRA L. MARTIN

Bioarchaeology, the study of human skeletal remains from archaeological contexts (for example, Larsen 2002; Martin et al. 2013), and forensic anthropology, "the application of the science of physical or biological anthropology to the legal process" (American Board of Forensic Anthropology 2017), offer unique perspectives on studies of massacres and present opportunities to interpret human skeletal remains in a broader cultural context. Massacres and other forms of large-scale violence have been documented in many different ancient and modern contexts. Moving the analysis from the victims to the broader political and cultural context necessitates using social theories about the nature of massacres. Massacres can be seen as a process, that is, as the unfolding of nonrandom patterns or a chain of events that precede the massacre itself and continue long after (Klusemann 2012:479). Massacres have a cultural logic of their own that is shaped by social and historical dynamics. Massacres can have varying aims, including subjugation or total eradication of a group based on status, ethnicity, or religion. Massacres can also signal powerful messages to witnesses and/or survivors about power dynamics and can be used a tool for social control.

This volume is among the first to bring together bioarchaeological and forensic anthropologists as well as cultural anthropologists to focus specifically on both archaeological and modern examples of massacres and how they can be interpreted and understood through the application of social theory. Bioarchaeology and forensic anthropology are complementary subdisciplines of biological anthropology. They both excavate and analyze human skeletal remains and utilize the same methodologies in their approach. In addition, the long-standing history of professionals practicing both bioarchaeology and forensic anthropology is being continued by many researchers today (Buikstra and Beck 2006; Komar and Buikstra 2008). The main difference between these approaches to the study of massacres is that in more contemporary contexts they may have legal implications (for example, see Kimmerle and Baraybar 2008). An integrated approach to bioarchaeology and forensic anthropology is adopted here, as the two subdisciplines have much to offer each other in studies of violence. For example, the incorporation of forensic perspectives may aid in the interpretation of bioarchaeological massacre assemblages, such as in chapter 3 by Marin A. Pilloud and Al W. Schwitalla. The consideration of bioarchaeology can also aid in the understanding of contemporary instances of massacres because bioarchaeology provides time depth and a cross-cultural perspective. This can help illuminate patterns of human behavior across time and space as well as variations in behavior due to cultural context.

This volume began as a symposium, presented at the 85th annual meeting of the American Association of Physical Anthropologists in Atlanta, Georgia (April 13–16, 2016). The thematic cohesion offered by this set of diverse studies provided the impetus for the book. The inclusion of both bioarchaeologists and forensic anthropologists affords a broad range of approaches to the study of massacres and shows both the similarities and differences through the cross-cultural and temporal approaches taken.

This introductory chapter presents some of the theoretical frameworks used by anthropologists to get at the poetics of massacres: the meaning that cultures ascribe to that particular form of violence. Massacres are deeply symbolic and are performed through ritual or passed on in codes of conduct in indigenous systems such as those discussed here. We have adopted the working definition of massacre offered by Dwyer and Ryan (2012:xv): the "killing by one group of people by another group of people, regardless of whether the victims are armed or not, regardless of age or sex, race, religion and language, and regardless of political, cultural, racial, religious or economic motives for the killing." The breadth expressed in this definition is important, because too often readers have particular massacres in mind, which then makes it easy to rule out other multiple homicides and mass killings.

How Do We Define Massacres?

Many researchers apply the term "massacre" without specifying how this type of large-scale violence differs from others, such as warfare. Does the application of the term merely depend on the number of individuals killed?

Semelin (2009:4) defines massacres as "a form of action that is most often collective and aimed at destroying non-combatants." Kuckelman et al. (2000) also propose a definition of massacres, which is adapted from Keeley (1996:67) and LeBlanc (1999:149). This definition states that "the term 'massacre' implies a surprise attack initiated to annihilate an enemy social unit" (Kuckelman et al. 2000:158). These definitions are important for the present discussion, as these authors put forth the idea that the destruction of the "social unit" is an important factor, including "non-combatants." This would suggest actions directed against entire families or communities, including women and children, and can be compared with the patterns seen in the archaeological record across time and space. Also, the idea that massacres are performed by a "collective" is significant, suggesting that massacres are not the actions of a few individuals but of a larger community with underlying social structures that allow for and justify the destruction of the enemy.

Massacres are largely carried out by males and are common to times of war from ancient times to the present (Gat 2006). Most scholars attempt to grapple with the fundamental question of why groups take this particular route to killing, usually in addition to more traditional hand-to-hand combat, raiding, and other forms of early and modern warfare (Martin and Harrod 2015). The study and understanding of massacres, then, does not focus on warriors or soldiers as in warfare. Massacres entail no demarcation between adult males and other members of the society and are rarely male-on-male violence. Massacres are necessarily relational and dynamic. Killing a particular demographic (such as women and children) or destroying bodies becomes all the more powerful because it communicates the symbolic nature of these acts and forms social memories carried over hundreds of years (Martin 2016).

How cultures use and react to violence and who is protected or at risk are global concerns with potentially dire consequences for the world's populations today. It would be helpful for more scholars to understand non-Western forms of violence and warfare in order to make sense of the kinds of things regularly written about in the media today, such as the horrific executions by the Islamic State in the Near East or the rape and murder of young girls by the Boko Haram in Africa. Simply identifying the death of males in warfare is only the tip of the iceberg in the problem of massacres. It is perhaps even more important to understand how forms of violence such as massacres target women and children.

Throughout this volume the authors apply a range of ways of defining and conceptualizing massacres. It is not our goal to try to apply one definition to all of the case studies but rather the opposite. We aim to explore the variation in this form of violence. In each chapter the authors present their own ways of identifying and defining massacre or mass violence and show how they are applicable to the specific period and/or social context in question. For example, in chapter 2 William E. De Vore, Keith P. Jacobi, and David H. Dye discuss the issues surrounding the criteria that researchers often use to identify massacres, including problems with the number of victims considered necessary for a massacre to have occurred. Their study demonstrates the importance of examining the cultural context and population size when forming interpretations of massacres. In chapter 10 Cate E. Bird demonstrates that mass death resulting from structural violence may also be considered a massacre by examining the ways in which U.S. government policies result in the high number of deaths of Undocumented Border Crossers (UBCs) along the U.S.-Mexico border. These are two of the many examples of ways that we can expand our understanding of massacres and the variability inherent in this kind of violence while recognizing that some similarities may also exist, such as the inclusion of noncombatants among the victims.

Structural Violence as a Form of Massacre

This important idea that structural violence resulting in poor health and early death may also be considered a form of massacre merits further consideration. One way that institutionalized inequalities and their effects on health have been theorized is through the idea of structural violence. Farmer (2004:307) presents a definition: "Structural violence is violence exerted systematically—that is, indirectly—by everyone that belongs to a certain social order." This structural violence against some groups but not others leads to differential access to resources, resulting in illness, injury, and early death, among other things (Farmer 2004:308). Farmer points out that while structural violence can lead to what we as a society more commonly think of violence, armed conflict, and terrorism, it most often leads to weakened bodies, often through disease. He demonstrates, for example, that global economic, political, and social structures that target specific groups of people (for example, the poor) have led to increased morbidity and mortality from infectious diseases among these groups in the modern era (Farmer 1996, 1999, 2003, 2004). So can these structures of oppression that lead to differential mortality also fall under the purview of a massacre?

Going back to the variety of definitions of massacres, including the one by Dwyer and Ryan (2012) adopted here, massacres consist of one group targeting another social group, often including noncombatants who pose no immediate harm to the perpetrators, such as women and children. Massacres are also performed by the society as a whole, or collective as Semelin (2009) states, not just individuals. Keeping these in mind, it seems that cases where mass death results from these structures of oppression targeted against a particular group of people (based on poverty, racism, gender inequality, or any other classification used to justify persecution in a society) should also be viewed as a form of massacre. This does not operate outside the realm of violence simply because the violence is indirect: it results in the same loss of life as violent events more commonly identified as massacres. It also arises from the same social processes as more "conventional" massacres, such as the processes of othering and dehumanization of those viewed as other (addressed in greater detail below).

Why Massacre: Understanding the Process of Massacres through Contemporary Examples

Some recent studies of contemporary examples of massacres provide insights into how these violent acts unfold in different contexts. One of the important insights that is apparent from these modern examples is that massacres are processes, not singular events. They are often characterized by patterns of violence that unfold over time and are manifested in a variety of ways (Klusemann 2012). Thus it is crucial to understand the history leading up to and after massacres. According to Klusemann (2012:469), these processes are impacted by the "situational *emotional dynamics*, which determine how massacres are actually enacted" (emphasis in the original). Massacres occur when a weaker, emotionally dominated enemy is attacked. Massacres are often preceded by other acts of destruction, which serve to provide emotional momentum for the perpetrators and to frighten the victims. In addition to these acts of destruction, the targeting of certain people, such as particularly weak individuals or selected elites (Klusemann 2012:474–475), as well as capture, torture, and theatrics may also precede a massacre (Osterholtz 2013). This contributes to the emotional conditions necessary for a massacre (Klusemann 2012:474–475). Once the violence begins, it is most often perpetrated by large groups of individuals, although not everyone will necessarily participate in the actual killing of victims.

This collective provides the necessary "emotional energy" (Klusemann 2012) to facilitate the violence (Dwyer and Ryan 2012).

In keeping with ideas of massacres as processes, Semelin (2009) argues that massacres have a mental development that includes debasing and destroying the victims that are viewed by the perpetrators as in some way "other." It is only after this process that the victims are killed (Semelin 2009:9). The occurrence of massacres cannot be linked to regional tension, which does not necessarily result in violence. Rather it is the buildup of multiple reasons that results in a situation where violence may occur, often directed against a group toward which negative attitudes already exist. In this situation leaders blame this group for the suffering and hardships present in society and suggest that the situation will improve if this group is eliminated (Semelin 2009:13). This occurs through channeling community anxiety into fear of the targeted group, which is subsequently viewed as dangerous. This leads to hatred for the group identified as the other. This hatred is then transformed into a desire to eliminate the feared other, which is referred to by Semelin (2009:17) as the "*imaginaire* of death."

One important social aspect that can contribute to the massacre of innocent noncombatants is the process of identity construction and dehumanization. For example, Semelin (2009:38) discusses the impact of the "animalization" of the other, which leads to questioning the very humanity of this group of individuals. This process can include rhetoric that associates the targeted social group with some sort of animal, generally one that is regarded negatively. This "animalization" process is intertwined with ideas about purity and cleansing society of these nonhuman beings (Semelin 2009). The fear and perceived threat of the members of this dehumanized other group lead to the idea that they must be destroyed in order to save society. This is not a linear process, however: identity construction and the process of assigning stigma, notions of purity and dehumanization of the other, and the fear of danger leading to action are all linked and serve to strengthen each other (Semelin 2009:49).

This process of dehumanization and fear can result in the desire to eradicate the targeted social group or a subset of that group, depending on the goals of the perpetrators in a specific context. Based on the study of contemporary massacres, Semelin (2009:327) points out that the death of everyone in the social unit is not the intent of all massacres. Instead, a massacre of some individuals can occur in order to force the submission of those that remain. In this scenario the perpetrators rely on the fear that they have instilled in the surviving witnesses in order to dominate them

(Semelin 2009:327). In these instances it is really this communication of a message to the witnesses through the performance of violent acts that demonstrates the power of the perpetrators and has a lasting impact (Schröder and Schmidt 2001). These processes of group identity construction, dehumanization, and resulting violence can be identified and examined through direct observation of human skeletal remains.

ORGANIZATION OF THIS VOLUME

In order to explore massacres and their social and political contexts, ten chapters highlighting case studies of massacres and/or innovative ways of examining or theorizing massacres are presented. These chapters cover a wide range of periods and geographic locations. Following these chapters, a thought-provoking conclusion by Ryan P. Harrod (chapter 12) explores the theme of the volume and the contributions of the individual chapters toward forming a better understanding of massacres.

Chapters in This Volume

William E. De Vore, Keith P. Jacobi, and David H. Dye (chapter 2) analyze mass graves from the Middle Tennessee River Valley and highlight problems in the way massacres are defined and identified in bioarchaeology. These contributors explore definitions of mass graves and the utility of using these features to identify massacres in the past. They suggest that there are different types of massacres and that a three-tiered definition of massacres may be more appropriate. This revised approach to studying massacres is then applied to several human skeletal assemblages in this region in order to form a more complete understanding of whether or not they represent the victims of massacres. This study raises important questions about the lack of standardization in defining and recognizing massacres archaeologically and cautions us not to overlook small-scale massacres.

Marin A. Pilloud and Al W. Schwitalla (chapter 3) look at mass graves from multiple archaeological sites in central California in order to examine larger patterns of massacres. These contributors compare these prehistoric cases of violence with modern examples to look for patterns of behavior. They demonstrate that most mass graves contain only adult males, but children may also be included when adult females are present. They also show the variability in terms of numbers of victims in mass graves, with a range of one victim to hundreds. The number of victims in the prehistoric central California mass graves tends to be small, indicating that they represent victims of intergroup violence that is not related to religious or ethnic differences. This review of prehistoric violence in central California illustrates the variability that exists among massacre skeletal assemblages and the need to incorporate forensic anthropology research into bioarchaeological analyses.

J. Marla Toyne (chapter 4) applies a gendered approach to studying mass violence among the Chachapoya in Peru. While the results of her analysis of the mass death assemblage at Kuelap demonstrate that both adults and subadults were among the victims, they also show a relatively low number of adult females. This suggests that men were specifically targeted by the perpetrators and that some of the women may have been abducted. This act of violence indicates that the goal of the perpetrators was likely the destruction of this community, specifically the men and children. Thus the experience of violence among the Chachapoya at this site may have varied based upon gender. This study demonstrates that it is important to examine the roles that different members of a society may play in acts of violence, either as victims or perpetrators, and to consider the social meaning behind these decisions.

Ashley E. Kendell (chapter 5) explores an innovative data-mining approach in order to show that archived data can be used to answer important anthropological questions about mass violence. She shows that the use of archived data allows for the collection of larger sample sizes and the exploration of broader patterns of violence. The method is demonstrated through the examination of a large sample size of Arikara individuals from ten archaeological sites gathered from the Smithsonian Institution database. Through the application of this method, evidence for perimortem trauma was discovered for several males, females, and subadults, including evidence of mutilation of some victims. This research shows that the use of data-mining techniques contributes to the study of massacre and mass death processes by allowing for the collection and comparison of large amounts of skeletal data from assemblages that may no longer be available to researchers.

Anna J. Osterholtz (chapter 6) examines the social significance of extreme processing at the Sacred Ridge massacre site in the American Southwest. In her analysis of the skeletal remains, she demonstrates that all of the victims were similarly processed and that processing of the body did not vary based on the age or sex of the victims. This similar processing indicates that this entire group of victims was viewed as the dehumanized other. This othering created a lack of empathy among the perpetrators for the victims, leading to their ability to perform the massacre. The psychological and emotional factors affecting the different groups (victims, perpetrators, and witnesses) are explored, highlighting how these dynamics can impact power relations. This careful analysis demonstrates how violence, and particularly the complete destruction of the bodies of the victims, played a significant social role in this case.

P. Willey (chapter 7) reexamines some of the human skeletal remains from Crow Creek, which contained the mutilated remains of hundreds of victims of a massacre. In this study he compares the human skeletal remains from the Bone Bed and the Village contexts at this site. Through careful, detailed osteological analysis, this research demonstrates the extent to which the perpetrators deliberately processed the victims. This would have taken some time, which suggests that the perpetrators did not leave immediately after the attack. This study demonstrates the importance of careful collection and interpretation of perimortem alterations in order to reconstruct human behaviors associated with the process of mass violence and mutilation. It is also an important case study demonstrating that this type of violence often goes beyond simply killing the victims and also can include complete destruction of the body of the enemy.

Julie M. Fleischman, Sonnara Prak, Vuthy Voeun, and Sophearavy Ros (chapter 8) discuss the impact of the Khmer Rouge regime on the people of Cambodia and the importance of documenting the evidence of violence. This study focuses on the important work being done at the Choeung Ek Genocidal Center analyzing the skeletal remains of the victims. In particular they discuss a recent study performed on a sample of Khmer Rouge victims and, through analysis of the perimortem trauma, confirm eyewitness accounts that blunt force trauma to the base of the skull was often utilized to execute the victims. The authors highlight the need to situate skeletal evidence for mass violence within the social and political context and how these factors impact the way the bodies are regarded. It also reveals the long-lasting impact of massacres on the community and the social significance of the bodies of the victims.

Tricia Redeker Hepner, Dawnie Wolfe Steadman, and Julia R. Hanebrink (chapter 9) discuss the social impacts of the war in Uganda and in particular the interactions between the survivors and the victims of violence who are seeking proper burial. They show how the bones of the Acholi massacre victims continue to assert their agency and hamper community healing. The authors also illustrate the persistent suffering experienced by those who survived the massacres and the dilemma that they face in placating the unknown dead. The ability to solve this issue is complicated by a number of factors, including the often unknown identities of the deceased and the lack of resources required to perform the necessary burial rituals. This careful anthropological analysis of the mass violence in Uganda and its aftermath highlights the complex processual nature of massacres and the social significance of the dehumanization of the dead through improper burial.

Cate E. Bird (chapter 10) examines the large-scale death of migrants in southern Arizona and the reasons why this should be viewed as an extended massacre. This mass violence against migrants is perpetrated by the state through U.S. government policies and the militarization of the U.S.-Mexico border. These policies affect the routes used by migrants, often funneling them through some of the harshest areas of the Sonoran Desert, resulting in many exposure-related deaths. The funneling of migrants into dangerous terrain is intentional and aimed at deterring unauthorized migration. In this case the desert itself is the weapon that is used against the victims. This careful analysis challenges some of the traditional definitions of massacre by demonstration that structural violence resulting in large-scale death over time constitutes a massacre and should be treated as such.

Krista E. Latham, Alyson O'Daniel, and Justin Maiers (chapter 11) explore undocumented migrant deaths on the U.S. Mexico border. They discuss how recent changes to border policies have led to an increase in migrant deaths. In order to make sense of this humanitarian crisis, they apply political economic theory that considers power and structural inequalities. They carefully review how historical trajectories in Latin America and the rise of neoliberalism have led to increases in social inequality and violence, resulting in increased migration as the oppressed flee in the hopes of finding a different life. Due to the dangerous conditions encountered along the journey, many migrants die every year attempting to find this new life. Through their discussion on the complexities of identifying and returning the remains of the deceased, the authors present a thoughtful discussion about the role of forensic scientists in this modern mass death crisis. Their discussion illuminates the social and political impact of these scientists as they seek to humanize the victims and raise public awareness of the crisis.

References

American Board of Forensic Anthropology. 2017. American Board of Forensic Anthropology. http://theabfa.org/.

Buikstra, J. E., and L. A. Beck (editors). 2006. *Bioarchaeology: The Contextual Analysis of Human Remains*. Academic Press, Boston.

Dwyer, P. G., and L. Ryan. 2012. Introduction: The Massacre and History. In *Theatres of Violence: Massacres, Mass Killings and Atrocity throughout History*, edited by P. G. Dwyer and L. Ryan, pp. xi–xxv. Berghahn Books, New York.

Farmer, P. 1996. On Suffering and Structural Violence: A View from Below. *Daedalus* 125(1):261–283.

———. 1999. Pathologies of Power: Rethinking Health and Human Rights. *American Journal of Public Health* 89(10):1486–1496.

———. 2003. *Pathologies of Power: Health, Human Rights, and the New War on the Poor*. University of California Press, Berkeley.

———. 2004. An Anthropology of Structural Violence. *Current Anthropology* 45(3):305–325.

Gat, A. 2006. *War in Human Civilization*. Oxford University Press, Oxford.

Keeley, L. H. 1996. *War before Civilization*. Oxford University Press, New York.

Kimmerle, E. H., and J. P. Baraybar (editors). 2008. *Skeletal Trauma: Identification of Injuries Resulting from Human Rights Abuses and Armed Conflict*. CRC Press, Boca Raton, FL.

Klusemann, S. 2012. Massacres as Process: A Micro-sociological Theory of Internal Patterns of Mass Atrocities. *European Journal of Criminology* 9(5):468–480.

Komar, D. A., and J. E. Buikstra. 2008. *Forensic Anthropology: Contemporary Theory and Practice*. Oxford University Press, Oxford.

Kuckelman, K. A., R. R. Lightfoot, and D. L. Martin. 2000. Changing Patterns of Violence in the Northern San Juan Region. *Kiva* 66(1):147–165.

Larsen, C. S. 2002. Bioarchaeology: The Lives and Lifestyles of Past People. *Journal of Archaeological Research* 10(2):119–166.

LeBlanc, S. A. 1999. *Prehistoric Warfare in the American Southwest*. University of Utah Press, Salt Lake City.

Martin, D. L. 2016. Hard Times in Dry Lands: Making Meaning of Violence in the Ancient Southwest. *Journal of Anthropological Research* 72(1):1–23.

Martin, D. L., and R. P. Harrod. 2015. Bioarchaeological Contributions to the Study of Violence. *American Journal of Physical Anthropology* 156:116–145.

Martin, D. L., R. P. Harrod, and V. R. Pérez. 2013. *Bioarchaeology: An Integrated Approach to Working with Human Remains*. Springer, New York.

Osterholtz, A. J. 2013. Hobbling and Torture as Performative Violence: An Example from the Prehistoric Southwest. *Kiva* 78(2):123–144.

Schröder, I. W., and B. E. Schmidt. 2001. Introduction: Violent Imaginaries and Violent Practices. In *Anthropology of Violence and Conflict*, edited by B. E. Schmidt and I. W. Schröder, pp. 1–24. Routledge, New York.

Semelin, J. 2009. *Purify and Destroy: The Political Uses of Massacre and Genocide*. Columbia University Press, New York.

2

Rethinking Massacres

A Bioarchaeological and Forensic Investigation of Prehistoric Multiple Burials in the Tennessee River Valley

WILLIAM E. DE VORE, KEITH P. JACOBI, AND DAVID H. DYE

The Tennessee River in prehistory was the scene of multiple diverse Native American cultures. These groups did not always exist in peace (Bridges et al. 2000; Jacobi 2007; Smith 2003). Direct and indirect exposure to violence was part of the daily lives of every individual who inhabited the river valley. Bioarchaeological evidence for conflict from the middle section of the Tennessee River Valley, which runs across the northern part of the state of Alabama, ranges from the recovery of isolated body parts to both single and multi-individual interments. Here we reexamine mass graves found in the Middle Tennessee River Valley, taking a different interpretative approach to what constitutes a massacre episode and how different lines of evidence can impact our thinking about and understanding of past cultures and past interpersonal and intrapersonal conflict.

Research on massacres tends to focus on the grandiose, and often most gruesome, single episodes of violent encounters that resulted in the murder of a large number of people (Zimmerman et al. 1981). These events are often considered "large-scale" based on the minimum number of individuals (MNI) involved. Following the same logic, "small-scale" massacre events, which are more common and often overlooked in the bioarchaeological record, have lower MNIs. The arbitrary use of the term "massacre," often based on the apparent scale of the violent episode (as assigned by an MNI), leaves wiggle room and gray areas that make understanding the day-to-day effects of violence on the inhabitants of the Tennessee River Valley in pre-history difficult.

The study of massacres has always been the study of mass graves or, at the very least, the study of settlements that appear to have been wiped out in a single instance, with the victims scattered among the structures and site as a whole. In this later line of evidence the entire site is treated as a de facto mass grave. There are problems with the use of mass graves as a foundation for the recognition of massacres in prehistory. First, many researchers (Egaña et al. 2008; Kendell and Willey 2014; Owsley and Bass 1979; Turner II and Morris 1970) only focus on high-MNI mass graves as evidence of massacres and disregard low-MNI mass graves, under the presumption that they do not constitute a massacre. Second, there is no currently clear and immutable definition of what a mass grave actually is (Haglund et al. 2001; Skinner 1987). Bioarchaeologists often develop their own definition of a mass grave based on what they think is an appropriate MNI. They often go to great lengths to distinguish differences between what they term "multiple burials" (several individuals within the same grave) and "mass graves" (again, several individuals within the same grave). In some cases they use existing definitions for a mass grave, but even then the original definition is fraught with problems.

The cases presented here highlight the very problematic nature of defining massacres using just mass grave evidence and also highlight the tenuous nature of defining mass graves using MNI. Other attributes, including the interrelationships of the victims and the assailants as well as the timing between conflict events, also influence whether the term "massacre" is truly applicable to an episode of violence. Our goal is to take a critical look at what signifies a massacre and rethink the underlying concepts central to the interpretation and understanding of massacres and conflict in prehistory.

MATERIALS

The skeletal remains examined and reviewed were excavated in the 1930s and 1940s before the construction of hydroelectric dams in the middle section of the Tennessee Valley was completed (Webb 1938, 1939; Webb and DeJarnette 1942, 1948; Webb and Wilder 1951).

CASE DESCRIPTIONS

Case 1 (Mulberry Creek–1Ct27): Individual 83 (Male, 45–55), 84 (Male, 25–35), 85 (Male, 18–20)

This burial has an MNI of 3. Cutmarks, indicative of scalp removal, were present on all three skulls. In addition, postcranial trauma included multiple rib-neck and posterior and lateral rib fractures and sharp force trauma to the lateral ribs of all three victims. Two of the three individuals, 84 and 85, had embedded projectile points in their vertebral column. The embedded points would not have been immediately lethal but would have paralyzed the individuals from the mid-back down. The trajectory of both points was the same, coming from the left side in an inferior to superior orientation. Fracturing to the upper cervical vertebrae of all three individuals suggests that they had their throats cut and their heads bent backward. Excavation drawings and photos indicate that all three heads were in anatomical position, suggesting they were never fully severed from the body (Webb and DeJarnette 1942:plates 274–275).

Due to a lack of repetitive patterns in the cutmark types, locations, and intensities, Hoskins (2015) determined that at least three assailants tortured and killed these three individuals.

Case 2 (Columbus City Landing–1Ms91–Unit 2): Individual 12 (Male, 25–35), 13 (Male, 20–25), 14 (Female, 50+), 15 (Female, 20–30—graphite), 16 (Female, 20–25—graphite), 17 (Female, 20–25—graphite), 31 (Male, 40–45), 32 (Male, 40–55)

This burial has an MNI of 8. Individuals 13, 14, and 31 are headless. Individuals 12 and 32 had their heads. Individual 32 has cutmarks on the cranial vault consistent with scalping. Individuals 15, 16, and 17 had graphite painted decorations on their skeletons, including the skulls. All three skulls, in addition to being decorated, had expanded foramen magnums, indicating the placement of the skull onto a pole for display. All three skulls also show scattered cutmarks on the cranial vault that do not allow for differentiation between mortuary defleshing and conflict-related soft tissue mutilation.

The burial pit was large and oval shaped, tapering toward the bottom. The limbs and skeletons of the individuals were intermingled as a result of having their bodies piled one on top of the other during placement in the grave.

Case 3 (Harris Site–1Ms80): Individual 33 (Child, 1–2), 34 (Male, 20–30), 35 (Female, 25–35)

This grave has an MNI of 3. Based on the cutmark evidence it appears that the victims were killed for adultery, representing a case of capital punishment (Boyer and Gayton 1992:83; De Vore and Jacobi 2015; Ewers 1958:108). Individual 34 has cutmarks on the frontal, parietals, and left temporal of the cranial vault. Cutmarks also are found on both the left and right zygomatic arches and on the right maxilla of the face. Individual 35 has cutmarks on both temporals and the occipital. She also has cuts on the left and right maxillae.

Based on the type of soft tissue that would have been mutilated as a consequence of the cutmark locations, ethnohistoric accounts reinforce the idea that this is a case of punishment for adultery. Inclusion of the small child seems to support this interpretation and is again consistent with ethnohistoric accounts (De Vore and Jacobi 2015).

Case 4 (Harris Site–1Ms80): Individual 76 (Male, 20–25), 77 (Female, 35–45—red paint), 78 (Female, 30–40—red paint), 79 (20–30—red paint)

This burial has an MNI of 4. It is a complete and fully articulated individual surrounded by three skulls painted with red ochre. The whole individual (76) showed no signs of conflict-related trauma. One of the three skulls (78) had cutmarks on it. Given the red decoration, it is impossible to determine whether the cutmarks are related to scalping/trophy taking or defleshing for curation.

DISCUSSION

The use of evidence from mass graves has been central to the study of massacres. There is no clear understanding, however, of what characterizes a mass grave. Additionally, the term "massacre" itself is applied arbitrarily. No set of criteria has been developed to use in the examination of evidence of conflict when trying to establish whether or not a massacre or some other episode of violence has occurred. This tenuous foundation does not account for all the cultural variability observed in the archaeological record.

In reexamining the defining attributes of a mass grave, Jaeger (2013) suggests the adoption of an MNI of 3 as the threshold. Again, this definition proves slippery when scrutinized further. As our above cases demonstrate, three or more individuals can end up in the same grave in multiple ways. The case of 1Ms80-33, 34, and 35 is likely an example of capital punishment for criminal activity, based on ethnohistorical records. The case of 1Ms80–76, 77, 78, and 79 is probably a single individual interred with three previously curated skulls. The case of 1Ms91–Unit 2–12, 13, 14, 15, 16, 17, 31, and 32 is a mix of individuals who show signs of either violent death or curation prior to final burial. Finally, the case of 1CT27-83, 84, and 85 involves three individuals who were tortured, killed, and buried. In all of these cases the MNI is 3 or more, but the number of primary and secondary individuals is different. Here we define primary individuals as those for whom the grave was dug. Secondary individuals are represented in several ways. First, some individuals were included in the grave, by the persons conducting the burial, as mortuary inclusions for the primary individuals. These can be whole bodies representing retainers or human body parts that may or not have been modified. Second, secondary individuals can be represented in a grave through unintentional inclusion/mixing of parts of other people. Because of these different possibilities, determining whether an individual is primary or secondary is a difficult task that requires a bioarchaeologist's interpretations as to the thought processes of the individual(s) who dug the grave.

It must be recognized that there are multiple ways to look at MNI in regard to calling a burial a mass grave. When making a final determination concerning mass graves, it is necessary to answer two questions. First, how do we determine MNI? Second, what is an appropriate threshold number to differentiate mass graves from those burials that are not mass graves?

We have two ways of looking at MNI. We can "lump" or we can "split." If we lump, MNI is defined by the number of individuals, irrespective of how much material from an individual's body is present and how it came to be in the grave. If we split, MNI is determined through the separation of individuals based on their primary or secondary status within the grave. To settle this debate, we argue for the use of three different MNIs. "Total MNI" is a count of every individual recovered from the grave. "Primary MNI" is a count of only those individuals who appear to be the intended recipient(s) of the efforts of those who dug the grave. "Secondary MNI" is a count of individuals considered to be secondary to the primary individuals within the grave. Again, these determinations must be made by the bioarchaeologist based on the remaining evidence and a "cultural" interpretation of the events surrounding the final interment of the deceased individual(s). This teasing out of different types of MNI allows for a more refined interpretation of the archaeological record and past cultural practices.

Any discussion on mass graves should factor in the roles that each of the interred individuals is performing. The general principle is that mass graves have multiple primary individuals in a single pit who died around the same time or in a single episode of violence. This definition eliminates all secondary individuals. We argue that any grave with an MNI of 2 or more primary individuals, irrespective of the number of secondary individuals, is a mass grave. By this reasoning, case 4 (1Ms80–76, 77, 78, and 79) does not constitute a mass grave. It has a total MNI of 4, a primary MNI of 1, and a secondary MNI of 3. Refining our methodology for the identification of mass graves has the most impact on our interpretation of small-scale massacres. For years bioarchaeologists have looked at mass graves and said, "Yep, that's a massacre all right." But what criteria are we using? What set of standards are we employing?

A strict definition of the word "massacre" is "the unnecessary, indiscriminate killing of a large number of human beings" (Webster 1996). As previously stated, the application of the term to bioarchaeological evidence is ambiguous. Developing criteria for the determination of massacres is not cut-and-dried. The structure of any society is multilayered. A victim's political/cultural community (as identified based on their social structure: family-level groups versus local groups), secondary affiliations (sodalities/moieties and so forth), and potential temporary groupings that reinforce/support daily social life (raiding parties, hunting/gathering groups) must be taken into consideration.

Our three-tier definition for massacres excludes motivation and focuses on the political/cultural affiliations of the victims. Genocide, the destruction of most or all of a cultural community, represents the highest form. Large-scale massacres, the middle form, are the destruction of most or all of a political community within a broader cultural community. Small-scale massacres, the lowest tier and likely the most common, are the destruction of some subcomponent (small group) within a political community. Therefore, massacres involve only events at the political community level, while genocides involve events at the cultural level. Timing between discrete events allows for large-scale massacres to be individual episodes of a broader genocide and small-scale massacres to be individual episodes of a larger massacre.

Case 1 (1Ct27–83, 84, and 85) meets the criteria for a mass grave because it has more than two primary individuals. Our interpretation, based on the circumstances (they were tortured to death), is that these individuals were probably not from the site where they were found. If we make the logical assumption that they were together when captured, then they could have been a hunting party or raiding party that was taken captive. Based on the "temporary group" idea, interpreting the evidence in that light would mean that this burial represents the massacre of a small hunting group of men and would fall into the category of small-scale massacre because the temporary group identity would be subservient to a larger political community.

Case 2 (1Ms91–Unit 2–12, 13, 14, 15, 16, 17, 31, and 32) includes the burial of eight people within the framework of a mass grave and massacre. However, the roles of the people within the mass grave are not all the same. We believe that the grave contains five primary interments and three secondary interments. In this instance our separation of the primary and secondary individuals within the grave is based upon the presence and absence of flesh on the bodies at the time of burial. Three of the five primary interments (flesh on the body) are headless, and cutmarks were observed on several. This is a clear indication of violent death and therefore a small-scale massacre of the primary individuals. The origin of the three secondary interments (defleshed skeletal remains), with signs of decoration on their entire skeletons, eludes us. They may or not constitute a separate small-scale massacre. If they represent venerated ancestors they likely are not massacre victims. If they represent vanquished enemies, then they very well could represent a massacre of three individuals not unlike the three people in case 1. In a similar case from 1Lu92 (Koger's Island) burials 101 and 102 show evidence of mutilation associated with adultery (De Vore and Jacobi 2015). Burial 101 (a 35- to 45-year-old adult female) was defleshed, disarticulated, and had her foramen magnum expanded in order to display her skull on a pole. This case calls into question the interpretation of the graphite-decorated skeletal remains of 1Ms91 Unit 2 as venerated ancestors.

An alternative interpretation for the grave in case 2 is that the three graphite-decorated individuals might in fact also be primary recipients of the burial effort. This burial is intriguing because of the intermingled nature of the individuals and the apparent attempt at "rearticulation" of the decorated skeletal remains, which also was observed in Burials 101 and 102 from 1Lu92. Could this grave represent the massacre of a lineage group and the subsequent burial of that lineage's ancestral power base? This idea is plausible, as the intermingling of the two types of individuals suggests an "equal" standing. Considering the importance often associated with rare objects, of which decorated human remains are the perfect example, we might wonder why the surviving population had no desire to continue curation of the three graphite individuals. Could it be that the individuals in the grave were the only ones within the community who had the knowledge and capability to hold and wield the power that the graphite-decorated skeletons represented and possessed?

Case 3 (1Ms80–33, 34, and 35) brings up an important issue. Should instances of capital punishment be considered massacres? All three individuals (adult male, adult female, and child) are represented by skulls only. All three show evidence of perimortem craniofacial mutilation. If the interpretation of the victims as people who were executed for criminal activity (adultery) is correct, then this was a "state"-sanctioned punishment of an illegal family unit. So does this case represent a massacre?

Case 4 (1MS80–76, 77, 78, and 79) is not a massacre. This burial has one complete individual with no evidence of violence and three additional ochre-painted skulls. The origin of the three skulls, like that of the graphite-painted individuals, remains open to debate. If these represent venerated ancestors then they are not likely the result of a massacre. If they represent trophy items, then they could be the result of a massacre.

SUMMARY

When bioarchaeologists use the term "massacre" they instill images of violent encounters, families and friends dying together, and merciless attackers. Most often this image takes on the form of grandiose destruction of villages and towns; rarely does it venture into the realm of the small groups. The cases considered here were chosen to highlight what we see as two major areas that have received little attention. First, what is the nature of the evidence of massacres? Second, what are the criteria that we use to determine massacres?

Mass graves, unlike isolated burials, provide the quickest reliable proof of massacres. This form of evidence has unique underlying attributes that have seldom been fully examined. The differences in how MNI is defined and used as a criterion for "mass graves" have an effect on the mortuary interpretation by bioarchaeologists when they encounter multiple individuals buried in the same pit. All graves with multiple individuals have a Total MNI. Failure to separate primary and secondary roles within a mass grave can result in an erroneous interpretation of the mortuary record.

Beyond the issues surrounding mass graves, bioarchaeologists have all too often overlooked the critical step of disseminating their exact criteria for whether or not the material that they are studying is a massacre. This ambiguity, whether intentional or accidental, makes true cross-comparison of massacre episodes difficult; especially considering the general neglect of small massacres. Having a clear understanding of the cultural/political spheres in which conflict victims existed when they were alive also makes a difference in massacre interpretations. The killing of a family of five within a cultural community whose main political subunits were small family-level groups should be considered a large-scale massacre. Some might not see it as such, because at first glance it does not appear to involve a grandiose loss of life. If that same family of five existed as a subcomponent of a larger political entity within a larger cultural community, then their murders represent a small-scale massacre. A large-scale massacre would entail the annihilation of most or all of the larger political entity of which the family was a subcomponent.

Another dilemma facing the bioarchaeologist trying to interpret mass graves as massacres is the inclusion or exclusion of executed criminals within the purview of massacres. For example, if episodes of capital punishment are not included within the scope of massacres then some mass graves with evidence of violence fail to meet the criteria of a massacre simply because these individuals were put to death for criminal activity by people in their own community and were not victims murdered by enemies.

Bioarchaeologists rely on criteria, including criteria for massacres, whether large or small. The consistency and the transparency of those criteria are essential to the reliable evaluation of the evidence that is presented as a massacre.

ACKNOWLEDGMENTS

We would like to thank Emily Hoskins for her assistance in the analysis and interpretations of the multiple burials and for the use of the detailed illustrations of the red-painted skulls.

REFERENCES CITED

Boyer, R. M., and N. D. Gayton. 1992. *Apache Mothers and Daughters.* University of Oklahoma Press, Norman.

Bridges, P. S., K. P. Jacobi, and M. L. Powell. 2000. Warfare-Related Trauma in the Late Prehistory of Alabama. In *Bioarchaeological Studies in the Age of Agriculture: A View from the Southeast*, edited by P. M. Lambert, pp. 35–62. University of Alabama Press, Tuscaloosa.

De Vore, W. E., and K. P. Jacobi. 2015. Facial Mutilations Associated with Scalpings from the Middle Tennessee River Valley. Paper presented at the 72nd Annual Meeting of the Southeastern Archaeological Conference, November 18–21, Nashville. http://www .southeasternarchaeology.org/wp-content/uploads/Bulletin_58_Camera_Ready_Final .pdf.

Egaña, S., S. Turner, M. Doretti, P. Bernardi, and A. Ginarte. 2008. Commingled Remains and Human Rights Investigations. In *Recovery, Analysis, and Identification of Commingled Human Remains*, edited by B. J. Adams and J. E. Byrd, pp. 57–80. Humana Press, Totowa, NJ.

Ewers, J. C. 1958. *The Blackfeet: Raiders of the Northwestern Plains*. University of Oklahoma Press, Norman.

Haglund, W. D., M. Connor, and D. D. Scott. 2001. The Archaeology of Contemporary Mass Graves. *Historical Archaeology* 35(1):57–69.

Hoskins, E. 2015. Reassessing Evidence of Conflict in Mass Graves for Minimum Number of Assailants. Paper presented at the 72nd Annual Meeting of the Southeastern Archaeological Conference, November 18–21, Nashville.

Jacobi, K. P. 2007. Disabling the Dead: Human Trophy-Taking in the Prehistoric Southeast. In *The Taking and Displaying of Human Body Parts as Trophies by Amerindians*, edited by R. J. Chacon and D. H. Dye, pp. 299–338. Springer, New York.

Jaeger, J. H. 2013. *Mass Grave or Communal Burial? A Discussion of Terminology*. Department of Prehistoric Archaeology, SAXO Institute, University of Copenhagen.

Kendell, A., and P. Willey. 2014. Crow Creek Bone Bed Commingling: Relationship between Bone Mineral Density and Minimum Number of Individuals and Its Effect on Paleodemographic Analyses. In *Commingled and Disarticulated Human Remains: Working toward Improved Theory, Method, and Data*, edited by A. J. Osterholtz, K. M. Baustian, and D. L. Martin, pp. 85–104. Springer, New York.

Owsley, D. W., and W. M. Bass. 1979. A Demographic Analysis of Skeletons from the Larson Site (39WW2) Walworth County, South Dakota: Vital Statistics. *American Journal of Physical Anthropology* 51(2):145–154.

Skinner, M. 1987. Planning the Archaeological Recovery of Evidence from Recent Mass Graves. *Forensic Science International* 34(4):267–287. Smith, M. O. 2003. Beyond Palisades: The Nature and Frequency of Late Prehistoric Deliberate Violent Trauma in the Chickamauga Reservoir of East Tennessee. *American Journal of Physical Anthropology* 121(4):303–318.

Turner, C. G., II, and N. Morris. 1970. A Massacre at Hopi. *American Antiquity* 35(3):320–331.

Webb, W. S. 1938. *An Archaeological Survey of the Norris Basin in Eastern Tennessee*. Smithsonian Institution, Bureau of American Ethnology, Bulletin 118. Government Printing Office, Washington, DC.

———. 1939. *An Archaeological Survey of Wheeler Basin on the Tennessee River in Northern Alabama*. Smithsonian Institution, Bureau of American Ethnology, Bulletin 122. Government Printing Office, Washington, DC.

Webb, W. S., and D. L. DeJarnette. 1942. *An Archaeological Survey of Pickwick Basin in the Adjacent Portions of the States of Alabama, Mississippi and Tennessee*. Smithsonian Institution, Bureau of American Ethnology, Bulletin 129. Government Printing Office, Washington, DC.

———. 1948. *The Perry Site, Lu25, Units 3 and 4, Lauderdale County, Alabama*. Alabama Museum of Natural History, Museum Paper 25. University, AL.

Webb, W. S., and C. G. Wilder. 1951. *An Archaeological Survey of Guntersville Basin on the Tennessee River in Northern Alabama*. University of Kentucky Press, Lexington.

Webster. 1996. *Webster's New Universal Unabridged Dictionary*. Barnes and Noble Books, New York.

Zimmerman, L. J., T. E. Emerson, P. Willey, M. Swegle, J. B. Gregg, P. Gregg, E. White, C. Smith, T. Haberman, and M. P. Bumstead. 1981. The Crow Creek Site (39BF11) Massacre: A Preliminary Report. Prepared by the University of South Dakota Archaeology Laboratory for the Omaha District, U.S. Army Corp of Engineers.

3

Forensic Perspectives on Massacres in Prehistoric and Historic Central California

MARIN A. PILLOUD AND AL W. SCHWITALLA

Violence in prehistoric societies has been well documented using the bio-archaeological record (e.g., Allen and Jones 2014; Knüsel and Smith 2013; Lambert 2007; Martin and Frayer 1997; Martin and Harrod 2015). Such practices are seen throughout prehistoric California in the form of blunt and sharp force trauma and evidence for trophy taking (Andrushko et al. 2005; Bartelink et al. 2013; Lambert 1997; Pilloud et al. 2014; Schwitalla, Jones, Pilloud, et al. 2014; Schwitalla, Jones, Wiberg, et al. 2014; Walker 1989). Violence has been argued to be the result of environmental and resource stress, colonization, population density, and the introduction of new technology as well as to serve as a means of maintaining social harmony, among other explanations (e.g., Jones and Schwitalla 2008; Schwitalla, Jones, Pilloud, et al. 2014; Weiss 2002).

In central California prehistory there are a few instances of massacres, which have a different taphonomic signature from other instances of violence. These contexts typically include burials of multiple individuals with extensive evidence of perimortem injury (including cutmarks around the cranial vault, craniofacial blunt force trauma, and cutmarks around major ligamentous and tendinous attachments of the postcranial skeleton). While work in the region has focused on large patterns of violence in relation to geography, time period, population density, and trauma type (e.g., Andrushko et al. 2005; Andrushko et al. 2010; Bartelink et al. 2013; Jones and Schwitalla 2008; Jurmain 2001; Pilloud 2006; Pilloud et al. 2014; Schwitalla, Jones, Pilloud, et al. 2014; Schwitalla, Jones, Wiberg, et al. 2014) there has been less focus on the implications of burials with multiple individuals interred together and what the patterns of these burials can reveal about the motivations behind these violent encounters and killings.

In this chapter we reevaluate these instances of mass graves as evidence of massacres within prehistoric central California, relative to other forensically documented contexts of mass fatalities. In particular, we focus on type of injury in addition to age and sex of the affected individuals and the types of graves encountered in these settings. The goal is to compare and contrast these prehistoric contexts to what is observable in the modern world with known conditions and motivations to aid in interpretations of the archaeological record.

Defining Massacres

The goal of this study is to identify instances of massacres in prehistoric central California. Episodes of mass physical violence resulting in death (i.e., massacres) may be difficult to reconstruct from the archaeological record alone. For this treatment we place much of the identification of this level of violence in the interpretation of mortuary practices, such that mass graves equate to evidence for massacres when at least one individual within the mass grave exhibits evidence of trauma indicative of physical violence. While some studies on the evidence of mass violence and massacres are based on the archaeological record (e.g., Bridges 1996; Duncan and Schwarz 2015; Meyer et al. 2015), here we draw on the forensic literature to define massacres and mass graves and to draw parallels and conclusions about prehistoric central California.

For forensic purposes, mass graves are typically investigated by forensic specialists to gather evidence to prosecute war crimes and human rights violations as well as in certain other medico-legal contexts. The investigation of such graves dates back to World War II, when the Germans investigated the massacre of Polish soldiers committed by the Soviets in the Katyń forest in 1940 (Haglund et al. 2001; Raszeja and Chróścielewski 1994). These investigations have continued since the 1940s and have spread to other regions around the world. Multiple organizations currently investigate these types of mass graves and human rights violations (e.g., the Argentine Forensic Anthropology Team, Guatemalan Forensic Anthropology Foundation, Physicians for Human Rights, and International Commission on Missing Persons, among others).

While mass graves have been investigated across the globe (e.g., Cabo et al. 2012; Juhl 2005; Juhl and Einar Olsen 2006; Primorac et al. 1996; Skinner et al. 2003; Tuller and Đurić 2006), there is currently no consensus on the definition of the term "mass graves" (Haglund et al. 2001). Mass graves have been defined as single inhumations with two individuals in contact with each other (Mant 1987), as four or more individuals buried together (Connor 2009), or as containing at least six individuals (Skinner 1987). Aside from the number of individuals in each inhumation, consideration should also be given to the context of the bodies and how they are arranged. Haglund (2002) identified various configurations of modern mass graves: (1) in a single, large body mass, (2) in individual body masses, or (3) in stratigraphic layers. These configurations are closely tied to number of bodies in the inhumation; however, they also identify the importance of relationships between the bodies within the inhumation. Alternatively, Sprague (1968) defines a mass grave as one containing *disarticulated bodies* with only fragments of articulated remains; he instead uses the term "multiple graves" to refer to those that contain "several articulated bodies" (Sprague 2005:74). Schmitt (2002:279), in contrast, argues that the focus in defining mass graves should be on the "anthropological context" and that the defining characteristic should be a commonality in cause and manner of death between at least two individuals buried together.

There are also legal definitions to consider in the study of mass graves. After investigations into war crimes in the former Yugoslavia, the United Nations special rapporteur defined a mass grave as containing three or more victims who died from extrajudicial executions outside of combat (ICTY 1996). An advantage to this definition is that it differentiates mass graves from natural disasters from those that are criminal or violent in nature (Jugo and Wastell 2015). Jessee and Skinner (2005:56), in a review of these anthropological and legal definitions, offer the following as a definition of mass graves: "any location containing two or more associated bodies, indiscriminately or deliberately placed, of victims who have died as a result of extra-judicial, summary or arbitrary executions, not including those individuals who have died as a result of armed confrontations or known major catastrophes."

Clearly delineating what constitutes a mass grave is of the utmost importance to this study. However, within this archaeological context, consideration must also be given to the population densities of prehistoric California and those associated with hunting and gathering practices. Therefore, for the purposes of this analysis, a mass grave is defined as any interment with two or more individuals where at least one displayed skeletal evidence of trauma (sharp and/or blunt force) and the archaeological

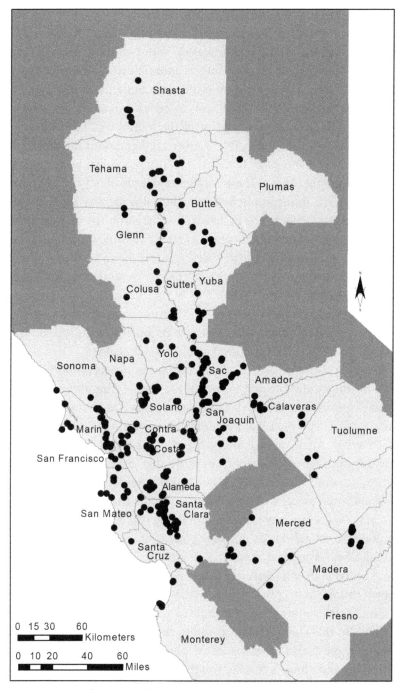

Figure 3.1. Map of central California with sites used in text.

context indicates that they were buried at the same time. This definition broadly follows that of Schmitt (2002), which incorporates social context by acknowledging that the remains share a commonality in time of death and likely cause and manner. This definition is favored in the current study because it has the benefit of excluding individuals who died of nonviolent causes and has also been applied in contemporary cases of mass violence and massacres, allowing for broad comparisons.

MATERIALS AND METHODS

This study used the Central California Bioarchaeological Database (CCDB) compiled by the second author over the last seventeen years from existing burial data housed at regional repositories. Data were compiled from a total sample size of approximately 17,898 individuals excavated from 355 sites that span a large time period (3050 BC–AD 1899) throughout central California (Schwitalla, Jones, Wiberg, et al. 2014). We define central California here as extending across the entirety of the east-west dimensions of the state with a northern limit of Shasta County and a southern limit of Fresno County (figure 3.1).

Sex and age estimates were available for all individuals following standard osteological recording procedures (Buikstra and Ubelaker 1994; see also Schwitalla, Jones, Pilloud, et al. 2014 for more details on osteological analyses). Data were separated into time periods based on recent updates to the California taxonomic system outlined in Schwitalla et al. (2014). These time periods are Early, 3050–500 BC; Early Middle, 500 BC–AD 420; Late Middle, AD 420–1010; Middle–Late Transition, AD 1010–1390; Late Prehistoric, AD 1390–1720; and Protohistoric/Historic, AD 1720–1899.

The CCDB was culled for individuals belonging to a mass grave (two or more individuals) where at least one of them displayed evidence for sharp and/or blunt force trauma. Sharp force trauma includes projectiles embedded in bone and evidence of cutmarks on skeletal elements that occurred during the perimortem interval. Blunt force trauma included perimortem and antemortem trauma to the skull. The inclusion of antemortem cranial and mandibular trauma was a recognition that these individuals were more likely to engage in violent behaviors and could be included in this treatment based on the context of the finding as well as the possibility for perimortem trauma not to be captured in skeletal tissue.

Results

These results are divided by blunt force and sharp force trauma. There is some overlap (albeit minimal) between the two categories (such that a mass grave could contain an individual with blunt force and sharp force trauma); therefore, we analyze each type of trauma separately. Additionally, the data are presented only in terms of mass graves (that is, we do not also present the total number of burials in the region for each period). Our intent is to outline general trends in mass graves observed in the archaeological record; therefore, we compare neither all interments in the region nor other instances of group interment that do not contain evidence of violence (e.g., mass burials with evidence of death from disease). Figure 3.2 is an example of a central California mass grave of three adult males.

Figure 3.2. Three young adult males with evidence of sharp and blunt force trauma at CA-SCL-478 (500 BC–AD 420). (Courtesy of Randy Wiberg of Holman and Associates, Inc.)

Blunt Force Trauma

Individuals with evidence of perimortem blunt force trauma in mass graves include 16 females, 28 males, and 2 of indeterminate sex, out of a total of 174 interred individuals. All of these individuals were adult. The number of individuals interred in mass graves ranged from 2 to 17 and varied over time (table 3.1). The Middle–Late Transition (AD 1010–1390) had the highest number of mass graves (n = 14); however, the Protohistoric/Historic period (AD 1720–1899) had the largest number of individuals interred in mass graves (n = 51, in multiple graves). The single largest grave was dated to the Late Middle period (AD 420–1010) and contained 17 individuals. By far the most common finding is an interment containing 2 individuals (n = 28), followed by 3 (n = 8), and then 4 (n = 4).

Sharp Force Trauma

Of those individuals buried in mass graves who also exhibit evidence of sharp force trauma 27 were female, 74 were male, and 20 were of indeterminate sex, out of a total of 197 individuals. All of these were adult individuals, with the exception of 1 female adolescent, 1 male adolescent, and 5 adolescents of indeterminate sex.

The number of individuals interred in mass graves ranged from 2 to 12 and varied by time period (table 3.2). The Early Middle period (500 BC–AD 420) had the highest number of mass graves (n = 22); however, the Middle–Late Transition (AD 1010–1390) had the highest number of individuals buried in mass graves (n = 63), as well as the largest mass graves (one with 8 and one with 12 individuals). Of all of the mass graves, again the most common finding is 2 individuals buried together (n = 45), followed by 3 (n = 8), 4 (n = 5), and 5 (n = 4).

DISCUSSION

Central California

Overall, there are more mass graves and individuals included with evidence of sharp force trauma. The number of double interments with sharp force trauma is nearly twice that of individuals with blunt force trauma. Such a finding may speak to a preference for sharp force trauma in instances of massacres, including the use of projectiles and postmortem trophy taking.

While temporal variation exists, there is evidence for mass graves in every period. In terms of blunt force trauma, the highest numbers of

Table 3.1. Distribution of mass graves with evidence of blunt force trauma over time

Time Period	Double	Triple	Quadruple	Quintuple	Sextuple	Septuple	Octuple	Decuple+	Totals Mass Graves	Individuals
3050–500 BC	3	1	1	0	0	0	0	0	5	6
500 BC–AD 420	7	4	0	0	1	0	0	0	12	32
AD 420–1010	4	0	1	0	0	0	0	1	6	29
AD 1010–1390	10	1	1	0	0	0	1	1	14	47
AD 1390–1720	2	0	0	1	0	0	0	0	3	9
AD 1720–1899	2	2	1	1	1	1	1	1	10	51
TOTALS	28	8	4	2	2	1	2	3	50	174

Table 3.2. Distribution of mass graves with evidence of sharp force trauma over time

Time Period	Double	Triple	Quadruple	Quintuple	Sextuple	Septuple	Octuple	Decuple+	Totals Mass Graves	Individuals
3050–500 BC	1	0	1	0	0	0	0	0	2	6
500 BC–AD 420	18	2	1	0	1	0	0	0	22	52
AD 420–1010	7	1	1	1	0	0	0	0	10	26
AD 1010–1390	11	4	1	1	0	0	1	1	19	63
AD 1390–1720	8	1	1	1	1	0	0	0	12	34
AD 1720–1899	0	0	0	1	0	0	0	1	2	16
TOTALS	45	8	5	4	2	0	1	2	67	197

individuals and mass graves are from the Early Middle period (500 BC–AD 420), the Middle–Late Transition (AD 1010–1390), and the Protohistoric/Historic period (AD 1720–1899). Sharp force trauma also sees an increase during the Early Middle period and the Middle–Late Transition. However, there is a marked decrease in mass graves with sharp force trauma in the Historic period (AD 1720–1899). Increases in violence during the Early Middle period in central California have been correlated to intrusions of different tribal groups into the region (Andrushko et al. 2010; Schwitalla, Jones, Pilloud, et al. 2014). Increases during the Middle–Late Transition may be related to the introduction of the bow and arrow in central California in AD 1200 (Schwitalla, Jones, Pilloud, et al. 2014), particularly with respect to sharp force trauma during this time. There is also some evidence for climatic changes at this time (Stine 1994), which could have led to an increase in violent behavior (Pilloud et al. 2014; Schwitalla 2013); however, there is likely regional variation in severity and response to this climatic instability (Pilloud 2006). The decrease in mass graves with evidence of sharp force trauma along with a slight increase of those with blunt force trauma during the Historic period is interesting. Such a shift may indicate a change in combat during massacres or could relate to different burial practices at this time, as individuals were also being interred in the missions across central California (Skowronek 1998).

An earlier study by Schwitalla, Jones, Pilloud, et al. (2014) based on these same data showed that in the bioarchaeological record of central California around 7.3 percent (462/6,287) of individuals show evidence of sharp force trauma and 4.3 percent (264/6,202) show evidence of blunt force trauma. These numbers are generally low; while changes in patterns of violence over time and space are related to cultural and environmental phenomena, the pattern of violence throughout the region may speak to a broad acceptance of low levels of violence of both males and females.

Comparisons to Forensic Cases of Massacres

To interpret the presence of these mass graves in prehistoric California, they were compared with demographic results of forensic cases of mass graves across the globe. Here we provide a brief summary of such reports in the literature with a focus on the age, sex, and total number of individuals in each mass grave. There can be many constraints on the analysis of remains from these contemporary mass graves, and we have attempted to highlight those that may be most comparable to our study in a range of contexts.

Early in the Balkan war, in 1992, a cave in the Hrgar region of Bosnia was used as a means to dispose of executed individuals. When this cave was excavated in 1997, 70 males between 16 and 65 years of age were recovered. A few bones of a single child aged between 3 and 5 years were also recovered (Simmons 2002). The village of El Mozote in El Salvador was witness to a massacre in 1981 during the civil war between guerrilla forces and the El Salvadorian government. When the convent there was excavated in 1992, the bodies of 131 children under the age of 12 as well as 12 adults were recovered. The sex of the adults was not reported, but 1 was documented as a pregnant female (Scott 2001). In 2006 and 2007 a site in northeastern Syria was excavated that was believed to be a mass grave containing Armenians killed at a nearby concentration camp in 1915. Analyses of the remains indicated that 80 individuals were buried at 30 loci, including 42 adults and 31 juveniles, with the rest being indeterminate in age. Sex was largely indeterminate based on the condition of the remains, but both males and females appear to be represented in the limited number of skeletons with observable traits to estimate sex (Ferllini and Croft 2009). A mass grave (KB-G1) in Rwanda was excavated in 1995–1996. Osteological analyses indicated that 454 individuals were present, 44 percent of whom were under the age of 15 (Juhl 2005); however, only a small percentage of these were positively identified (Haglund 2002).

In a review of recent and well-published human rights violations, Komar (2008) outlined the demographic distribution of multiple and mass graves from Bosnia and Iraq. In Bosnia the graves were overwhelmingly composed of male adults, although some females and subadults were present. These graves also ranged in the number of individuals interred from 1 to 460. The majority (58 percent) contained single individuals, followed by graves with 2–9 individuals (38 percent) and mass graves with 10+ individuals (4 percent). Komar (2008) argues that such demographic indicators (along with several others) are suggestive of genocide: the systematic destruction of an ethnic, racial, or religious group.

The forensic examples outlined above highlight the range of mass graves in terms of number of individuals interred, varying from a single individual to several hundred. However, some commonalities were observed in terms of the demographic profile of these mass graves, the majority of which contained adult males. When females were included, however, children were also present. California mass graves with evidence of sharp force or blunt force trauma are mostly males ($n = 102$), although females are also present

(n = 43), and they are all adults. Such results may indicate that these acts of violence in central California were not motivated by racial, ethnic, or religious differences—as they likely were in these modern cases. Additionally, multiple and mass graves in California tended to be of smaller groups of individuals, which also may be further evidence that they were not the result of large-scale institutionalized violence.

CONCLUSIONS

Overall, these findings point to a prehistoric/historic culture that did not employ structural violence at a large scale, as these mass graves are not overly biased to a particular group or sex and contained only adults. Furthermore, the evidence of what could be ritualized trophy taking in a few instances (see Schwitalla, Jones, Pilloud, et al. 2014; and Schwitalla, Jones, Wiberg, et al. 2014 for more discussion) might point toward low levels of culturally sanctioned violence (Martin and Harrod 2015:135). Massacres in prehistoric and historic central California occurred in low numbers and indicate a group that tolerated low levels of violence toward both males and females. Motivations for violent behavior and massacres varied over time and space and are likely related to changes in the environment, technological advances, migration, and colonization.

Incorporating forensic anthropological research into this bioarchaeological study made it possible arrive at interpretations about motive and intent. Careful analyses are required in bioarchaeological studies, and it is important not to overstate findings. This study has attempted to highlight the complementary relationship of bioarchaeology and forensic anthropology, particularly in studies of trauma, taphonomy, and context. This type of analysis also provides perspective on violent behaviors in prehistory and the complexity and variation that is involved in interpreting violence from skeletal remains.

ACKNOWLEDGMENTS

We thank the many archaeologists, physical anthropologists, and Native Americans who have contributed to the CCBD over these past 100 years. We would like to thank our colleague Randy Wiberg of Holman and Associates, Inc., for figure 3.2.

REFERENCES

Allen, M. W., and T. L. Jones. 2014. *Violence and Warfare among Hunter-Gatherers.* Left Coast Press, Walnut Creek, CA.

Andrushko, V. A., K. A. Latham, D. L. Grady, A. G. Pastron, and P. L. Walker. 2005. Bioarchaeological Evidence for Trophy-Taking in Prehistoric Central California. *American Journal of Physical Anthropology* 127:375–384.

Andrushko, V. A., A. W. Schwitalla, and P. L. Walker. 2010. Trophy-Taking and Dismemberment as Warfare Strategies in Prehistoric Central California. *American Journal of Physical Anthropology* 141:83–96.

Bartelink, E. J., V. A. Andrushko, V. Bellifemine, I. Nechayev, and R. Jurmain. 2013. Violence and Warfare in the Prehistoric San Francisco Bay Area, California: Regional and Temporal Variations in Conflict. In *The Routledge Handbook of the Bioarchaeology of Human Conflict*, edited by C. Knüsel and M. Smith, pp. 285–307. Taylor and Francis, Oxford.

Bridges, P. S. 1996. Warfare and Mortality at Koger's Island, Alabama. *International Journal of Osteoarchaeology* 6(1):66–75.

Buikstra, J. E., and D. H. Ubelaker (editors). 1994. *Standards for Data Collection from Human Skeletal Remains.* Research Series No. 44. Arkansas Archeological Survey, Fayetteville.

Cabo, L. L., D. C. Dirkmaat, J. M. Adovasio, and V. C. Rozas. 2012. Archaeology, Mass Graves, and Resolving Commingling Issues through Spatial Analysis. In *A Companion to Forensic Anthropology*, edited by D. C. Dirkmaat, pp. 175–196. John Wiley and Sons, New York.

Connor, M. A. 2009. Mass Grave Investigation. In *Wiley Encyclopedia of Forensic Science.* John Wiley and Sons, New York.

Duncan, W. N., and K. R. Schwarz. 2015. A Postclassic Maya Mass Grave from Zacpetén, Guatemala. *Journal of Field Archaeology* 40(2):143–165.

Ferllini, R., and A. M. Croft. 2009. The Case of an Armenian Mass Grave. *Journal of Human Rights* 8(3):229–244.

Haglund, W. D. 2002. Recent Mass Graves, an Introduction. In *Advances in Forensic Anthropology: Method, Theory, and Archaeological Perspectives*, edited by W. D. Haglund and M. H. Sorg, pp. 243–261. CRC Press, Boca Raton, FL.

Haglund, W. D., M. Connor, and D. D. Scott. 2001. The Archaeology of Contemporary Mass Graves. *Historical Archaeology* 35(1):57–69.

International Criminal Tribunal for the Former Yugoslavia (ICTY). 1996. *International Criminal Tribunal for the Former Yugoslavia Bulletin.* N.p., n.d.

Jessee, E., and M. Skinner. 2005. A Typology of Mass Grave and Mass Grave–Related Sites. *Forensic Science International* 152(1):55–59.

Jones, T. L., and A. Schwitalla. 2008. Archaeological Perspectives on the Effects of Medieval Drought in Prehistoric California. *Quaternary International* 188(1):41–58.

Jugo, A., and S. Wastell. 2015. Disassembling the Pieces, Reassembling the Social: The Forensic and Political Lives of Secondary Mass Graves in Bosnia and Herzegovina. In *Human Remains and Identification: Mass Violence, Genocide, and the "Forensic Turn,"* edited by E. Anstett and J.-M. Dreyfus, pp. 142–174. Manchester University Press, Manchester, UK.

Juhl, K. 2005. *The Contribution by (Forensic) Archaeologists to Human Rights Investigations of Mass Graves*. Museum of Archaeology, Stavanger, Norway.

Juhl, K., and O. Einar Olsen. 2006. Societal Safety, Archaeology and the Investigation of Contemporary Mass Graves. *Journal of Genocide Research* 8(4):411–435.

Jurmain, R. 2001. Paleoepidemiological Patterns of Trauma in a Prehistoric Population from Central California. *American Journal of Physical Anthropology* 115(1):13–23.

Knüsel, C., and M. Smith (editors). 2013. *The Routledge Handbook of the Bioarchaeology of Human Conflict*. Routledge, London.

Komar, D. 2008. Patterns of Mortuary Practice Associated with Genocide Implications for Archaeological Research. *Current Anthropology* 49(1):123–133.

Lambert, P. 2007. The Osteological Evidence for Indigenous Warfare in North America. In *North American Indigenous Warfare and Ritual Violence*, edited by R. J. Chacon and R. G. Mendoza, pp. 202–221. University of Arizona Press, Tucson.

Lambert, P. M. 1997. Patterns of Violence in Prehistoric Hunter-Gatherer Societies of Coastal Southern California. In *Troubled Times: Violence and Warfare in the Past*, edited by D. L. Martin and D. W. Frayer, pp. 77–110. Routledge, New York.

Mant, A. K. 1987. Knowledge Acquired from Post-War Exhumations. In *Death, Decay and Reconstruction: Approaches to Archaeology and Forensic Science*, edited by A. Boddington, A. N. Garland, and R. C. Janaway, pp. 65–78. Manchester University Press, Manchester, UK.

Martin, D. L., and D. W. Frayer (editors). 1997. *Troubled Times: Violence and Warfare in the Past*. Routledge, New York.

Martin, D. L., and R. P. Harrod. 2015. Bioarchaeological Contributions to the Study of Violence. *Yearbook of Physical Anthropology* 156:116–145.

Meyer, C., C. Lohr, D. Gronenborn, and K. W. Alt. 2015. The Massacre Mass Grave of Schöneck-Kilianstädten Reveals New Insights into Collective Violence in Early Neolithic Central Europe. *Proceedings of the National Academy of Sciences* 112(36):11217–11222.

Pilloud, M. A. 2006. The Impact of the Medieval Climatic Anomaly in Prehistoric California: A Case Study from Canyon Oaks, Ca-Ala-613/H. *Journal of California and Great Basin Anthropology* 26(2):57–69.

Pilloud, M. A., T. Jones, and A. W. Schwitalla. 2014. The Bioarchaeological Record of Craniofacial Trauma in Central California. In *Re-examining a Pacified Past: Violence and Warfare among Hunter-Gatherers*, edited by M. W. Allen and T. L. Jones, pp. 257–272. Left Coast Press, Walnut Creek, CA.

Primorac, D., S. Andelinovic, M. Definis-Gojanovic, I. Drmic, B. Rezic, M. M. Baden, M. A. Kennedy, M. S. Schanfield, S. B. Skakel, and H. C. Lee. 1996. Identification of War Victims from Mass Graves in Croatia, Bosnia, and Herzegovina by Use of Standard Forensic Methods and DNA Typing. *Journal of Forensic Science* 41(5):891–894.

Raszeja, S., and E. Chróścielewski. 1994. Medicolegal Reconstruction of the Katyń Forest Massacre. *Forensic Science International* 68(1):1–6.

Schmitt, S. 2002. Mass Graves and the Collection of Forensic Evidence: Genocide, War Crimes, and Crimes against Humanity. In *Advances in Forensic Anthropology: Method,*

Theory, and Archaeological Perspectives, edited by W. D. Haglund and M. H. Sorg, pp. 277–292. CRC Press, Boca Raton, FL.

Schwitalla, A. W. 2013. *Global Warming in California: A Lesson from the Medieval Climatic Anomaly (A.D. 800–1350)*. Center for Archaeological Research at Davis No. 17. University of California Davis, Davis.

Schwitalla, A. W., T. Jones, M. A. Pilloud, B. F. Codding, and R. S. Wiberg. 2014. Violence among Foragers: The Bioarchaeological Record from Central California. *Journal of Anthropological Archaeology* 33:66–83.

Schwitalla, A. W., T. L. Jones, R. S. Wiberg, M. A. Pilloud, B. F. Codding, and E. C. Strother. 2014. Archaic Violence in Western North American: The Bioarchaeological Record of Dismemberment, Human Bone Artifacts, and Trophy Skulls from Central California. In *Violence and Warfare among Hunter-Gatherers*, edited by M. W. Allen and T. L. Jones, pp. 273–295. Left Coast Press, Walnut Creek, CA.

Scott, D. D. 2001. Firearms Identification in Support of Identifying a Mass Execution at El Mozote, El Salvador. *Historical Archaeology* 35(1):79–86.

Simmons, T. 2002. Taphonomy of a Karstic Cave Execution Site at Hrgar, Bosnia-Herzegovina. In *Advances in Forensic Taphonomy: Method, Theory and Archaeological Perspectives*, edited by W. D. Haglund and M. H. Sorg, pp. 264–275. CRC Press, Boca Raton, FL.

Skinner, M. 1987. Planning the Archaeology Recovery of Evidence from Recent Mass Graves. *Forensic Science International* 34:20.

Skinner, M., D. Alempijevic, and M. Djuric-Srejic. 2003. Guidelines for International Forensic Bio-archaeology Monitors of Mass Grave Exhumations. *Forensic Science International* 134(2–3):81–92.

Skowronek, R. K. 1998. Sifting the Evidence: Perceptions of Life at the Ohlone (Costanoan) Missions of Alta California. *Ethnohistory* 45(4):675–708.

Sprague, R. 1968. A Suggested Terminology and Classification for Burial Description. *American Antiquity* 33(4):479–485.

———. 2005. *Burial Terminology: A Guide for Researchers*. AltaMira Press, New York.

Stine, S. 1994. Extreme and Persistent Drought in California and Patagonia during Mediaeval Time. *Nature* 369:546–549.

Tuller, H., and M. Đurić. 2006. Keeping the Pieces Together: Comparison of Mass Grave Excavation Methodology. *Forensic Science International* 156(2–3):192–200.

Walker, P. L. 1989. Cranial Injuries as Evidence of Violence in Prehistoric Southern California. *American Journal of Physical Anthropology* 80(3):313–323.

Weiss, E. 2002. Drought-Related Changes in Two Hunter-Gatherer California Populations. *Quaternary Research* 58:393–396.

4

Only the Men Will Do

A Bioarchaeological Exploration of Gender in an Andean Mass Death Assemblage

J. MARLA TOYNE

Feminist scholars invite us to broaden our theoretical approach in the construction of gender in bioarchaeological investigations of past societies (Geller 2005). In the case of warfare and social conflict, this does not necessarily mean to look for evidence of female violence but to explore the gendered experience of violence in human history. Violence is generally seen as a male purview and warfare as a male-dominated social activity, where political leaders and warriors engage in violent assaults on other groups (Hutchings 2008; Kirby and Henry 2012; Wies and Haldane 2011). Cross-culturally men are more frequently involved in warfare and social conflict (Hutchings 2008; Parpart and Zalewski 2008) and greatly outnumber women combatants even today, although women do participate (Dietrich Ortega 2012). Bioarchaeological studies have shown that women were not always exempt from physically violent encounters and attacks. Beyond cases classified as intimate partner assaults or domestic violence, women have also been targeted during wartime and not spared the same fate as men (Frayer 1997; Tung 2014). Yet archaeological evidence for warfare often leaves ephemeral traces: only rarely do we discover a clear record of strategically violent events and exactly who was involved (Knüsel 2005; Vencl 1984).

Demographic profiles of large collections of skeletal remains can be used as a characteristic to interpret violence in the past and define war activities (Bishop and Knüsel 2005). Few studies of the association between gender and violence in the Andean past have gone beyond identifying the victims and how they died (Torres-Rouff and Costa Junqueira 2006; Tung 2014). Moreover, some definitions of massacres (the theme of this volume) suggest that violence should be experienced indiscriminately rather than being age or gender specific (Stewart and Zimmerman 1989). Therefore, a gendered approach to the bioarchaeology of violence serves to enrich our understanding of the social context of massacres in the past.

The Chachapoya of the northeastern highlands of Peru have been colloquially touted as the "warriors of the clouds" due to misinterpretation and the mythologizing of early historical documents (Church and von Hagen 2008; Nystrom and Toyne 2014). This specter of warfare has also shaped archaeological explanations of the sociopolitical organization and the defined roles of men and women in Chachapoya society. When a mass death assemblage was discovered at the major occupational center of Kuelap, the possible massacre suggested that violence was an important social strategy, especially during the social and political upheaval in the late fifteenth and early sixteenth centuries. Yet the biased sample distribution toward children and adult male victims would seem to suggest that gender as a construct of social identity also influenced the outcome of this mass killing. Due to the more selective victim profile, I prefer to call this a mass killing rather than a massacre. A bioarchaeological examination of these remains provides details of who was killed as a possible key to determining the motivation behind the attack and the broader impact of what happened at Kuelap and in the broader region in the protohistoric period.

The analysis presented here focuses on the demographic profile from the fragmentary and commingled remains as well as patterns of perimortem cranial trauma. The extensive and consistent pattern in blunt force cranial vault trauma is interpreted as lethal and was recorded for 117 individuals including a large proportion of children, but only 9 of the 55 adults were probable females. Using this context, this chapter explores gender and violence in the Andean past and how this impacts the interpretation of such violent historical events. The mass killing at Kuelap was likely motivated by broader changing sociopolitical conditions; but the demographic data reflect a sex-based bias, suggesting that the attack was focused on eliminating the men and perhaps the male children in the group.

Chachapoya Culture and Sociopolitical Organization

Regionally Chachapoya archaeology is emerging, but only a few of the hundreds of sites in the broader geographic landscape have been mapped or excavated (Church and von Hagen 2008). While early manifestations of Chachapoya material culture are poorly defined, there is a coalescence of architectural and iconographic materials across a widespread area beginning in about 900 AD. Yet current interpretations of the sociopolitical nature of the Chachapoya are highly debated (Schjellerup 1997). There is some evidence of highly elaborate and individualized tombs but limited evidence of disparity in residential construction to confirm the existence of a singular leadership (such as kings or chiefs) (Guengerich 2014). While the Chachapoya society is not defined as a polity, political complexity was likely based on certain family lineages and larger centers achieving significant influence over other groups.

Recent early historical research argues that prior to the arrival and conquest of the Inca in AD 1470 the Chachapoya sites or a small group of nearby sites represented generally autonomous and self-sufficient communities (Schjellerup 1997). Groups such as the Chilcho, or the Chillao, are named and geographically localized communities, but archaeological correlates have yet to been determined (Ruiz 2011; Schjellerup 2008). The Inca's occupation and redefinition of local politics may have been responsible for the creation of "Chachapoya" as an aggregated regionally defined group. If distinctive group identities existed prior to the Inca conquest then it is possible that social competition for resources including lands and labor (people) existed. Such local competition may have resulted in warlike activities, such as physical attacks, raiding, and even massacres. At the same time, the major sociopolitical and cultural upheaval associated with the expansion of the Inca Empire into the region also may have created new tensions among communities and impacted gender ideologies.

Kuelap, Chachapoyas

The monumental archaeological complex of Kuelap is located in the center of the Amazonas Department of northeastern Peru (map 4.1). While other large settlements exist in the region, Kuelap is unique in that the over 400 circular houses are situated upon a massive fortress-like masonry walled platform up to 20 meters high (figure 4.2). Additionally, access to the site is restricted to three narrow, high-walled passages (figure 4.1). The site has

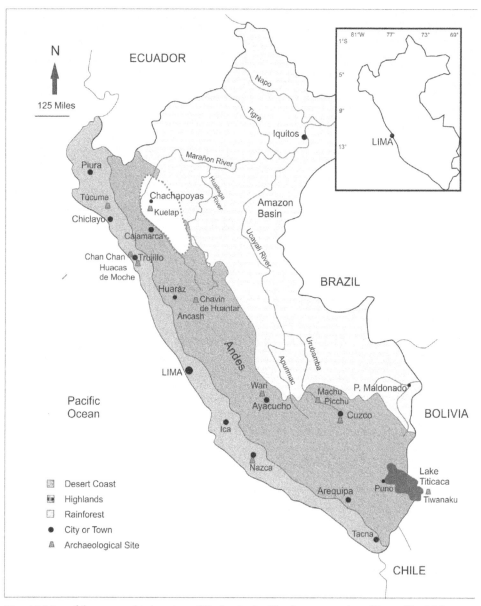

Map 4.1. Map of the geographic location of Kuelap in the Chachapoyas region. (Created by J. M. Toyne.)

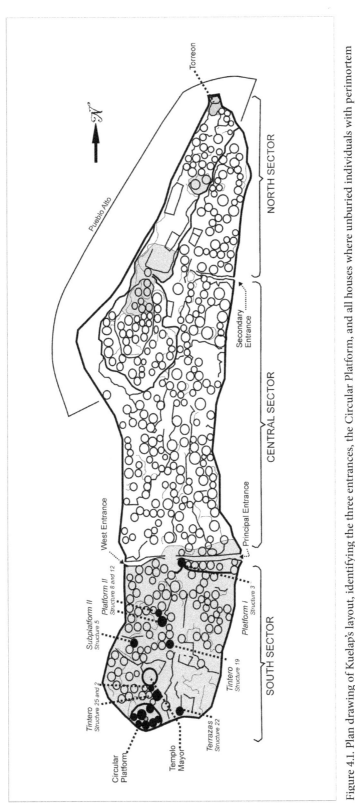

Figure 4.1. Plan drawing of Kuelap's layout, identifying the three entrances, the Circular Platform, and all houses where unburied individuals with perimortem cranial trauma have been recovered to date (filled-in circles). Excavated areas of the site are in light gray. (Redrawn by J. M. Toyne.)

Figure 4.2. Photograph of Kuelap's principal entrance and circular house structures (a modern reconstruction) at the southern end of the site. (Photo by J. M. Toyne.)

a long history of exploration, and these architectural features have been interpreted as defensive in nature. Over the last ten years concentrated excavations have defined major sectors of the residential areas, especially at the southern end of the site. Kuelap has been reinterpreted as a citadel, a large fortified community housing a regionally significant religious building, the Templo Mayor; therefore the walls are inferred to be protective and restrictive rather than necessarily built to keep out military threats (Narváez 1996, 2013).

The Mass Killing Event at Kuelap

Excavations in 2007 focused on a distinctive architectural feature called the Circular Platform. While circular houses at the site are often group along linear platforms or organized around a small central patio, this large elevated platform over 30 meters across was created using massive cut stone blocks fit together with great precision. Architecturally it is similar to the nearby Templo Mayor ritual structure in terms of the quality of the platform's construction and also the inverted angle of the walls. Narváez (personal communication, 2008) argues that the parallels indicate a direct relationship between the two structures: the Circular Platform housed an elite lineage whose sociopolitical power was derived from control of rituals performed at the Templo Mayor. Excavations revealed an abundance of human skeletons scattered across the terminal occupational floor inside and along the corridors outside the six buildings on the Circular Platform.

Unburied and Demolished

Kuelap has well-defined but variable burial treatments across the site. Traditionally individuals were interred in floors and walls either in primary (tightly flexed body positions) or secondary condition (bundled skeletal remains) or in collective or individual tombs (Narváez 2013; Ruiz 2009). The individuals on the Circular Platform showed no signs of mortuary treatment or burial individually or in a mass grave. For those that were better preserved, body and limb positioning was irregular and a number of individuals were superimposed.

Archaeological evidence suggests that the residential stone walls were intentionally knocked down and a substantial area of the southern end of the site was burned. This required a concerted effort because the masonry walls were well built and up to 4 meters high. The conical house roofs were constructed out of wood beams, and thick straw matting providing substantial material to burn. It is difficult to determine exactly when this further destruction took place, but it was apparently soon after the violent attack. Subsequent taphonomic damage due to the site's recent historical use as a corral for cattle resulted in substantial fragmentation of the osteological remains and further dismantling of remaining house walls.

While the majority of the victims were located here, later osteological analysis identified other individuals from previous field seasons whose bodies were similarly not buried in traditional mortuary contexts. These remains were recovered scattered across floor surfaces in eight other household contexts adjacent to the Circular Platform, on the Platform I, Tintero, Subplatform II, and Terrazas sectors (figure. 4.1). These 14 individuals also demonstrate similar evidence of perimortem cranial trauma. No other skeletal remains with similar features have been recovered from the more northern areas of the site with archaeological interventions, such as the Pueblo Alto or Pueblo Bajo sectors. Current evidence confines this pattern of mortuary context and skeletal trauma to the region south of the principal entrance and concentrated on the Circular Platform.

Osteological Analysis

Archaeologists initially interpreted these remains as an early historic epidemic, but evidence for interpersonal violence was quickly identified in subsequent laboratory analysis. In addition to the archaeological context and traumatic injuries, the demographic profile of the sample also supports an alternative interpretation than disease even though it does follow expectations for a mass death assemblage (Bishop and Knüsel 2005; Margerison and Knüsel 2002). Aging and sexing estimations followed accepted protocols identified in *Standards* (Buikstra and Ubelaker 1994); tentative estimations were made where the skeletal materials were incompletely recovered or highly fragmented. Sex was not assigned to juvenile remains. Table 4.1 shows the age estimations for the entire assemblage (see also figure 4.3), grouping the categories of "possible males" with "males" from the Circular Platform and "possible females" with "females." The minimum number of individuals is 103. The sample total, including the additional individuals with similar contextual and perimortem trauma ($n = 14$), is estimated at 117. The adult sex ratio of males to females is 6:1.

When the age and sex distribution of these remains is compared to the skeletal sample recovered from the Kuelap attritional mortuary sample

Table 4.1. Distribution by age category from the mass death assemblage context compared to local site cemetery

| | Kuelap Circular Platform | | | | Kuelap Site | | | |
Age Category (years)	n	n of males	n of females	% of total sample	n	n of males	n of females	% of total sample
NB (newborn)	2	—	—	2	6	—	—	1.3
INF (0 to 1)	2	—	—	2	32	—	—	7.2
CH (2–5)	8	—	—	7	19	—	—	4.3
JUV (6–10)	18	—	—	15	66	—	—	14.8
EADO (11–14)	22	—	—	19	13	—	—	2.9
LADO (15–19)	10	—	—	9	20	6	2	4.5
YA (20–34)	38	32	6	32	126	75	48	28.3
MA (35–49)	16	14	2	14	101	50	49	22.6
OA (50+)	1	0	1	1	21	9	12	4.7
SUB (age indeterm.)	0	—	—	0	2	—	—	0.4
ADU (age indeterm.)	0	—	—	0	40	18	8	9.0
Total	117	46	9		446	158	119	
% of total sample		39.3%	7.7%			35.4%	26.7%	

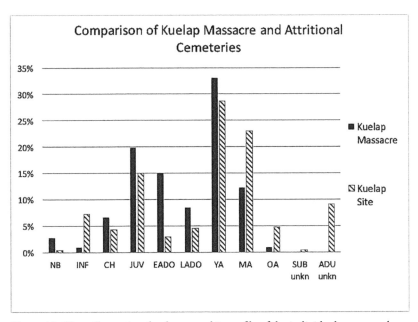

Figure 4.3. Chart illustrating the demographic profile of the individuals recovered with perimortem trauma compared to other burials from Kuelap (age categories follow table 4.1).

(which includes a broad age range of individuals from very young and very old) there is a statistical difference in all age categories ($X^2 = 67.69$, df 11, $p <$ 0.05). The rest of the site also has a more even sex ratio of males to females of 1.32:1, which is significantly different from the mass death assemblage ($X^2 = 32.10$, df 1, $p < 0.0001$) (figure 4.3). The calculation of the Juvenility Index D5-14/D20-w, where D equals the number of people dying at age x and w is the maximum age achieved before death (Bocquet-Appel and Masset 1996) results in 0.945 (52/55) for the Circular Platform and 0.479 (138/288) for the rest of Kuelap. This indicates a significant number of juveniles in this mass death sample, almost equal to the number of adults. The noticeable absence of an equal portion of adult females distinguishes this sample from the rest of Kuelap's mortuary sample. Compared to expectations developed by Bishop and Knüsel (2005), the Kuelap site sample predicts a living population, but the mass death assemblage around the Circular Platform is also distinct from other historically derived warfare-related samples. This deviation is mostly due to high a proportion of juvenile remains.

Perimortem cranial trauma was identified in 74.1 percent of the observable cranial remains recovered from the Circular Platform (figure 4.4). Most crania were highly fragmented, and incomplete reconstructions may underestimate the number and location of some cranial injuries especially to the facial region. Perimortem postcranial injuries also were found, but significant postmortem fragmentation and incomplete archaeological recovery limited observations. Cranial trauma was evenly observed between juveniles and adults, although juveniles were more likely to have multiple impact sites on the cranial vault.

Inferences about the location of injuries across the vault have been explored (Toyne and Narváez 2014). While adults were slightly more likely to receive blows to the front of the head and juveniles to the posterior aspect of the vault, injuries were not restricted to the "hat-brim line" as suggested from forensic analysis of lethal interpersonal attacks (Berryman and Haun 1996). This variation in location and the identification of multiple impacts across the vault would suggest that the victims were not always facing their attackers; nor was the intention simply to incapacitate them with nonlethal blows. A few perimortem fractures of the distal ulna suggest that individuals attempted to protect themselves, but the identification of perimortem fractures of the lower legs indicates that some may have been knocked down and then struck in the head. It is unclear if the victims had their own weapons or if the remains include any attackers that may have been killed in defense.

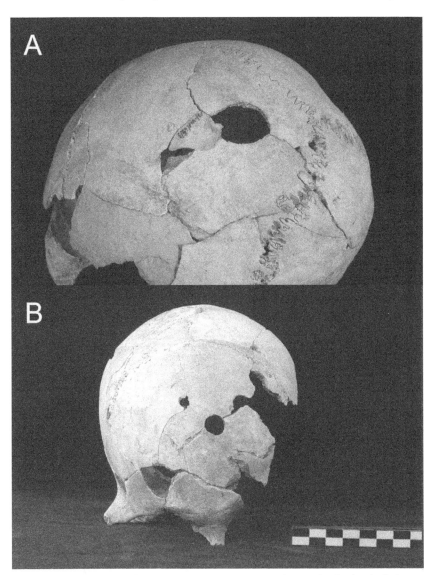

Figure 4.4. Photographs of perimortem penetrating cranial wounds of individuals from the Circular Platform, Structure 5. (A) Ent 47 (adolescent possible male, left lateral view parietal bone); (B) Ent 66c (middle-aged male, anterior view frontal bone). (Photo by J. M. Toyne.)

The perimortem injuries are also clearly weapon-related trauma. The moderate-sized (~1–2 cm) circular penetrations into the cranial vault and circular perforations with adjacent circular hinge fractures are consistent with the star-shaped stone maces found at the site and fairly common in the broader region (Toyne and Narváez 2014: figures 5 and 6). Additional

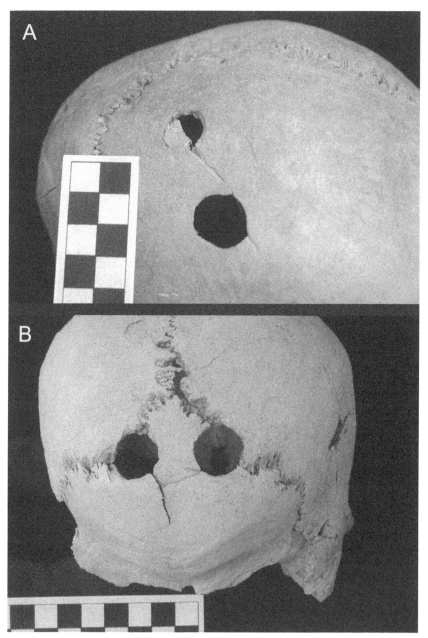

Figure 4.5. Photographs of perimortem cranial trauma from nearby houses. (A) Subplatform Structure 5, Ent 3 (young adult male, right lateral view posterior parietal bone); (B) Terrazas Structure 22, Ent 1a (young adult male, posterior view occipital bone). (Photo by J. M. Toyne.)

fracturing of the cranial vault is consistent with a more widely distributed impact of blunt force such as a flat surface, wall, or floor. There is no clear evidence of perimortem sharp force trauma injuries. The interpretation of these skeletal lesions is consistent with a lethal interpersonal assault against a large number of individuals. The 14 individuals from nearby house structures also demonstrate the same pattern in cranial trauma (figure 4.5).

From a more forensic perspective, the reconstructed patterns of contextual features observed suggest that this event was carried out with a great deal of violence and potentially excessive use of force. The murder of the youngest individuals, who were generally not likely to have been combatants in civil conflicts, also suggests that the aim was annihilation. However, the general absence of women may indicate that they were captured or separated from the men and children, who were directly killed. Based on the concentration of the bodies in and about the southern end of the site, this may have been a surprise attack within the settlement. Those who were killed were ill prepared for combat, perhaps even fleeing together toward one area of the site, trying to escape the attackers. The proposed defensive architectural features with limited access to the complex also meant limited escape routes. This mass death assemblage follows patterns ascribed to massacres due to the large number of victims and nature of the systematic violence (Stewart and Zimmerman 1989). Yet, with the more selective victim profile, I prefer to call this a mass killing rather than a massacre.

ANALYSIS OF THE CONTEXT

Rarely are we able to pinpoint the exact dates of massacres to be able to identify victims, perpetrators, and motives (but see Fiorato et al. 2007). Evidence should coalesce, however, to be able to interpret the context. Unfortunately, due to radiocarbon calibration curve inconsistencies, the absolute dating of this mass killing ranges almost 200 years, from approximately AD 1450–1640 (350 ± 30 BP, BETA-30630; human bone; 2 sigma standard error) (Toyne and Narváez 2014). This includes the original Chachapoya cultural occupation (ca. AD 900–1470), the Inca conquest (AD 1470), and the early European colonial period (AD 1535). Therefore, understanding the exact chronology of the mass killing is a challenge. While it is possible to use the bioarchaeological data to refine the time frame, it is difficult to rule out interpretations.

Essential to interpreting this context is trying to elucidate the nature of the Chachapoya's sociopolitical organization and their cultural responses to subsequent conquest processes. Unfortunately, based on limited archaeological research in the region, pre-Inca Chachapoya cultural structure and institutions are poorly known. If the Chachapoya lived in autonomous settlements, then an attack at Kuelap could reflect intracommunity violence that had escalated to the destruction of one of the largest sites in the region. This is unlikely to have been a small nearby community but a large force or possibly even several groups together. While weapon signatures are consistent with local stone maces, it seems unlikely that this was an intracommunity or intercommunity Chachapoya period massacre-like event. Within the site, this mass killing and destruction made this entire area unlivable, so it was not a site takeover or part of a territorial expansionist strategy. This area of the site, if not the whole site, was abandoned soon after the event. If it was retaliation for a perceived egregious social offense, then this might make sense (Boehm 2011). While there is no clear archaeological evidence to deny such a possibility, however, the presence of Inca ceramic materials and architectural constructions suggests that the event was post–Inca conquest.

If this mass killing took place during the latter part of the fifteenth or early sixteenth century, it was possibly during the Inca occupation or early historic period. There is abundant evidence for Inca occupation, but the nature of the conquest (as peaceful or conflictive) remains uncertain. Ethnohistoric records suggest that the Chachapoya resisted Inca occupation and rebelled at various times against their imposed rule (Cieza de León 1984 [1553]). This resulted in retaliation and reconquest of the region using physical violence. While the Inca were known to use military force against groups, others argue that their alternative strategies focused on economic extraction. Killing these Chachapoya would not benefit the long-term goals of the empire. In fact that very warrior strength was coopted by the Inca, who incorporated the Chachapoya as a significant part of their army (Garcilaso de la Vega 2004 [1609]). The Inca also used the strategy of relocating a substantial quantity (>50 percent) of the local population to distant locations across the empire (Espinoza Soriano 1967; Schjellerup 2002). This strategy may have served as an example to reduce previous intercommunity hostilities, but it could also have led to new conflicts with the remaining groups.

One feature of the archaeological context that remains problematic is the discovery of a single fragment from a colonial-period ceramic vessel mixed within the archaeological remains at the Circular Platform. One sherd from a commingled context is insufficient to confirm an early historic date for this mass killing, but it does potentially shift the circumstances around it. The early colonial period was clearly a tumultuous time for all indigenous communities in the Andes. After their arrival the Europeans began to colonize and take control of territories and resources while dismantling the Inca Empire. Death in large numbers occurred due to political resistance but also due to infectious diseases, poor living conditions, and overwork (Cook 1998; Klaus and Tam 2009). Massacres may have been part of these historical processes, but no documented examples exist. But why would the Spanish destroy such a large part of a community's viable workforce, when taxes and labor tribute were the main economic benefits? The Spanish may have used this violence as a short-term political measure to achieve longer-term control over the people or in light of a specific rebellion (Murphy et al. 2010), but there is no historical record of Chachapoya violent resistance to colonial rule. Alternatively, local indigenous hostilities may have resurfaced, as reported in other areas of the Americas (Stodder and Martin 1992).

While no early historical documents specifically mention a site named Kuelap or reference such a mass killing or the circumstances around it, a local legend alludes to it. Early in the twentieth century Bandelier (1907) recorded the story of a war between Kuelap and the neighboring communities of Huancas (an Inca relocated community) and Levanto. The legend mythologizes the actions of a powerful shaman who jumped from mountain peak to mountain peak, arrived at Kuelap in the night, and slaughtered them all while they were sleeping, using a hammer. The circumstantial features of this story parallel the evidence identified at Kuelap and would seem to suggest that an intracommunity conflict lead to this mass killing, not some overarching colonial manifesto. Yet the legend does not describe the particular motive or explain why so few females were recovered within the sample. Considering the degree of violence, it is surprising that the event was not more directly recorded historically or in other oral traditions.

A GENDERED EXPERIENCE OF VIOLENCE AT KUELAP

In the Andean past, as elsewhere, archaeological evidence for direct physical violence associated with warfare is scarce, even though social conflict clearly played an important role in many ancient societies (Arkush and Stanish 2005; Arkush and Tung 2013; Owsley 1994; Scherer and Golden 2014; Smith 2003; Willey 1990). Only rarely do we find in situ remains of mass death assemblages, especially where the bodies are not buried by survivors or victors (Knüsel 2005; Komar 2008). Kuelap may be the only site in the Andean region. This shows that even in a short period of later prehistory there are many interpretations for even a single event linked to various environmental, social, political, and religious factors. But the evidence is more consistent with a conflict situation rather than with sacrifice, cannibalism, or explicit genocide.

It is the demographic profile of the assemblage, however, that provides an important window into the nature of this event and its possible motivations and outcomes. The estimation of age and sex for this collection is skewed toward adult males over adult females but also includes a large proportion of indeterminate sex juveniles. This bias is pervasive in other massacre events (Bishop and Knüsel 2005) and also in several other contexts where ritual violence or other political violence took place (Šlaus et al. 2010; Smith 1998; Toyne 2011; Verano and Toyne 2011). Catastrophic death assemblages should include indiscriminate age at death and both sexes of individuals due to random events like plague epidemics, famine, or massacres (Margerison and Knüsel 2002).

Following the model developed by Stewart and Zimmerman (1989), the bioarchaeological evidence at Kuelap appears to include the defined massacre features such as potential for a history of mutual hostility, a surprise attack, and destruction of the massacre site. But it does not support indiscriminate slaughter even though there is clear perimortem trauma consistent with emotionally impassioned rage. The demographic profile and interpretation of the physical violence at Kuelap do not show random killing of all community members but a selection toward men and children in the group. Therefore, this mass killing had an explicit motivation, which also included destroying this area of the site by dismantling building walls. The men were targeted for physical violence and death. This demonstrates power and dominance to any surviving members of the community, including the women who may have been taken captive or escaped. These women served as witnesses to the violence and its aftermath, but not all them were spared. They may have suffered indirect violence via the loss of their community and families, but it is unknown what else happened to them, whether they were kept as slaves or killed elsewhere. Thus, this is a case of a clear political message: the goal was not domination of the site but rather the elimination of Kuelap—or at least this large sector of the community.

The Chachapoya men are described as fierce warriors in historical texts (Guaman Poma de Ayala 1980 [1615]; Salinas Loyola 1965 [1571]), which say nothing about the nature of the women except to mention their physical beauty. According to Garcilaso de la Vega (2004 [1609]:67), the men were very valiant and ready with weapons to die for the defense of their liberty. If the Chachapoya were the "warriors of the clouds," then we might expect that warfare, raiding, and physical violence were part of their everyday existence in a localized competitive environment. While the definition of children is not a cultural universal (Perry 2006), neither is the earliest age for participation in war or social conflict (Rosen 2005). These juvenile individuals may have been considered participants, so that their deaths were deliberate and part of the attack.

Examples of female combatants are found in many different societies across time (Cohen 2013; Dietrich Ortega 2012; Redfern 2008; Warner et al. 2005), and perhaps the presence of a few adult females reflects their active participation in defense of their homes or just being randomly killed in the mayhem. According to Otterbein's (2000) analysis, men were more likely to be killed fighting attackers so that women and children could escape. He also determined that male survivors were less likely to be taken captive. If taking captives was the goal in this attack, we would also expect that only a few children were killed, but juvenile skeletal remains (<15 years) make up a large portion (44 percent) of the sample recovered. This attack appears to have been targeted at eliminating the group's men and children and retaining the women alive. Alternatively, perhaps the females with babies-in-arms escaped the attack altogether, but why would the other children not also have fled with them? Capture seems more plausible. Or perhaps they were just left alone as survivors. The mortality profile at Kuelap is similar to the identified reprisal killing at Punta Lobos on the central coast of Peru during the Late Intermediate Period (~AD 1350). But we found no evidence of any females there and the killing was a more systematic and almost ritualized execution of men and boys (Verano and Toyne 2011).

If raiding and capture of women or children were a common part of the regional warfare program, then perhaps we would also see similar features of nonlethal cranial trauma consistent with such attacks. Work by Wilkinson (1997) suggests that an analysis of antemortem violence can demonstrate the nature of social conflict within a group and identify contexts where women were captured and made slaves. High percentages of nonlethal cranial trauma could be associated with raiding and abduction practices. As men are incapacitated, women are attacked and taken captive. They may also be exposed to additional abuse and physical violence as captives, resulting in high frequencies of cranial trauma similar to that of the males in the group. Rather than being participants or aggressors in violent encounters, women are the victims. Considering the rates and distribution of antemortem cranial injuries among the earlier Chachapoya period cranial sample, males clearly have more healed cranial fractures. But there is no significant difference between males (26/66, 39.4 percent) and females with interpersonal cranial injuries (16/49, 32.7 percent). These calculations suggest a fairly high rate of interpersonal trauma at the site, however, and may reflect regular social conflict in the region, including raiding or female participation in warfare.

Warfare has directly and indirectly been observed to have a gendered impact in other areas of the Andes. Tung (2012, 2014) argues that Wari (AD 600–1100) empire building involved violence, militarism, and abductions to expand and maintain imperial authority. The investigation of cranial trauma and strontium isotope tracers of geographic origins suggest that women were preferentially mistreated and likely captured as part of expansionist state strategies. But women may have shifted to a more active role in military action and defense of their communities during post-Wari times (AD 1000–1400). Other research also shows higher prevalence in perimortem trauma among males during a time frame similar to the Kuelap Late Horizon/early colonial period on the coast near Lima (Murphy et al. 2010).

Conclusions

Violence and violent events have shaped past societies, yet men are overwhelmingly more often associated with physical violence and trauma, including contexts with evidence for explicitly male-dominated skeletal assemblages: men as victims of violent attacks. This unique mass death assemblage at Kuelap demonstrates that it had a significant impact on the site and likely the surrounding area. This included not just a demographic impact by reducing the population and eliminating most of the following generation but also the displacement of those living at Kuelap, including a large number of adult females.

The nature of sociopolitical change and the power struggle among the various factions in Chachapoyas in the protohistoric period is still little understood, but raiding and warlike activities may have played a significant role in shifting the balance. The lack of chronological precision is challenging, considering the range of possible perpetrators or motivations for the attack. More excavations at additional sites will help elucidate interpretations of the role of violence and its impact on both women and men. This isolated mass killing in the community of Kuelap alone does not define the Chachapoya as an inherently violent people, as proposed by the early historic documents. Many other conflict situations may have been negotiated peacefully. It does illustrate, however, that at least in this case women and men experienced violence differently.

ACKNOWLEDGMENTS

Funding for this research was provided by the National Geographic Society (EC0374-08) as well as the Peruvian Ministry of Culture, COPESCO from the Peruvian Ministry of Trade and Tourism, the World Monuments Fund, and the Ambassador Fund from the American Embassy in Peru for excavations at Kuelap. This research would have not been possible without the collaboration of the Kuélap Archaeological Project and especially the director Alfredo Narváez Vargas. I also acknowledge many engaging discussions with John W. Verano, Haagen D. Klaus, Warren Church, Klaus Koshmeider, Armando Anzellini, and Kenneth C. Nystrom on the nature of violence among the Chachapoya. I thank Cheryl Anderson and Debra Martin for the invitation to participate in the volume and for their editorial suggestions.

REFERENCES

Arkush, E. N., and C. Stanish. 2005. Interpreting Conflict in the Ancient Andes: Implications for the Archaeology of Warfare. *Current Anthropology* 46(1):3–28.

Arkush, E. N., and T. A. Tung. 2013. Patterns of War in the Andes from the Archaic to the Late Horizon: Insights from Settlement Patterns and Cranial Trauma. *Journal of Archaeological Research* 21(4):307–369.

Bandelier, A. 1907. *The Indians and Aboriginal Ruins near Chachapoyas in Northern Peru.* Historical Records and Studies, New York.

Berryman, H. E., and S. J. Haun. 1996. Applying Forensic Techniques to Interpret Cranial Fracture Patterns in an Archaeological Specimen. *International Journal of Osteoarchaeology* 6:2–9.

Bishop, N. A., and C. Knüsel. 2005. A Palaeodemographic Investigation of Warfare in Prehistory. In *Warfare, Violence and Slavery in Prehistory: Proceedings of a Prehistoric Society Conference at Sheffield University,* edited by M. Parker Pearson and I. J. Thorpe, pp. 201–216. Archaeopress, Oxford.

Bocquet-Appel, J. P., and C. Masset. 1996. Paleodemography: Expectancy and False Hope. *American Journal of Physical Anthropology* 99:571–583.

Boehm, C. 2011. Retaliatory Violence in Human Prehistory. *British Journal of Criminology* 51(3):518–534.

Buikstra, J. E., and D. H. Ubelaker (editors). 1994. *Standards for Data Collection from Human Skeletal Remains: Proceedings of a Seminar at the Field Museum of Natural History*. Research Series No. 44. Arkansas Archaeological Survey, Fayetteville.

Church, W. B., and A. von Hagen. 2008. Chachapoyas: Cultural Development at an Andean Cloud Forest Crossroads. In *Handbook of South American Archaeology*, edited by H. Silverman and W. H. Isbell, pp. 903–926. Springer, New York.

Cieza de León, P. d. 1984 [1553]. *La crónica del Perú*. Historia 16, Madrid.

Cohen, D. K. 2013. Female Combatants and the Perpetration of Violence: Wartime Rape in the Sierra Leone Civil War. *World Politics* 65(3):383–415.

Cook, N. D. 1998. *Born to Die: Disease and New World Conquest, 1492–1650*. Cambridge University Press, New York.

Dietrich Ortega, L. M. 2012. Looking beyond Violent Militarized Masculinities. *International Feminist Journal of Politics* 14(4):489–507.

Espinoza Soriano, W. 1967. Los senorios étnicos ee Chachapoyas y la alianza Hispano-Chacha: Visitas, informaciones y memoriales inéditos de 1572–1574. *Revista Histórica* (Lima) 30:224–333.

Fiorato, V., A. Boylston, and C. Knüsel (editors). 2007. *Blood Red Roses: The Archaeology of a Mass Grave from the Battle of Towton AD 1461*. Oxbow Books, Oxford.

Frayer, D. W. 1997. Ofnet: Evidence for a Mesolithic Massacre. In *Troubled Times: Violence and Warfare in the Past*, edited by D. L. Martin and D. W. Frayer, pp. 181–216. Gordon and Breach, Amsterdam.

Garcilaso de la Vega, I. 2004 [1609]. *Comentarios reales de los Incas*. Biblioteca, Ayacucho.

Geller, P. L. 2005. Skeletal Analysis and Theoretical Complications. *World Archaeology* 37(4):597–609.

Guaman Poma de Ayala, F. 1980 [1615]. *El primer nueva crónica y buen gobierno*. Translated by J. I. Urioste. Colección América Nuestra, 31. Vol. 1. Siglo Veintiuno Editores, S.A., México City.

Guengerich, A. 2014. The Architect's Signature: The Social Production of a Residential Landscape at Monte Viudo, Chachapoyas, Peru. *Journal of Anthropological Archaeology* 34:1–16.

Hutchings, K. 2008. Making Sense of Masculinity and War. *Men and Masculinities* 10(4):389–404.

Kirby, P., and M. Henry. 2012. Rethinking Masculinity and Practices of Violence in Conflict Settings. *International Feminist Journal of Politics* 14(4):445–449.

Klaus, H. D., and M. E. Tam. 2009. Contact in the Andes: Bioarchaeology of Systemic Stress in Colonial Mórrope, Peru. *American Journal of Physical Anthropology* 138:356–368.

Knüsel, C. J. 2005. The Physical Evidence of Warfare—Subtle Stigmata? In *Warfare, Violence and Slavery in Prehistory*, edited by M. P. Pearson and I.N.J. Thorpe, pp. 49–65. BAR International Series 1374. BAR, Oxford.

Komar, D. 2008. Patterns of Mortuary Practice Associated with Genocide: Implications for Archaeological Research. *Current Anthropology* 49(1):123–133.

Margerison, B. J., and C. J. Knüsel. 2002. Paleodemographic Comparison of a Catastrophic and an Attritional Death Assemblage. *American Journal of Physical Anthropology* 119(2):134–143.

Murphy, M. S., C. Gaither, E. Goycochea, J. W. Verano, and G. Cock. 2010. Violence and Weapon-Related Trauma at Puruchuco-Huaquerones, Peru. *American Journal of Physical Anthropology* 142:636–649.

Narváez Vargas, A. 1996. La Fortaleza de Kuelap. *Arkinka* 13:90–98.

———. 2013. Kuelap: Centro del poder político y religioso de los Chachapoyas. In *Los Chachapoyas: Colección Arte y Tesoros del Perú*, edited by F. Kauffman-Doig, pp. 87–160. Banco de Crédito del Perú, Lima.

Nystrom, K. C., and J. M. Toyne. 2014. "Place of Strong Men": Skeletal Trauma and the (Re)Construction of Chachapoya Identity. In *The Bioarchaeology of Human Conflict: Traumatised Bodies from Earliest Prehistory to the Present*, edited by C. J. Knüsel and M. Smith, pp. 371–388. Routledge Press, New York.

Otterbein, K. F. 2000. Killing of Captured Enemies: A Cross-Cultural Study. *Current Anthropology* 41(3):439–443.

Owsley, D. W. 1994. Warfare in Coalescent Tradition Populations of the Northern Plains. In *Skeletal Biology in the Great Plains: Migration, Warfare, Health, and Subsistence*, edited by D. W. Owsley and R. L. Jantz, pp. 333–344. Smithsonian Institution Press, Washington, DC.

Parpart, J. L., and M. Zalewski (editors). 2008. *Rethinking the Man Question: Sex, Gender and Violence in International Relations*. Zed Books, London.

Perry, M. A. 2006. Redefining Childhood through Bioarchaeology: Toward an Archaeological and Biological Understanding of Children in Antiquity. In *Archaeological Papers of the American Anthropological Association*, edited by J. E. Baxter, pp. 89–111. University of California Press, Berkeley.

Redfern, R. 2008. A Bioarchaeological Analysis of Violence in Iron Age Females: A Perspective from Dorset, England (Fourth Century BC to the First Century AD). Paper presented at the Changing Perspectives on the First Millennium BC: Proceedings of the Iron Age Research Student Seminar 2006, Oxford.

Rosen, D. M. 2005. *Armies of the Young: Child Soldiers in War and Terrorism*. Rutgers University Press, Piscataway, NJ.

Ruiz Estrada, A. 2009. Sobre las formas de sepultamiento prehispánicas en Kuelap, Amazonas. *Arqueología y Sociedad* 20:1–16.

———. 2011. La mita de Chachapoyas del año 1586. *Investigaciones Sociales* 15(27):359–374.

Salinas Loyola, J. d. (editor). 1965 [1571]. *Historia Indica. Vol. II, Obras completas*. Biblioteca de Autores Españoles, Madrid.

Scherer, A. K., and C. Golden. 2014. War in the West: History, Landscape, and Classic Maya Conflict. In *Conflict, Conquest, and the Performance of War in Pre-Columbian America*, edited by A. K. Scherer and J. W. Verano, pp. 57–92. Dumbarton Oaks Research Institute, Washington, DC.

Schjellerup, I. 1997. *Incas and Spaniards in the Conquest of Chachapoyas*. Archaeological and Ethnohistorical Research in the Northeastern Andes of Peru, Gotarc, Series B, Gothenburg Archaeological Theses, 7. Göteborg University, Göteborg, Sweden.

———. 2002. Reflections on the Chachapoya in the Chinchasuyu. In *Identidad y transformación en el Tawantinsuyu y en los Andes coloniales: Perspectivas arqueológicas y ethnohistóricas, Primera parte*, edited by P. Kaulicke, G. Urton, and I. Farrington, pp. 43–56. Boletín de Arqueología PUCP, Lima.

———. 2008. Sacando a los caciques de la oscuridad del olvido: Etnias Chachapoya y Chilcho. *Bulletin de L'Institut Français d'Études Andines* 37(1):111–122.

Šlaus, M., M. Novak, V. Vyroubal, and Z. Bedic. 2010. The Harsh Life on the 15th Century Croatia-Ottoman Empire Military Border: Analyzing and Identifying the Reasons for the Massacre in Cepin. *American Journal of Physical Anthropology* 141(3):358–372.

Smith, A. 1998. Trauma Most Foul: The Human Remains from Kintbury, Berkshire. In *Current and Recent Research in Osteoarchaeology: Proceedings from the Third Meeting of the Osteoarchaeological Research Group*, edited by S. Anderson and K. Boyle, pp. 27–30. Oxbow Books, Oxford.

Smith, M. O. 2003. Beyond Palisades: The Nature and Frequency of Late Prehistoric Deliberate Violent Trauma in the Chickamauga Reservoir of East Tennessee. *American Journal of Physical Anthropology* 121(4):303–318.

Stewart, J. R., and L. J. Zimmerman. 1989. To Dehumanize and Slaughter: A Natural History Model of Massacre. *Great Plains Sociologist* 21:1–16.

Stodder, A.L.W., and D. L. Martin. 1992. Native Health and Disease in the American Southwest before and after Spanish Contact. In *Disease and Demography in the Americas*, edited by J. W. Verano and D. H. Ubelaker, pp. 55–73. Smithsonian Institution Press, Washington, DC.

Torres-Rouff, C., and M. A. Costa Junqueira. 2006. Interpersonal Violence in Prehistoric San Pedro de Atacama, Chile: Behavioral Implications of Environmental Stress. *American Journal of Physical Anthropology* 130(1):60–70.

Toyne, J. M. 2011. Interpretations of Pre-Hispanic Ritual Violence at Tucume, Peru, from Cut Mark Analysis. *Latin American Antiquity* 22(4):505–523.

Toyne, J. M., and A. Narváez Vargas. 2014. The Fall of Kuelap: Bioarchaeological Analysis of Death and Destruction on the Eastern Slopes of the Andes. In *Conflict, Conquest, and the Performance of War in Pre-Columbian America*, edited by A. K. Scherer and J. W. Verano, pp. 345–368. Dumbarton Oaks Research Institute, Washington, DC.

Tung, T. A. 2012. Violence against Women: Differential Treatment of Local and Foreign Females in the Heartland of the Wari Empire, Peru. In *The Bioarchaeology of Violence*, edited by D. L. Martin, R. P. Harrod, and V. R. Pérez, pp. 180–198. University Press of Florida, Gainesville.

———. 2014. Gender-Based Violence in the Wari and Post-Wari Era of the Andes. In *The Bioarchaeology of Human Conflict: Traumatised Bodies from Earliest Prehistory to the Present*, edited by C. J. Knüsel and M. Smith, pp. 333–354. Routledge Press, New York.

Vencl, S. 1984. War and Warfare in Archaeology. *Journal of Anthropological Archaeology* 3:116–132.

Verano, J. W., and J. M. Toyne. 2011. Estudio bioantropológico de los restos humanos del Sector II, Punta Lobos, Valle De Huarmey. In *Arqueología de la costa de Ancash*, edited by M. Giersz and I. Ghezzi, pp. 449–474. ANDES: Boletin del Centro de Estudios Precolombinos de la Universidad de Varsovia, Lima.

Warner, J., K. Graham, and E. Adlaf. 2005. Women Behaving Badly: Gender and Aggression in a Military Town, 1653–1781. *Sex Roles* 52(5/6):289–298.

Wies, J. R., and H. J. Haldane (editors). 2011. *Anthropology at the Front Lines of Gender-Based Violence*. Vanderbilt University Press, Nashville, TN.

Wilkinson, R. G. 1997. Violence against Women: Raiding and Abduction in Prehistoric Michigan. In *Troubled Times: Violence and Warfare in the Past*, edited by D. L. Martin and D. W. Frayer, pp. 21–44. Gordon and Breach, Amsterdam.

Willey, P. S. 1990. *Prehistoric Warfare on the Great Plains: Skeletal Analysis of the Crow Creek Massacre Victims*. Garland Publishing, New York.

5

Applications of Coded Osteological Data from the Smithsonian Repatriation Database for the Study of Violence in the Past

ASHLEY E. KENDELL

Since the passage of the National Museum of the American Indian Act (NMAIA), Public Law 101–185, in 1989 and the Native American Graves Protection and Repatriation Act (NAGPRA), Public Law 101–601, in 1990, museums, laboratories, and universities have been focused on documenting their collections of Native American human remains before materials are offered for repatriation to culturally affiliated descendants. Before repatriation legislation, documentation at the Smithsonian Institution (SI) was not systematic and was often dependent on curator interests (Ousley et al. 2005). Likewise, other museums and institutions across the country collected skeletal data in idiosyncratic formats with little effort devoted to data standardization. The field of physical anthropology was forward-thinking in creating a set of standards to record basic information about each skeleton so that data could be collected and placed into databases for use by future researchers. *Standards for Data Collection from Human Skeletal Remains* (*Standards*, Buikstra and Ubelaker 1994) was developed in response to repatriation legislation to minimize the loss of data and maximize comparability of data between institutions across the country (Ousley et al. 2005). The value of standardized data is apparent when one considers the significance of large-scale comparisons. Unlike specialized data, which can only be used to answer specific research questions, large standardized datasets can increase the breadth of research and our understanding of human history by uncovering unexpected or previously unknown patterns within a skeletal collection that only emerge in large-scale datasets (Ousley et al. 2005).

This research provides a geographic and temporally expansive analysis of violence, using a large dataset of Arikara-related skeletal materials and artifacts inventoried at the SI. The Arikara material was selected because this is one of the best-documented tribes (in terms of both the literature and previous bioarchaeological analyses) and one of the largest samples curated at the Smithsonian Institution. This chapter explores possible applications of data mining and using osteological coded data for studying violence in prehistoric and historic populations when access to osteological collections is no longer available.

CONTEXT

Anthropological research has historically utilized traditional data collection methods, which involve independent analysis and data collection from existing skeletal assemblages. The data in a collection may be analyzed and recorded dozens if not hundreds of times in a university or museum setting. The traditional method of data collection begs the question: is reanalysis and independent data collection necessary? Enactment of repatriation legislation has forced this question, as access to skeletal collections is drastically reduced by the reburial of human skeletal remains or constraints placed upon collections following the offer of repatriation. The development of *Standards* provided a means of ensuring comparability of data collected by different institutions and individuals and increased the percentage of skeletons analyzed in the United States from roughly 30 percent to nearly 100 percent (Rose et al. 1996). *Standards* also minimized interobserver error as researchers were prompted to utilize generalized categories of data collection instead of independent analysis without standard protocols. Most importantly, repatriation prompted the development of relational databases for the curation of osteological data, which allow current and future researchers to assess the work of our predecessors. While the curation of digitized osteological data is becoming more commonplace in physical anthropology, practitioners have yet to maximize potential extraction and manipulation of coded osteological data curated in relational databases. This chapter aims to demonstrate that reanalysis and independent collection of osteological data are not a necessary component of an anthropological research design.

The SI dataset used for the current study is widely varied both geographically and temporally, allowing for a more nuanced view of the changing patterns of violence directly proceeding, during, and following violent human interactions. Using digitized archival data, it may be possible to infer causative mechanisms and outcomes of violence on past population structure by assessing change through time. Finally, with the enactment of NMAIA, NAGPRA, and the repatriation of Native American human remains and associated artifacts, the creation and utilization of large digital data repositories may provide the only opportunity for future researcher to study historic Native American populations.

ARIKARA HISTORY AND WARFARE ON THE PLAINS

The Arikara Tribe is emphasized in this research. While the Arikara form a single tribal entity in the twenty-first century, tracing their lineage back into the eighteenth century reveals an aggregate of Caddoan-speaking bands and villages (Parks 2001). The Arikara are the northernmost member of the Caddoan language family and are thought to have diverged from the Pawnee after AD 1400 (Rogers 1990). Ancestors of both the Arikara and the Pawnee have been traced to the Upper Republican phase of the Central Plains tradition (Parks 2001).

Historically, the Arikara were a farming tribe, inhabiting earthlodge villages throughout the Missouri River Valley (Billeck et al. 2005). Agricultural settlements developed in the valley, where the tribe grew corn, beans, and squash. In addition to these horticultural practices, the Arikara subsistence economy was largely dependent upon bison hunting. Earthlodge villages were typically occupied from spring through the middle of summer. After the corn was planted in midsummer, the tribe typically left the village for a time to participate in an extended bison hunt on the prairie (Billeck et al. 2005). Villages were then reoccupied as the harvest approached and were likely continuously inhabited throughout the winter.

During the eighteenth century the land occupied by the Arikara tribe was on the edge of European knowledge. Therefore, few direct references can be found in the literature. The first recorded direct contact between a European and the tribe was in 1743, when Chevalier de La Verendrye visited an Arikara settlement (Smith 1980:112). While direct European contact was infrequent in the eighteenth century, historical records of European contact were also recorded by Jean-Baptiste Truteau in 1794–1795, John Mackay and John Thomas Evans in 1796–1797, Pierre Antoine Tabeau in

1804–1805, and Meriwether Lewis and William Clark in 1804–1806 (Billeck et al. 2005:5). European contact with the tribe throughout the eighteenth century was mostly indirect and involved the exchange of Euro-American goods through the vast trade network. Although both French and Spanish traders traveled northward up the Missouri River, most direct trade terminated in Nebraska with the Omaha and Ponca tribes (Billeck et al. 2005:5). European references to the Arikara in the eighteenth century report the tribe living along the Missouri River in South Dakota (Billeck et al. 2005). The Arikara resided in South Dakota until the 1830s, when they migrated north into North Dakota (Billeck et al. 2005:4).

Historic records indicate a rapid decrease in Arikara populations in the eighteenth and nineteenth centuries. In a report by Veniard de Bourgmond written in 1714, the trader mentions two contiguous Arikara villages lying north of Omaha in present-day Nebraska and another forty villages of "Caricara" higher up the Missouri River (Billeck et al. 2005:5; Norall 1988:110). The number of villages and the tribe's population size rapidly diminished because of disease and warfare. The Arikara were particularly susceptible to disease because their involvement in the fur trade put them in direct contact with carriers of infectious diseases, such as smallpox, against which they had no conferred immunity. Because the tribe was primarily horticultural, with individuals living in multifamily dwellings, the dissemination of infectious disease was rampant. Decimation of Native American populations due to the spread of epidemic disease stands out as one of the most significant impacts of early contact (McGinnis 1990).

The integration of the horse and gun into Native American life following European contact also resulted in a tremendous amount of cultural change for the tribe. It is impossible to specify an exact date for the contact period in the Plains, primarily because European excursions into the region were widely separated both geographically and temporally at the northern and southern reaches of the territory (Lehmer 2001). Participation in the trade network and attainment of the horse and gun facilitated hunting and access to European goods (Wedel 1972). However, this period of cultural climax was short-lived. Both the ethnohistoric and archaeological records indicate an eastward retreat of Plains village groups as highly mobile bison hunters began to dominate the Western and Central Plains, outcompeting the horticulturalists for food and access to trade goods (Wedel 1972). The Arikara, once forty-three villages strong, were depleted to only two villages by 1790. The survivors were forced to move north, away from the path of the Sioux migration (Calloway 1982). Plains tribes were faced with serious consequences of white settlement, including near-complete depletion of the bison herds, spread of epidemic disease, warfare with both European-American and Native American neighbors, and finally confinement on reservations (Fowler 2001). Both hunters and farmers underwent cultural attrition as white contact increased and the reservation destroyed what was left of Native American social institutions and traditions (Fowler 2001; Wedel 1972).

Following smallpox epidemics in 1792, 1836, and 1837, the Arikara, Mandan, and Hidatsa tribes had so few surviving members that they were forced to establish a single society at Like-a-Fishhook Village, to maintain cultural continuity (Schneider 2001). The Arikara tribe in the twenty-first century is one of the Three Affiliated Tribes, also known as the Mandan, Hidatsa, and Arikara Nation (Mandan Hidatsa Arikara Nation 2016). The Three Affiliated Tribes settled on the Berthold Indian Reservation in New Town, North Dakota, in 1936 (Schneider 2001). The reservation now represents a small portion of the land reserved for the tribe in the Fort Laramie Treaty of 1851 (Parks 2001:367).

MATERIALS

Osteoware

A database to store and manage data curated by the SI became a necessity with the enactment of the NMAIA (Dudar 2011). For the SI, repatriation legislation required that over 19,000 catalogue numbers for human remains be inventoried and documented, and the data had to be collected quickly (Dudar 2011:2). The SI's Repatriation Osteology Laboratory (ROL) was established in 1991. Efforts to create a database to manage the data generated by the documentation process began shortly after (Dudar 2011). The original storage repository was a DOS-based Paradox system with text screens and a flat file, nonrelational database (Dudar 2011:3). In 1998 Dr. Stephen D. Ousley, newly appointed director of the ROL, transitioned the Osteoware software into the first Windows-based data entry program (Dudar 2011:3). The Osteoware software program was designed to provide an easy-to-use interface for the collection of both qualitative and quantitative observations of human skeletal remains (Dudar 2011). Osteoware works in conjunction with a separate database manager, Advantage Data Architect (Advantage) version 9.1 by Sybase, Inc. Links across data tables are established by a unique identifier or primary key, allowing extraction of data using Structured Query Language (SQL; Dudar 2011).

The Osteoware program is primarily based upon the protocols outlined in *Standards*. Osteoware has a total of twelve modules: Inventory, Age and Sex, Pathology, Taphonomy, Postcranial Metrics, Dental Inventory/Deviation/Pathology, Dental Morphology, Cranial Nonmetrics, Macromorphoscopics, Cranial Deformation, Craniometrics, and Summary Paragraph. Each module represents a digital data entry form for a specific skeletal attribute. The modules provide a graphic user interface: the analyst uses a series of radio buttons and text boxes to enter quantitative and qualitative information following skeletal analysis. All osteological data input into the Osteoware program are subsequently coded and curated in a relational database (RDB) controlled by Advantage. For a more detailed description of the Osteoware software, modules, and coding system refer to Kendell (2016).

Skeletal Materials

For this study, data were exported from Osteoware, using SQL, for 1,221 Arikara individuals. Independent data collection was not performed in this study. Osteological data collected by the SI between the years 1993 and 2012 was analyzed. Because the focus of this research was on changing patterns of violence within the Middle Missouri region, data were extracted from the following tables: Inventory, AgeSex, CulturalAffiliation, Pathology, and SummPara (Summary Paragraph). The completeness of each skeleton was based upon the data recorded in the Inventory and Summary Paragraph modules. To account for differential preservation of the skeletal remains, which bias the reported frequencies of trauma by overenumerating or underenumerating the results, only crania that were at least 50 percent complete were included in the study. Postcranial remains were removed from the sample if they were recorded as fragmentary or commingled. After eliminating partial and commingled remains, the sample was reduced to 990 individuals.

In the database 508 adult individuals were assigned a sex: 266 were males and 242 were females. All individuals assigned a "probable" sex were lumped in with that particular sex category (e.g., "probable males" were included in the male category). Sex could not be determined in 14 cases because of the incompleteness of the remains or the fragmentary nature of the cranium and pelvis. The remaining 468 individuals were subadults, ranging in age from intrauterine months to young adolescents, whose sex was not assessed. Sex was estimated by the original data recorder following sex determination methods outlined in *Standards*.

Skeletal ages were reported in Osteoware in two different formats. Some individuals' ages were reported as an age range in a single column (e.g., 17–20), while other ages were reported in two columns in the form of a minimum and maximum. Additionally, individuals could also have both an age range and a minimum and maximum age. Due to the differences in age reporting, individuals were assigned an age-point estimate (either the midpoint of the age range selected or the average of the minimum and maximum reported ages). Once established, the midpoint was assigned to broad age categories based on *Standards* (Buikstra and Ubelaker 1994:9): fetal (< birth), infant (birth–2.5 years), child (3–11.5 years), adolescent (12–19.5 years), young adult (20–34.5 years), middle adult (35–49.5 years), and old adult (50+ years).

Sample Provenience

The sample represents the remains recovered from ten archaeological sites in the Middle Missouri River Basin in South Dakota, many of which were obtained under the auspices of the River Basin Surveys (RBS) Program (figure 5.1). The RBS emerged under the larger Interagency Archaeological Salvage Program, a cooperative archaeological effort to save the nation's archaeological resources threatened by a comprehensive water resource development project that was set to flood a large part of the nation's watercourses at the end of World War II. "During its lifespan RBS archaeologists conducted surveys and excavations in at least 273 reservoir areas, recorded more than 5,000 archaeological sites, and conducted excavations at more than 576 of them" (as of 1965; Stephenson 1967:4).

The ten archaeological sites included in this sample were geographically divided into two adjacent regions lying along the Missouri River and defined by Lehmer (1971) as the Bad-Cheyenne Region and the Grand-Moreau Region. Following Lehmer (1971:29), the Middle Missouri, a sub-area of the Great Plains, can be further subdivided into smaller units or regions: Big Bend, Bad-Cheyenne, Grand-Moreau, Cannonball, Knife-Heart, and Garrison. The Bad-Cheyenne Region extends north from the mouth of the Bad River to roughly the old Cheyenne Indian Agency, South Dakota. The Grand-Moreau Region is north of and contiguous to the Bad-Cheyenne Region, extending upstream to 15 miles of the North Dakota–South Dakota border (Lehmer 1971:29). Sites in the Bad-Cheyenne Region

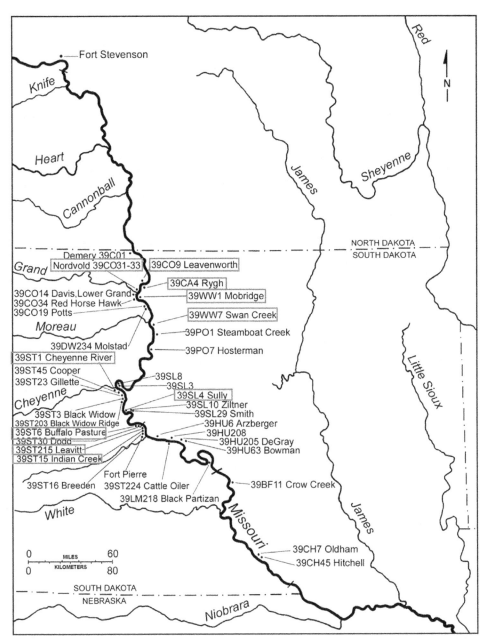

Figure 5.1. Geographic distribution of sites throughout the Missouri River Basin. (Figure 2 in Billeck et al. 2005: ii.)

Table 5.1. Site information for Arikara sample

Site Name	Period	Geographic Region	Number of Individuals
Leavenworth (39C09)	Postcontact Coalescent	Grand-Moreau	30
Mobridge (39WW1)	Extended Coalescent, Postcontact Coalescent	Grand-Moreau	308
Norvold (39C031, 39C032, 39C033)	Extended Coalescent, Postcontact Coalescent	Grand-Moreau	49
Swan Creek (39WW7)	Extended Coalescent, Postcontact Coalescent	Grand-Moreau	12
Cheyenne River (39ST1)	Extended Coalescent, Postcontact Coalescent	Bad-Cheyenne	78
Buffalo Pasture (39ST6, 39ST216)	Postcontact Coalescent	Bad-Cheyenne	26
Indian Creek (39ST15)	Postcontact Coalescent	Bad-Cheyenne	9
Leavitt Cemetery (39ST215)	Postcontact Coalescent	Bad-Cheyenne	22
Sully (39SL4)	Extended Coalescent, Postcontact Coalescent	Bad-Cheyenne	440
Anton Rygh (38CA4)	Extended Coalescent, Postcontact Coalescent	Grand-Moreau	16

include Cheyenne River (39ST1), Buffalo Pasture (39ST6, 39ST216), Leavitt (39ST215), Indian Creek (39ST15), and Sully (39SL4). The Grand-Moreau Region encompasses Leavenworth (39C09), Anton Rygh (39CA4), Mobridge (39WW1), Swan Creek (39WW7), and Norvold (39C031, 39C032, 39C033). The geographic division of sites made it possible to analyze violence in two regions of the Middle Missouri River Basin.

Chronologically, the sample is composed of individuals dating from the late prehistoric and protohistoric periods to the early historic period. The sites date from the Extended Coalescent (AD 1300–1650) and Postcontact Coalescent variants (AD 1600–1832) (table 5.1). Four of the sites (Leavenworth, Buffalo Pasture, Indian Creek, and Leavitt) date to a single variant, the Postcontact Coalescent (Billeck et al. 2005). The remaining six sites are multicomponent sites, with multiple dates of occupation that span two variants, the Extended Coalescent and the Postcontact Coalescent.

METHODS

Data were extracted from the SI RDB using a series of simple table join SQL statements and wildcard queries. SQL is a computer language designed to interact with databases. Its main function is to provide a simple and efficient way to both manage and query (search) a database (Forta 2013). For a detailed discussion of Osteoware, Advantage, and SQL codes, please refer to the Osteoware user manual (Dudar 2011) and Kendell (2016).

After the data were exported from the Relational Database Management System (RDBMS), it was necessary to clean and normalize the results. The following modifications were made to the osteological dataset; otherwise all data were kept in their original form for statistical analysis. Individuals in the sample were categorized as having cranial remains only, postcranial remains only, or both cranial and postcranial remains present. This categorization was necessary to establish trauma frequencies in the sample. Trauma data are recorded by element in Osteoware. Once exported, these data were recategorized by body region. The skeleton was divided into five regions: facial (splanchnocranium with the addition of the frontal), cranial vault (parietals, occipital, temporals, sphenoid), axial skeleton (vertebrae, ribs, and sacrum), upper appendage (bones of the shoulder, arm and hand), and lower appendage (innominates and bones of the leg and foot). Additionally, injuries were identified by trauma type: (1) fracture of a long bone, (2) dislocation, (3) blunt force trauma, (4) sharp force trauma, and (5) projectile trauma.

Analysis of Interpersonal Violence

Trauma is broadly defined in the field of bioarchaeology. Traumatic injuries include defects of both an accidental and intentional nature. For this reason, the statistical analysis of trauma was subdivided into injuries potentially resulting from interpersonal violence. Investigation of interpersonal violence historically has focused on craniofacial trauma and injuries derived from projectile points or other weaponry (Bartelink et al. 2014:286). Several studies have included perimortem mutilation (such as trophy taking of body parts and scalping) as an additional indicator of interpersonal violence (Andrushko et al. 2005; Andrushko et al. 2010; Bartelink et al. 2014; Steadman 2008; Tung 2007, 2008; Tung and Knudson 2008; Verano 2003). For this study, markers of interpersonal violence include cranial trauma (both craniofacial and cranial vault), projectile injuries, and evidence of perimortem mutilation with no evidence of healing (specifically scalping and the taking of trophy skulls).

Interpersonal Violence Statistical Methods

Chi-square tests were calculated for all prevalence comparisons between the sexes, age categories, regions and periods, and Fischer's exact tests were applied when counts were less than five. Statistical analyses were calculated in SPSS 23.0 (SPSS, Inc., Chicago), with significance set at α = .05.

Results and Discussion

Within the SI RDB there was a lack of integration between the osteological data and archaeological and provenience data; therefore, qualitative observations of the skeletal remains could not be contextualized in a mortuary context. The analysis of trauma was heavily reliant on taking a population-based assessment of trauma patterns within the Arikara sample. While no significant differences were observed in skeletal markers of interpersonal violence when comparing the sexes, different age groups, temporal periods, or regional variants, some meaningful differences were found (table 5.2).

Table 5.2. Trauma frequencies and results of statistical analyses

Skeletal Marker	Group Comparison	Variables	Trauma Frequency	Chi-Square Value	Degrees of Freedom	P-value
Craniofacial trauma						
	Sex differences	Females	10.8% (19/176)	0.341	1	0.559
		Males	12.8% (25/196)			
	Age differences	Young adults	12.2% (16/131)	1.669	2	0.434
		Middle adults	12.0% (14/117)			
		Old adults	18.2% (12/66)			
	Temporal period	Extended Coalescent	6.3% (12/190)	0.143	1	0.705
		Postcontact Coalescent	7.1% (33/462)			
	Geographic location	Bad-Cheyenne	6.3% (23/366)	0.596	1	0.440
		Grand-Moreau	7.8% (23/294)			
Cranial vault trauma						
	Sex differences	Females	6.3% (11/176)	2.126	1	0.141
		Males	3.1% (6/196)			
	Age differences	Children	2.2% (2/89)	0.7578	4	0.944

Skeletal Marker	Group Comparison	Variables	Trauma Frequency	Chi-Square Value	Degrees of Freedom	P-value
		Adolescent	3.9% (3/76)			
		Young adult	3.8% (5/131)			
		Middle adult	4.2% (5/118)			
		Old adult	4.5% (3/66)			
	Temporal period	Extended Coalescent	3.7% (7/190)	0.343	1	0.558
		Postcontact Coalescent	2.8% (13/462)			
	Geographic location	Bad-Cheyenne	3.6% (13/366)	0.731	1	0.380
		Grand-Moreau	2.4% (7/294)			

PROJECTILE & BLADED WEAPON TRAUMA

Skeletal Marker	Group Comparison	Variables	Trauma Frequency	Chi-Square Value	Degrees of Freedom	P-value
	Sex differences	Females	0.83% (2/242)			Fisher's exact, p = 0.112
		Males	2.6% (7/266)			
	Age differences	Adolescent	0.81% (1/123)			Small sample size
		Young adult	2.7% (5/183)			
		Middle adult	1.7% (3/174)			Small sample size
		Old adult	1.3% (1/79)			
	Temporal period	Extended Coalescent	0.4% (1/236)			Fisher's exact, p = 0.263
		Postcontact Coalescent	1.2% (9/741)			
	Geographic location	Bad-Cheyenne	0.9% (5/575)			Fisher's exact, p = 0.415
		Grand-Moreau	1.2% (5/415)			

TROPHY TAKING

Skeletal Marker	Group Comparison	Variables	Trauma Frequency	Chi-Square Value	Degrees of Freedom	P-value
	Sex differences	Female	1.1% (2/176)			Small sample size
		Male	0.5% (1/196)			
	Age differences	Adolescent	3.9% (3/76)			Small sample size
		Young adult	0.8% (1/131)			
	Temporal period	Extended Coalescent	1.1% (2/190)			Small sample size
		Postcontact Coalescent	0.4% (2/462)			
	Geographic location	Bad-Cheyenne	0.6% (2/366)			Small sample size
		Grand-Moreau	0.7% (2/294)			

Sex and Age Differences

The analysis of markers of interpersonal violence between the sexes showed that males had higher frequencies of craniofacial trauma and projectile point trauma, while females had higher frequencies of cranial vault trauma and scalping. There were also differences when comparing the indicators of interpersonal violence among the age groups. Craniofacial and cranial vault injuries were most frequently observed in old adults, projectile injuries occurred most frequently in young adults, and evidence of trophy taking was observed most frequently in adolescents. Few children had skeletal markers of interpersonal violence ($n = 2$), while 9 adolescents had probable violent injuries. In most cases of injury in adolescents, the injuries were sustained in individuals over the age of 17. The pattern of injury closely mirrored the injury patterns observed in adults: males manifesting projectile and craniofacial injuries and females exhibiting injuries to the cranial vault. Of the 3 individuals with scalping cutmarks 2 were adolescent females. These findings suggest that adolescents were involved in the same activities and potentially violent encounters as their adult counterparts.

Most injuries observed in the Arikara sample were antemortem injuries. The age distribution of interpersonal violence markers therefore may not be reliable because injuries are cumulative during an individual's lifespan (Glencross 2011). Perimortem injuries are discussed in the remainder of this section because there is no definitive way to determine when an injury occurred in the antemortem interval. In this study only 12 individuals had perimortem injuries: 6 males, 4 females, 1 adolescent, and 1 child. Of the 4 females with perimortem injuries 3 exhibited depressed cranial fractures, 2 young adults and 1 middle adult. The fourth female with perimortem trauma was an adolescent exhibiting scalping cutmarks on the cranial vault. Of the 6 males with perimortem trauma 5 exhibited skeletal manifestations of weapon-related violence, including a musket-ball injury to the ilium of a young adult, blunt force cranial trauma and evidence of potential trophy taking (drill holes) on a middle adult, sharp force trauma to the cranium of a middle adult, and 2 cases of sharp force trauma to the axial skeletons of a young adult and middle adult. Only a single case of perimortem injury did not represent interpersonal violence: a middle adult male with perimortem vertebral compression fractures in thoracic vertebrae 11 and 12.

The increased incidence of lethal injuries in young and middle adults suggests a pattern of injury correlated with participation (both direct and indirect) in violent acts such as warfare, raiding, or village defense. The patterns of injury (females with depressed cranial fractures and trophy taking and males exhibiting weapon-related injuries) suggested a differential risk of injury based on sex and age. The data suggest that involvement in war or aggressive behavior was determined largely by an individual's age and sex. Young adult males were more engaged in forms of warfare than other demographic groups. Alternatively, the pattern of injury observed in young females suggested more passive involvement in war, likely as the result of victimization during village raids.

Most historic descriptions of Arikara women depict them as passive victims of warfare. Early travelers and traders reported that women were vulnerable while working in the fields near the village. Village raiding is also known to have included the shooting and scalping of female victims (Taylor 1897). Arikara women are thought to have been susceptible to violence inflicted by the Sioux, a neighboring nomadic tribe competing for land and trade system resources. A probable scalping at the Sully Site is cited as supporting evidence of violence against women during village raids. Other documentary sources suggest that the Sioux were known to beat or kill Arikara women during horse-stealing raids (Abel 1939). Tribal relations in the early historic period were volatile. Even on the day directly following a friendly exchange of goods, warriors of the nomadic tribes returned to raid for horses or other goods from the more sedentary village tribes, such as the Arikara (McGinnis 1990). Compared to their nomadic neighbors, village tribes were often small and vulnerable because of their immobility. Early historic accounts of intertribal relations could not comprehend this type of combat, as European rules of warfare did not permit killing civilians and discouraged the slaughter of women and children (McGinnis 1990:4). These ethnocentric views lent themselves to claims of savagery by Native Americans. Unlike European war tactics, intertribal warfare more often focused on individual bravery and spiritual power than on the outcome of a battle (McGinnis 1990). Tribal victories occurred through the defense of a village or the discovery that an opponent was weak (e.g., could not defend women and children: McGinnis 1990:4). It is possible that the perimortem injuries observed in the Arikara female sample resulted from nonlethal village raids by neighboring Native American tribes.

Unlike the female victims, males with skeletal markers of interpersonal violence mostly exhibited injuries related to weaponry. Many of the perimortem injuries sustained by male victims, such as sharp force trauma to the axial and cranial skeleton and a potential trophy skull, suggested hand-to-hand combat and direct involvement in warfare. Likewise, the musket-ball injury is not likely to have occurred within the village. However, male victims of domestic violence are often misidentified as victims of assault due to the high amount of overlap in wound patterning (Redfern 2017). Therefore, it is also possible that some of the perimortem injuries documented in male skeletal remains may have resulted from aggressive interactions within the village or between intimate partners.

Temporal and Regional Patterns

The frequency of all skeletal markers of interpersonal violence remained stable through time. None of the statistical analyses yielded significant results, but there were slight increases in the frequency of craniofacial and weapon-related trauma in the Postcontact period. When all indicators of interpersonal violence were combined, no significant difference between the temporal periods was found. One of the reasons for the increase in craniofacial and weapon-related trauma may be the changing pattern of warfare from the protohistoric through the historic period.

One of the earliest historical records of explorers in the Southern Plains comes from Francisco Vásquez de Coronado, who was followed by Spanish military expeditions in the 1600s and 1700s (McGinnis 1990:ix). While French traders traversed the Southern Plains in the 1700s, the Northern High Plains remained relatively unknown to Euro-Americans until the late 1700s and 1800s, when trading and exploratory expeditions began. Early European accounts reported that the Indians engaged in constant warfare (McGinnis 1990:ix). Continuous tribal migration and the acquisition of horses and firearms compounded intertribal hostilities in the Postcontact period. However, when compared to modern warfare practices, Native American conflict was limited. Hostilities were often set aside to establish a truce between nomadic and sedentary tribes who needed the goods that the other supplied (McGinnis 1990:x). Also, many tribes depended on male participation in hunting and recognized that they could not afford the high casualties associated with direct warfare.

From the earliest contact, Euro-Americans became involved in intertribal relationships, influencing and altering tribal interactions with firearms, trade goods, and newly established Euro-American/Native American alliances (McGinnis 1990:x). The two biggest contributing factors altering Native American relationships and lifeways were guns and horses. They provided tribes with more lethal forms of weaponry and increased mobility, forever changing the Precontact modes of warfare. Horses reached the Plains in the early 1700s, coming from Spain by way of the tribes west of the Rocky Mountains (McGinnis 1990:6). Firearms also arrived. After the 1730s guns and horses initiated gradual changes on the intertribal conflicts in the Northern Plains (McGinnis 1990:9).

As contact with Euro-American traders increased, so did the frequency and intensity of intertribal conflict. By the 1780s and 1790s Euro-American contact had altered intertribal relations to the point that a major shift in the balance of power occurred, which is said to have produced major changes in Plains culture and warfare practices (McGinnis 1990:10). A number of factors contributed to this shift in the balance of power in four ways. Increased mobility raised the level of competition for hunting grounds. Growing Euro-American settlement in the East initiated a chain of Native American migrations that reached the Plains tribes. Increased access to European goods altered Plains culture in terms of transportation, hunting, and war. And the fur trade brought new diseases that had a devastating impact on Native American population size. In addition to smallpox, cholera and other diseases killed more Native Americans than guns or war (McGinnis 1990:10).

To assess change over time, the sample used in this research was divided into two temporal groups, Precontact (Extended Coalescent variant) and Postcontact (Postcontact Coalescent variant), using the classification system of dividing the Coalescent into three variants: Initial, Extended, and Postcontact. According to Lehmer's (1971) taxonomic system, the Coalescent tradition can instead be divided into four variants: Initial, Extended, Postcontact, and Disorganized Coalescent. According to that classification system, the Leavenworth Site would be classified as Disorganized Coalescent. For the purposes of this research, the Disorganized Coalescent variant was absorbed into the Postcontact Coalescent, preventing a diminished sample size in the Disorganized Coalescent variant. However, if Leavenworth, as the only historic site included in the sample, is analyzed independently, an interesting pattern emerges. The Disorganized Coalescent yields a markedly elevated frequency of trauma (23.3 percent) when compared with the original Precontact (Extended Coalescent variant; 17.8 percent) and Postcontact (Postcontact Coalescent variant; 11.0 percent) temporal classification system.

Of the 30 individuals from Leavenworth, 7 individuals displayed trauma on their skeletons (23.3 percent): 3 females, 1 male, 2 adolescents, and 1 child. Interestingly, each of the 7 individuals with skeletal trauma displayed at least 1 skeletal marker of interpersonal violence (table 5.2). A higher proportion of females and children displayed skeletal markers of interpersonal violence than at any other site included in the sample. While the trauma observed at the site may reflect a single attack upon the village by the U.S. Army and the Sioux in 1823, this aggressive interaction marks a period of instability and hostility between Native American tribes and Euro-Americans. The distinct pattern of trauma is markedly different from the pattern of trauma observed in either the Extended or Postcontact Coalescent periods.

This discussion outlines the ever-changing nature of intertribal relations from the protohistoric through the historic period. Intertribal warfare and raids were a well-established practice in the Plains long before European contact. Contact and access to European trade goods changed the form of warfare but did not necessarily alter the frequency of warfare until later in the historic period, after the sample used in this research. While the Postcontact Coalescent variant extends into the 1880s, the sample used in this study only dates as late as 1832.

The comparable frequency of skeletal markers of interpersonal violence in the Extended Coalescent and Postcontact Coalescent variants may reflect the enduring nature of aggressive intertribal interactions. The increase in craniofacial and weapon-related trauma in the Postcontact group likely reflected the increased availability of European weapons and shift from warfare to intertribal raiding, with young men engaging in individual combat. The patterns of injury suggest that intertribal raiding was the most common method of warfare practiced in both the Precontact and Postcontact periods (Owsley 1994). Instead of an increase in the frequency of intertribal raiding after contact with Euro-Americans, there appears to be a continuance of long-standing violent engagements from the protohistoric to historic period. A general lack of evidence of high mortality in young adult males and the low frequency of perimortem trauma are also consistent with small-scale raiding as the primary form of aggressive intertribal interactions in the region (Owsley 1994).

There is no evidence to support regional differences in the Arikara sample. The frequencies of cranial, projectile, and mutilation injuries were roughly equivalent in the Bad-Cheyenne and Grand-Moreau Regions. The lack of regional differences may be due to the close geographical proximity of the ten sites used in this research. Each of the ten sites was likely subject to the same external pressures, resulting in comparable injury patterns in those two regions of the Middle Missouri River Valley.

The Future of Archival Data in Anthropology

The need for data mining and working with relational databases has traditionally been an impediment to anthropological research because anthropologists are not typically trained in data mining and SQL code writing. Mining osteological databases can help future researchers to identify previously unknown trends or patterns in the data. As we move from hypothesis-driven research toward exploratory research, we are likely to learn more about a population(s) or see temporal changes that would have not been predicted through reviewing the literature or previous bioarchaeological research. Incorporating data-mining methods can therefore lead to interpretations that are better informed, more accurate, and more empirically substantiated than was previously possible.

This research has also demonstrated the wide-ranging benefits of employing large-scale datasets and by extension digital relational databases in an assessment of human history. The SI collections represent some of the largest and most variable in the world. Utilization of the SI collections in this research has impacted the insights obtained through an analysis of violence by making readily available large-scale, time-space distributional data that are comparably recorded. Such large-scale digital samples are easily manipulated and analyzed, a previously unattainable approach (Kintigh 2006). The SI database allows researchers to address large-scale and long-term questions with a high level of empirical support because the data span the entirety of the United States and a wide range of temporal periods. The development of *Standards* and the integration of standard protocols into Osteoware promoted maximum comparability of data across the sample. Comparability of data allows researchers to integrate data drawn from multiple sites, collectors, and time frames. Data comparability thus enables researchers to identify patterns that become visible in samples larger and more widely geographically and temporally distributed than can be collected by any single individual (Steckel and Rose 2002). By increasing the temporal and geographic distributions of samples, we increase the breadth of understanding of the human past; large-scale analyses can reveal changes through time and space as well as evolving interpersonal interactions between and within populations. If additional data are desired in the future, a relational database can be expanded to include supplemental analytical tables, ensuring that data collection is never a static process.

In the past researchers have also been constrained by their abilities to compare their own data-driven results to those of other researchers due to a lack of primary data (Kintigh 2006:570). As a result, they have been forced to draw comparisons with the summary statistics of other projects that smooth over the details of the primary data, potentially minimizing the insights that could be ascertained from a data-driven comparison (Kintigh 2006). The comparability of data collected following *Standards* enhances our abilities to perform data-driven research integrating data from multiple samples drawn from both legacy datasets and modern collections. The digitization of osteological data and creation of digitally curated collections have increased the accessibility of anthropological data, thereby promoting access to primary data. However, many collections in the United States are still largely inaccessible to researchers because of either a lack of digitization efforts or limitations imposed on digitized data (due to a lack of knowledge of data-mining practices or restrictions by a university or institution).

Conclusions

With the development of *Standards* and the creation of Osteoware, the SI has preserved and made available large-scale databases to be used by future researchers of repatriated collections that are no longer accessible. Not only has digitization of osteological data led to long-term preservation of the bioarchaeological record, but the creation of large-scale databases has changed the way we conduct bioarchaeological research. Digitized osteological databases present opportunities to conduct macro-regional and macro-temporal analyses. By increasing the temporal and geographic range of our samples, we have increased the breadth of our understanding of the past. Bioarchaeologists can use large-scale databases to document changes through time and space as well as interpersonal interactions between, and not only within, a single population.

As demonstrated by this research, violence in the Arikara tribe was a long-standing cultural tradition that predated European contact. While injuries tended to accumulate with age in both sexes, there was a different pattern of injury for males compared to females. The injury patterns suggest that intertribal raiding was the most common method of warfare practiced in both the Precontact and Postcontact periods. Instead of contact with Euro-Americans increasing the frequency of intertribal raiding, long-standing violent engagements continued from the protohistoric through the early historic period. A general lack of evidence of high mortality in young adult males (when compared to other sex and age groups) and the low frequency of perimortem trauma were also consistent with small-scale raiding as the primary form of aggressive intertribal interactions in the Middle Missouri River Basin.

REFERENCES

Abel, A. H. 1939. *Tabeau's Narrative of Loisel's Expedition to the Upper Missouri.* University of Oklahoma Press, Norman.

Andrushko, V. A., K.A.S. Latham, D. L. Grady, A. G. Pastron, and P. L. Walker. 2005. Bioarchaeological Evidence for Trophy-Taking in Prehistoric Central California. *American Journal of Physical Anthropology* 127(4):375–384.

Andrushko, V. A., A. W. Schwitalla, and P. L. Walker. 2010. Trophy-Taking and Dismemberment as Warfare Strategies in Prehistoric Central California. *American Journal of Physical Anthropology* 141(1):83–96.

Bartelink, E. J., V. Andrushko, V. Bellifemine, I. Nechayev, and R. J. Jurmain. 2014. Violence and Warfare in the Prehistoric San Francisco Bay Area, California: Regional and Temporal Variations in Conflict. In *The Routledge Handbook of the Bioarchaeology of Human Conflict*, edited by C. Knüsel and M. J. Smith, pp. 285–307. Routledge Press, New York.

Billeck, W. T., E. Eubanks, A. Lockard, and P. C. Cash. 2005. *Inventory and Assessment of Human Remains and Funerary Objects Potentially Affiliated with the Arikara in the National Museum of Natural History, Smithsonian Institution.* Repatriation Office, National Museum of Natural History, Smithsonian Institution, Washington, DC.

Buikstra, J. E., and D. H. Ubelaker (editors). 1994. *Standards for Data Collection from Human Skeletal Remains: Proceedings of a Seminar at the Field Museum of Natural History.* Research Series, No. 44. Arkansas Archaeological Survey, Fayetteville.

Calloway, C. G. 1982. The Inter-tribal Balance of Power on the Great Plains, 1760–1850. *Journal of American Studies* 16(1):25–47.

Dudar, J. C. 2011. Extracting Data from the Database. In *Osteoware Software Manual, Volume I*, edited by C. A. Wilczak and C. J. Dudar, pp. 84–88. Smithsonian Institution, Washington, DC.

Forta, B. 2013. *Sam's Teach Yourself SQL in 10 Minutes.* 4th ed. Pearson Education, Indianapolis.

Fowler, L. 2001. History of the United States Plains since 1850. In *Handbook of North American Indians: Plains*, edited by R. J. DeMallie, pp. 280–299. Vol. 13. Smithsonian Institution Press, Washington DC.

Glencross, B. A. 2011. Skeletal Injury across the Life Course. In *Social Bioarchaeology*, edited by S. C. Agarwal and B. A. Glencross, pp. 390–409. Wiley-Blackwell, Oxford.

Kendell, A. E. 2016. Examining Skeletal Trauma on the North American Great Plains: Applications of Coded Osteological Data from the Smithsonian Repatriation Database. PhD dissertation, Anthropology Department, Michigan State University.

Kintigh, K. 2006. The Promise and Challenge of Archaeological Data Integration. *American Antiquity* 71(3):567–578.

Lehmer, D. J. 1971. *Introduction to Middle Missouri Archaeology*. National Park Service, Anthropological Papers 1. Department of the Interior, Washington, DC.

———. 2001. Plains Village Tradition: Postcontact. In *Handbook of North American Indians: Plains*, edited by R. J. DeMallie, pp. 245–255. Vol. 13. Smithsonian Institution Press, Washington, DC.

Mandan Hidatsa Arikara Nation. 2016. Mandan, Hidatsa, Arikara Nation: http://www.mhanation.com.

McGinnis, A. 1990. *Counting Coup and Cutting Horses: Intertribal Warfare on the Northern Plains, 1738–1889*. Cordillera Press, Evergreen, CO.

Norall, F. 1988. *Bourgmont, Explorer of the Missouri, 1698–1725*. University of Nebraska Press, Lincoln.

Ousley, S. D., W. T. Billeck, and R. E. Hollinger. 2005. Federal Repatriation Legislation and the Role of Physical Anthropology in Repatriation. *Yearbook of Physical Anthropology* 48:2–32.

Owsley, D. W. 1994. Warfare in Coalescent Tradition Populations of the Northern Plains. In *Skeletal Biology in the Great Plains: Migration, Warfare, Health, and Subsistence*, edited by D. W. Owsley and R. L. Jantz, pp. 333–344. Smithsonian Institution Press, Washington, DC.

Parks, D. R. 2001. Arikara. In *Handbook of North American Indians: Plains*, edited by R. J. DeMaille, pp. 365–390. Vol. 13. Smithsonian Institution, Washington, DC.

Redfern, R. C. 2017. Identifying and Interpreting Domestic Violence in Archaeological Human Remains: A Critical Review of the Evidence. *International Journal of Osteoarchaeology* 27(1):13–34.

Rogers, J. D. 1990. *Objects of Change: The Archaeology and History of Arikara Contact with Europeans*. Smithsonian Institution Press, Washington, DC.

Rose, J. C., T. J. Green, and V. D. Green. 1996. NAGPRA is Forever: Osteology and the Repatriation of Skeletons. *Annual Review of Anthropology* 25:81–103.

Schneider, M. J. 2001. Three Affiliated Tribes. In *Handbook of North American Indians: Plains*, edited by R. J. DeMaille, pp. 391–398. Vol. 13. Smithsonian Institution Press, Washington, DC.

Smith, G. H. 1980. *The Explorations of the La Vérendryes in the Northern Plains, 1738–43*. University of Nebraska Press, Lincoln.

Steadman, D. W. 2008. Warfare Related Trauma at Orendorf, a Middle Mississippian Site in West-Central Illinois. *American Journal of Physical Anthropology* 136(1):51–64.

Steckel, R. H., and J. C. Rose (editors). 2002. *The Backbone of History: Health and Nutrition in the Western Hemisphere*. Cambridge University Press, Cambridge.

Stephenson, R. L. 1967. *Reflections on the River Basin Surveys' Program*. Preprint Series No. 48. University of Nevada, Desert Research Institute, Las Vegas.

Taylor, J. H. 1897. *Sketches of Frontier Life*. The Author, Bismarck, SD.

Tung, T. A. 2007. Trauma and Violence in the Wari Empire of the Peruvian Andes: Warfare, Raids, and Ritual Fights. *American Journal of Physical Anthropology* 133(3):941–956.

———. 2008. Dismembering Bodies for Display: A Bioarchaeological Study of Trophy Heads from the Wari Site of Conchopata, Peru. *American Journal of Physical Anthropology* 136(3):294–308.

Tung, T. A., and K. J. Knudson. 2008. Social Identities and Geographical Origins of Wari Trophy Heads from Conchopata, Peru. *Current Anthropology* 49(5):915–925.

Verano, J. W. 2003. Mummified Trophy Heads from Peru: Diagnostic Features and Medicolegal Significance. *Journal of Forensic Sciences* 48(3):525–530.

Wedel, W. R. 1972. Culture Sequence in the Central Great Plains. *Plains Anthropologist* 17(57):291–352.

6

Each One the Same

Performance, Demography, and Violence at Sacred Ridge

ANNA J. OSTERHOLTZ

This chapter details the demographical analysis of the massacred assemblage at Sacred Ridge, a Pueblo I site in southwestern Colorado. This site is one of the few large well-excavated Pueblo I period (circa AD 700–900) sites in the Four Corners Region of the American Southwest. The period is notable for the reliance on agriculture and the transition from semi-subterranean pit structures to above-ground pueblos and the increasing sedentism and aggregation of populations into larger settlements. The period is also notable for the shared cultural ideology present at multiple sites throughout the region despite their diverse populations (Cordell and McBrinn 2012). It is generally accepted that these groups formed a coherent and persistent cultural system that extends to modern-day Puebloan groups living in Arizona and New Mexico (Martin 2015).

Dating to approximately AD 800, this site has the first example of *extreme processing*. Extreme processing has been identified in dozens of sites throughout the Southwest but tends to occur in the Pueblo I (PII, AD 900–1150) and Pueblo III (PIII, AD 1150–1350) periods (Kuckelman et al. 2000). The assemblage at Sacred Ridge is approximately 200 years earlier than the others and much larger in terms of number of bone fragments and individuals massacred.

Extreme processing has been identified in assemblages having the following characteristics by Turner and Turner (1999): (1) excellent preservation; (2) high degrees of fragmentation and possibly commingling, depending on the number of individuals processed; (3) high percentage of burned bones; (4) perimortem fracturing; and (5) tool marks. *Man Corn*

(Turner and Turner 1999) is the culmination of decades of reanalysis of southwestern assemblages and the codification of a checklist approach to the study of violence in this region. Beginning with the earliest analyses of commingled assemblages at Polacca Wash (1970), Turner and Turner used a checklist—if the characteristics listed above were present, the assemblage could be seen in terms of cannibalism. This checklist approach is alluring because it allows researchers to take subjective analysis and interpretation out of the equation. It has proven attractive to researchers since the early 1990s in terms of both analysis (e.g., Baker 1993; Billman et al. 2000; Flinn et al. 1976; Grant 1989; Kantner 1998; Marlar et al. 2000; Ortiz de Montellano 1978; Somers 1920; Turner and Turner 1992; White 1992) and critique (e.g., Bullock 1991; Darling 1999; Lambert 2002; Martin 2000). When excavators were confronted with the Sacred Ridge assemblage, this was the first natural research question to occur (Potter and Chuipka 2010). Because of the excavation and mapping methods employed, however, a greater variety of research questions can be approached with the Sacred Ridge data. The question of whether cannibalism occurred, in fact, becomes less interesting than examining the violence and processing. Violence on the scale seen at Sacred Ridge served a social purpose. When this violence is examined in a long view (in terms of the extreme processing that occurred later in Puebloan prehistory), it clearly continued to serve this purpose for a very long time. In effect, this violence was an effective social structure for hundreds of years, possibly allowing for the re-creation of Puebloan cosmology, the creation of group identity, and the negotiation of social status (Martin and Osterholtz 2015).

Did cannibalism occur at Sacred Ridge? Marlar (2010) tested various surfaces of cooking pots, ground stone, and flaked stone from two different pit structures (Features 58 and 104). All of the surfaces tested positive for both human hemoglobin and myoglobin, indicating that both human blood and muscle tissue residue were present. Ultimately this is evidence of where the processing took place, not the final disposition of those processed pieces. It is not possible for us to say whether cannibalism physically occurred or not at Sacred Ridge. But issues of processing and social control *can* be addressed with the extensive data set. These are the focus of this chapter.

Demography can be important in the interpretation of violence, particularly in the analysis of massacres and their social meaning in the Four Corners Region.

Context

The site of Sacred Ridge dates to the PI period (circa AD 800) and is located in southwestern Colorado. The site consists of clusters of structures along ridge tops within Ridges Basin outside Durango (map. 6.1). It is one of the larger PI sites in the Four Corners Region. In addition to its large size the architecture and artifact assemblages have led Potter and Chuipka (2007, 2010) to interpret it as a regional ritual center. The site has large amounts of ground stone and what has been identified as a "community-level ritual structure" (Potter and Chuipka 2010:512). This large pit structure has a vent doorway and appears to have been constructed in the late AD 700s. Potter and Chuipka (2010) have also identified a tower kiva, palisade, and several other large pit structures and middens identified as the Ridgetop complex. Based on the size and layout of the Ridgetop complex, Potter and Chuipka (2007, 2010) argue that the site held special significance in the region from the late AD 700s through the abandonment of the site around AD 800 (as evidenced by radiocarbon dates from numerous features and pit structures).

Two pit structures with large amounts of processed human remains were located in the viewshed of the Ridgetop complex (Features 104 and 58). Over 14,000 fragments of human and animal bone (both the normal food-animal refuse and the remains of at least 6 dogs) were recovered in a commingled and disarticulated state in the two pit structures. Within the two pit structures were fragments of at least 33 males and females of all ages as well as children and the remains of at least 6 dogs. These individuals were systematically disassembled without regard to age, sex, or species. Dogs and humans were similarly processed and deposited together. The deposition of the remains is likely one of the final activities to occur before site abandonment; the latest radiocarbon dates obtained for the site are from the commingled assemblage.

Bioarchaeological Evidence for Massacre

The concept of a massacre can be a difficult one to define. Betz et al. (2003:9) identify a massacre as "the mass murder or mutilation of innocent victims by an assailant or assailants immediately present at the scene." This definition brings to mind an immediacy and direct contact between the aggressors of the act and the victims of the act. It suggests indiscriminant killing, the killing of innocents. Massacres often involve the murder of women and

Map 6.1. Map of the Four Corners Region showing relevant sites. (Created by Anna J. Osterholtz.)

children, two groups usually not associated with active warfare or social threats.

Almost every fragment of bone from Sacred Ridge exhibits evidence of perimortem fracturing or processing. The perimortem fractures are very systematic and formulaic in location. The bones exhibit similar processing and fracturing, with only mild variations. Most individuals, for example, exhibit a large fracture to the right side of the skull. A few individuals have the same fracture on the left side of the skull, suggesting that multiple individuals were involved with the processing (perhaps indicating individual preference for the side of the skull fractured: figure 6.1). Frontal bones were also ubiquitously fractured, usually on the superior bosses and exhibiting the same pattern of mostly right with a few left side fractures (figure 6.2). This indicates the systematic disassembly of the human body from a living human into a pile of unidentifiable fragments of bone and flesh. The demography of the assemblage is important to this interpretation. Both males and females as well as children of all ages were included in the assemblage.

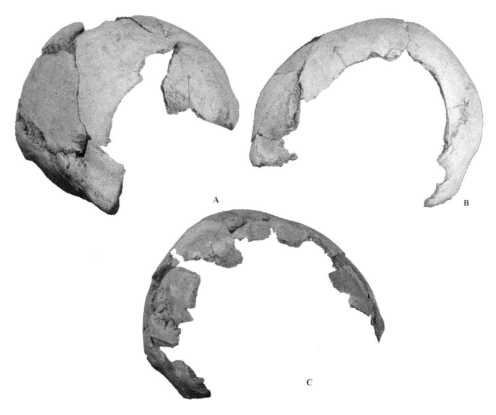

Figure 6.1. Lateral views of three skulls showing the systematic fracturing. (*A*) SKU-218, an adult male; (*B*) SKU-139, an adult female; (*C*) SKU-188, a subadult probable male. (Courtesy of SWCA Environmental Consultants.)

Individual of all ages and both sexes were treated the same in death: subjected to the same types and degrees of processing and deposited in a completely commingled state (Osterholtz 2014b; Stodder and Osterholtz 2010; Stodder et al. 2010).

Of the 33 individuals, 21 could be identified as being over the age of 18 at the time of death. The remaining 12 (36 percent) were under the age of 18 at death. Individuals under the age of 12 made up approximately 58 percent of the under-18 population and 21 percent of the total population (table 6.1). The inclusion and consistent treatment of all individuals indicates that they were not viewed as individuals with different social identities (such as man, woman, daughter, son, and so on) but were instead viewed as a collective *other*, distinctly removed from society and humanity.

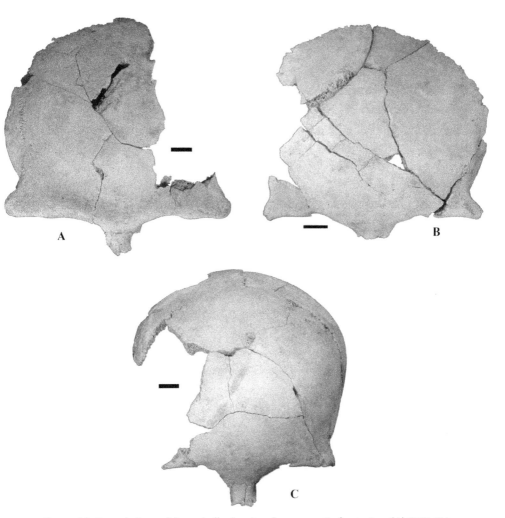

Figure 6.2. Frontal views of three skulls showing the systematic fracturing. (*A*) SKU-014, an adult male; (*B*) SKU-016, an adult of indeterminate sex; (*C*) SKU-004, a subadult of unknown sex. (Courtesy of SWCA Environmental Consultants.)

Table 6.1. Demography of the Sacred Ridge assemblage

Category	*n*	% of overall MNI
Infant (b–2 y)	4	12
Juvenile (2–12 y)	3	10
Nonadult (<18 y)	1	3
Subadult (12–18 y)	4	12
Y. Adult (18–35 y)	4	12
M. Adult (35–50 y)	7	21
Adult (18+ y)	10	30
Total	33	100

According to Douglas and Stodder (2010), individuals within the commingled assemblage are more closely related to each other than to other individuals recovered from other burial contexts at the site. This closer relatedness indicates the targeted killing of a clan or lineage.

Who committed the killing? Was it committed by groups from the surrounding settlements (as suggested for the Awat'ovi massacre) or by fellow community members? With the data currently available, it is not possible to determine who is responsible for the massacre at Sacred Ridge: fellow community members or members from the surrounding settlements.

Sacred Ridge in Larger Perspective

The Sacred Ridge assemblage has been the subject of discussion for several years. Potter and Chuipka (2010) interpret this as ethnic violence, while Osterholtz (2013) interprets it as a performative massacre with ritual overtones. The overall performativity of the massacre is indicated by the patterned processing of the individuals regardless of age or sex (Osterholtz 2014b). The patterning of the processing is evident in the consistent fracture patterning, consistent tool marks, and commingling of the remains (Osterholtz 2014b).

The demography of Sacred Ridge can be compared to two others—Polacca Wash and Mancos Canyon (Osterholtz and Martin 2017). The three sites have been used by Osterholtz and Martin (2017) to argue for persistent memory and cultural continuity in this region. All three sites have individuals of all age categories and both sexes represented in the assemblages (see Brooks 2016 for more on Polacca Wash; see White 1992 for a detailed description of the Mancos demography). All three assemblages also have consistent processing of the remains regardless of sex, indicating the total *othering* of massacred portion of the population. But how does this occur?

Two relationships are at play, one dependent upon a relationship between the two groups (the witnesses to the victims and aggressors). This cements the social control that the aggressors have over the witnesses by causing pain to the victims (e.g., hobbling and torture). Aggressors (those who perpetrate violence) can have physical and social control over the witnesses by causing pain to the victims. They gain social control over both groups by selectively targeting only a subset of individuals. The other relationship at play in a massacre is the us/them, in-group/out-group relationship. This is essentially dependent upon the lack of empathy or sense of community that an empathetic relationship entails.

This first relationship has been explored in terms of pain and performance with respect to hobbling and torture as a necessary step in establishing social control (Osterholtz 2013). Aggressors, in both physical and social control, are somehow psychologically able to inflict violence upon individuals. The victim group is easy to identify: it is their remains that end up being recovered archaeologically. The witness group is more amorphous and difficult to identify. The social control of the victims by the aggressors is maintained by the performance of violence upon some of the victim group for the benefit of the witnesses. Witnesses may be drawn from the surrounding community, may be subordinate members of the aggressors' social group, or may be future victims.

Examination of Whitehead's (2004, 2005, 2007) model of the poetics of violence is integral to understanding how this performance becomes an important cultural expression. Repetitive activities have the power to establish identity and group membership (Osterholtz and Harrod 2013), whether they be initiation rites or military drills. They create an in-group and an out-group. For massacres, these in-group and out-group identifications become more important than any other social identity (e.g., sex, gender, or age). Natural pathways to empathize with the out-group are limited. Singer et al. (2004) identify empathy as the ability to understand what it feels like when someone else experiences physical or emotional change. A lack of empathy is necessary for the creation of this out-group and for the massacre. This lack of empathy also allows for treatment of the out-group that might otherwise be considered impossible. This is particularly true when the role of inflicting pain in the maintenance of social control is examined.

BROADER ISSUES OF VIOLENCE: WHAT DOES DEMOGRAPHY TELL US ABOUT THE SOCIAL ROLE OF MASSACRE?

Massacres, like any other type of violence, must be seen to have cultural meaning. These are culturally and/or socially sanctioned acts that are seen as rational and reasonable by those making the decisions. Once the coupling of in-group/out-group status and the role of empathy is understood, the break between the aggressors and victims becomes even more distinct.

For the Four Corners Region in particular violence may have served significant social functions. In examining three assemblages with extreme processing (Sacred Ridge, Mancos, and Polacca Wash), Osterholtz and Martin (2017) show that extreme processing served similar social functions. Map 6.1 provides a representation of the geographical relationship between Polacca Wash, Mancos, and Sacred Ridge. As the final massacre assemblage included in that analysis, Polacca Wash may give a clue as to the overall meaning of these assemblages. Both Malotki (1993) and Brooks (2016) present detailed accounts of the destruction of the village of Awat'ovi by nearby Hopi village warriors. Jesse Fewkes (in the 1800s) and J. O. Brew (in the early 1900s) collected ethnographic accounts of this massacre indicating that destruction of the village became necessary because inhabitants had strayed from traditional practices and beliefs (they had adopted some elements of Christianity). This abandonment of traditional beliefs was believed to be causing large-scale problems, so the only remedy was the extreme violence and processing seen at Polacca Wash. All inhabitants of the village of Awat'ovi were either killed or taken captive. The massacre was seen as an act to balance the Hopi world. The males were in a kiva at the time of the attack and were easily killed there, except for the few who escaped and followed the aggressors who were leading the women and children away. In Polacca Wash a decision was ultimately made that the women and children should also be killed along with the few escaped males who attempted to free the women and children, explaining the skewed demography of this assemblage compared to either Mancos or Sacred Ridge. In effect, Polacca Wash is only half of the assemblage resulting from the massacre at Awat'ovi. If examined holistically as a process, this massacre exhibits demography similar to both Mancos and Sacred Ridge.

Importantly, Polacca Wash gives us a view into a possible explanation for the extreme processing seen at numerous Four Corners sites. Demography is consistent for the three assemblages, and the types of extreme processing and commingling are consistent through time. They may show individualized differences (see Osterholtz 2014a for a comparison of techniques for disarticulation at Mancos and Sacred Ridge), but these differences are likely due to individual preferences in disarticulation: disarticulation itself is still an important element in the overall processing. The three massacres show three different times in Puebloan history, but at all of them violence and annihilation of the body are an important vehicle for the creation of memory. This type of destruction is creative in terms of identity and memory formation and links the historic Puebloans to the Ancestral Puebloans of the past.

Analysis of violence must be nuanced and is culturally dependent. The role that violence plays in one society may be taken up by a different social structure in another. Many violent interactions help to enforce and negotiate social control within relationships and within society as a whole.

ACKNOWLEDGMENTS

I wish to thank SWCA Environmental Consultants, the Bureau of Reclamation, and the Ute Mountain Ute Tribe for their continued support of this research.

REFERENCES

Baker, S. A. 1993. Rattlesnake Ruin: The Question of Cannibalism and Violence in Anasazi Culture. *Canyon Legacy* 17:2–10.

Betz, J., C. Hughes, and J. Wong. 2003. The Definition of Massacre. *Social Philosophy Today* 17:9–19.

Billman, B. R., P. M. Lambert, and B. L. Leonard. 2000. Cannibalism, Warfare, and Drought in the Mesa Verde Region during the Twelfth Century A.D. *American Antiquity* 65(1):145–178.

Brooks, J. F. 2016. *Mesa of Sorrows: A History of the Awat'ovi Massacre.* W. W. Norton, New York.

Bullock, P. Y. 1991. A Reappraisal of Anasazi Cannibalism. *Kiva* 57(1):5–16.

Cordell, L. S., and M. E. McBrinn. 2012. *Archaeology of the Southwest.* 3rd ed. Left Coast Press, Walnut Creek, CA.

Darling, A. J. 1999. Review of *Man Corn: Cannibalism and Violence in the Prehistoric American Southwest* by C. G. Turner II and J. A. Turner. *Latin American Antiquity* 10(4):441–442.

Douglas, M. T., and A.L.W. Stodder. 2010. Skull Morphoology in the ALP Skeletal Series. In *Animas–La Plata Project: Volume XV—Bioarchaeology*, edited by E. M. Perry, A.L.W. Stodder, and C. A. Bollong, pp. 197–222. Vol. 15. SWCA Environmental Consultants, Phoenix.

Flinn, L., C. G. Turner II, and A. Brew. 1976. Additional Evidence for Cannibalism in the Southwest: The Case of LA 4528. *American Antiquity* 41(3):303–318.

Grant, S. S. 1989. Secondary Burial or Cannibalism? An Example from New Mexico. *American Journal of Physical Anthropology* 78:230–231.

Kantner, A. 1998. Survival Cannibalism or Sociopolitical Intimidation? Explaining Perimortem Mutilation in the American Southwest. Paper presented at the 62nd Annual Society for American Archaeology Annual meeting, March 25–29, Seattle, WA.

Kuckelman, K. A., R. R. Lightfoot, and D. L. Martin. 2000. Changing Patterns of Violence in the Northern San Juan Region. *Kiva* 66(1):147–165.

Lambert, P. M. 2002. Review of *Man Corn: Cannibalism and Violence in the Prehistoric American Southwest* by Christy G. Turner II and Jacqueline A. Turner. *American Journal of Physical Anthropology* 119:294–296.

Malotki, E. (editor). 1993. *Hopi Ruin Legends-Kiqotutuwutsi. Narrated by M. Lomatuway'ma, L. Lomatuway'ma and S. Namingha.* University of Nebraska Press, Lincoln.

Marlar, R. 2010. Appendix B: Residue Analysis of Human Myoglobin and Human Hemoglobin Protein Samples. In *Animas–La Plata Final Synthetic Report. SWCA An-*

thropological Research Paper No. 10, edited by J. Potter. Vol. 16. SWCA Environmental Consultants, Phoenix.

Marlar, R. A., B. L. Leonard, B. R. Billman, P. M. Lambert, and J. E. Marlar. 2000. Biochemical Evidence of Cannibalism at a Prehistoric Puebloan Site in Southwestern Colorado. *Nature* 407:74–78.

Martin, D. L. 2000. Book Review: *Man Corn: Cannibalism and Violence in the Prehistoric American Southwest. American Antiquity* 65:199–201.

———. 2015. Beyond Epidemics: A Bioarchaeological Perspective on Pueblo-Spanish Encounters in the American Southwest. In *Beyond Germs: Native Depopulation in North America*, edited by C. M. Cameron, pp. 99–118. University of Arizona Press, Tucson.

Martin, D. L., and A. J. Osterholtz. 2015. The Poetics of Processing: Deviant Performances and Memory Making in the Ancient Southwest. Paper presented at the 114th American Anthropological Association Annual Meeting, November 18–22, Denver, CO.

Ortiz de Montellano, B. R. 1978. Aztec Cannibalism: An Ecological Necessity? *Science* 200(4342):611–617.

Osterholtz, A. J. 2013. Hobbling and Torture as Performative Violence: An Example from the Prehistoric Southwest. *Kiva* 78(2):123–144.

———. 2014a. Extreme Processing at Mancos and Sacred Ridge: The Value of Comparative Studies. In *Commingled and Disarticulated Human Remains: Working toward Improved Theory, Method, and Data*, edited by A. J. Osterholtz, K. M. Baustian, and D. L. Martin, pp. 105–128. Springer, New York.

———. 2014b. Patterned Processing as Performative Violence at Sacred Ridge. Paper presented at the 79th Annual Meeting of the Society for American Archaeology, April 23–27, Austin, TX.

Osterholtz, A. J., and R. P. Harrod. 2013. Warrior, Soldier, Big Man: Warrior Ethos, Identity Formation and the Negotiation of Social Roles in Multicultural Settings. Paper presented at the 78th Annual meeting of the Society for American Archaeology, April 3–7, Honolulu, HI.

Osterholtz, A. J., and D. L. Martin. 2017. The Poetics of Annihilation: On the Presence of Women and Children at Massacre Sites in the Ancient Southwest. In *Bioarchaeology of Women and Children in Times of War: Case Studies from the Americas*, edited by C. Tegtmeyer and D. L. Martin, pp. 111–128. Springer, New York.

Potter, J., and J. P. Chuipka. 2007. Early Pueblo Communities and Cultural Diversity in the Durango Area: Preliminary Results from the Animas–La Plata Project. *Kiva* 72(4):407–430.

———. 2010. Perimortem Mutilation of Human Remains in an Early Village in the American Southwest: A Case for Ethnic Violence. *Journal of Anthropological Archaeology* 29(4):507–523.

Singer, T., B. Seymour, J. O'Doherty, H. Kaube, R. J. Dolan, and C. D. Firth. 2004. Empathy for Pain Involves the Affective But Not Sensory Components of Pain. *Science* 303:1157–1162.

Somers, A. N. 1920. Prehistoric Cannibalism in America. *Wisconsin Archaeologist* 19(1):20–24.

Stodder, A.L.W., and A. J. Osterholtz. 2010. Analysis of the Processed Human Remains from the Sacred Ridge Site: Methods and Data Collection Protocol. In *Animas–La*

Plata Project: XV—Bioarchaeology, edited by E. M. Perry, A.L.W. Stodder, and C. A. Bollong, pp. 243–278. J. Potter, general editor. SWCA Environmental Consultants, Phoenix.

Stodder, A.L.W., A. J. Osterholtz, K. Mowrer, and J. P. Chuipka. 2010. Processed Human Remains from the Sacred Ridge Site: Context, Taphonomy, Interpretation. In *Animas–La Plata Project: XV—Bioarchaeology*, edited by E. M. Perry, A.L.W. Stodder, and C. A. Bollong, pp. 279–415. SWCA Environmental Consultants, Phoenix.

Turner, C. G., II, and N. Morris. 1970. A Massacre at Hopi. *American Antiquity* 35(3):320–331.

Turner, C. G., II, and J. A. Turner. 1992. The First Claim for Cannibalism in the Southwest: Walter Hough's 1901 Discovery at Canyon Butte Ruin 3, Northeastern Arizona. *American Antiquity* 57(4):661–682.

———. 1999. *Man Corn: Cannibalism and Violence in the Prehistoric American Southwest.* University of Utah Press, Salt Lake City.

White, T. D. 1992. *Prehistoric Cannibalism at Mancos 5MTUMR-2346.* Princeton University Press, Princeton.

Whitehead, N. L. 2004. On the Poetics of Violence. In *Violence*, edited by N. L. Whitehead, pp. 55–78. SAR Press, Santa Fe.

———. 2005. War and Violence as Cultural Expression. *Anthropology News* 46(5):23–26.

———. 2007. Violence & the Cultural Order. *Daedalus* 136(1):40–50.

7

Bones in the Village

Fragmentary Human Bones and Scattered Contexts from the Crow Creek Village

P. WILLEY

Archaeological identification of warfare and raiding has employed several approaches. In the Middle Missouri River region, the potential for such hostilities has been inferred from archaeological settlement patterns such as the occupation of readily defendable locations, settings often further protected by dry moats and palisades (Caldwell 1964). As an example, this settlement pattern occurs at the Arzberger Site in central South Dakota (map 7.1). The actuality of violence is indicated by unusual deposition of skeletons in the Middle Missouri region, such as those remains discovered on lodge floors at the Fay Tolton (AD 1036–1258, Butler 1976; Johnson 2007:74; Wood 1976), Larson (ca. AD 1750–1786, Owsley et al. 1977), Helb (AD 1304–1433, Johnson 2007:68; Pringle 1998), and Tony Glas (Pringle 1998) sites (map 7.1). Finally, the occurrence of violence has also been suggested by fresh-bone alterations to human skeletal remains. At the Fay Tolton and Larson sites, burning and fresh-bone modifications have been identified (Bass and Berryman 1976; Holliman and Owsley 1994; Owsley et al. 1977). Scalping has been documented at several Coalescent Tradition sites (Kendell 2016:118; Owsley 1994) as well as Middle Missouri Tradition sites (Holliman and Owsley 1994; Pringle 1998). Fortifications, unusual contexts of skeletons, and skeletal alterations all converged at the Crow Creek Site to demonstrate the occurrence of a massacre.[1]

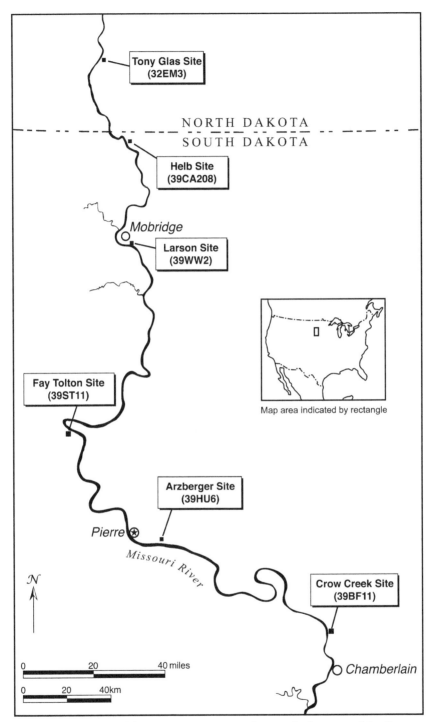

Map 7.1. Map of the Middle Missouri River region showing the locations of the Crow Creek Site and other sites mentioned in the text. (Drawn by Judy Stolen.)

Context

The Crow Creek Site (39BF11; map 7.1) was a large, well-fortified village in central South Dakota on the east bank of the Missouri River. It had two components (Kivett and Jensen 1976). The earlier one came from the Middle Missouri tradition, which began in the region about AD. 1000. About AD 1300 there was an intrusion into the Middle Missouri region from the Central Plains region to the south (Krause 2001; Lehmer 1971). The Central Plains tradition originated in that region about AD 900 and was similar to the Middle Missouri tradition in some ways. For more details concerning the Central Plains tradition, see Wedel's (2001) summary. The amalgamation of the Central Plains and Middle Missouri traditions resulted in the Coalescent tradition. The later component at Crow Creek represented the Initial Coalescent tradition.

Crow Creek is best known for the human bone bed (Bamforth 1994) in one end of the long, bastioned fortification ditch (figure 7.1). The deposit is generally attributed to the Initial Coalescent tradition in the early fourteenth century (see Bamforth and Nepstad-Thornberry 2007 for a later occupation date). Located in the extreme northwest corner of the site, the Bone Bed was discovered in 1978 when erosion exposed its western end (Zimmerman et al. 1981). The Bone Bed consisted of the partially articulated remains of at least 486 individuals, representing all age groups and both sexes (Willey 1990; Willey and Emerson 1993; Zimmerman 1997; Zimmerman et al. 1981).

The Bone Bed's context indicated that a single event produced the remains. The bodies had been mutilated, with many of the bones displaying indications of fresh-bone blunt force and sharp force modifications, and a few suggesting thermal alteration. The bodies had been exposed above ground and chewed by scavengers before being gathered and placed in the ditch then covered with a thin layer of dirt (Willey 1990; Willey and Emerson 1993; Zimmerman 1997; Zimmerman et al. 1981).

In addition to the striking indications of warfare portrayed by the context and remains of the Bone Bed, more subtle indications of the massacre occurred in the interior of the village itself. Excavations in the 1950s uncovered the village remains, but that evidence went largely unnoticed and misinterpreted. Without the 1978 discovery of the Bone Bed, misinterpretations of bones scattered in the village might have continued, and misunderstandings of the significance of those Village remains would have been perpetuated.

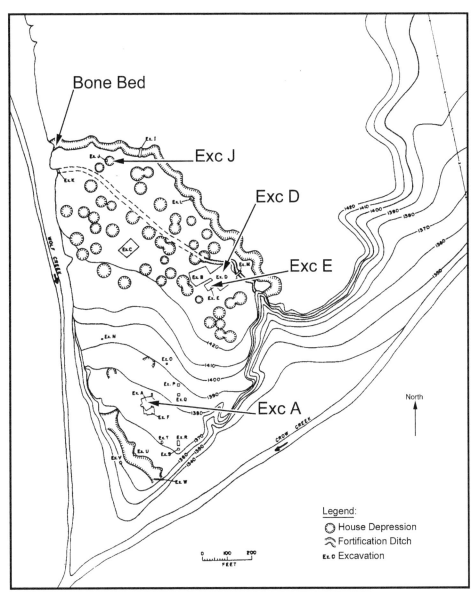

Figure 7.1. Map of Crow Creek Site showing location of Bone Bed and excavation units ("Exc") inside the Village where human bones were recovered. (Modified from Kivett and Jensen 1976:2, figure 1, published with permission of the Nebraska State Historical Society.)

The Crow Creek Site was surveyed and tested in the 1940s and 1950s by Smithsonian Institution–River Basin Survey crews and was more extensively tested by Marvin Kivett and crews from the Nebraska State Historical Society (NSHS) in 1954 and 1955 (Kivett and Jensen 1976). The later prehistoric occupation—the one of interest here—represented the Initial Coalescent tradition. The NSHS excavated five Initial Coalescent houses completely, sampled others, and tested sections of the fortification ditches. Despite the presence of burned lodges and disarticulated human remains, earlier researchers misinterpreted those materials.

As an example of misinterpretation, one of these earlier excavations (figure 7.1, Excavation J) exposed a partially disarticulated Initial Coalescent skeleton with cutmarks. It was found near the bottom of a pit (Feature 185) inside a house. Writing before the 1978 discovery of the Bone Bed, Kivett and Jensen (1976:27) claimed: "Considering the lack of care in interment and the possibility of mutilation, this individual was apparently not an important member of the Wolf Creek [Initial Coalescent] society and may have represented a member of another tribe." Following discovery of the massacre, it became probable that the skeleton represented a full-fledged Crow Creek village member and one of the massacre victims, not an unimportant person or from another tribe.

Considering this misinterpretation and the likelihood of other errors, it behooves us to reexamine the Crow Creek skeletal remains from the perspective of the massacre and in light of recent osteological improvements. Although the Bone Bed remains are no longer available (reburied in 1981), scattered remains from inside the village proper were available for examination. Here "Village" materials mean those elements found *inside* the Village, contrasted with remains from the fortification ditch's Bone Bed.

In addition to correcting erroneous conclusions of previous analyses, reexamination of the Crow Creek Village specimens enhances understanding of the massacre. Because nearly all of the previous conclusions concerning the massacre came from the Bone Bed materials, the Village elements offer an additional perspective on those events.

The Bone Bed elements presumably represented those bones and body parts gathered in or near the Village and placed in the fortification ditch. On the other hand, the Village remains were those that were overlooked during the gathering, or for other reasons went unrecovered during the collection that concentrated the bones in the Bone Bed. As a consequence, the two assemblages—the Bone Bed and the Village remains—should be complementary. When they are not complementary, processes other than the gathering—such as scavenging, trophy taking, and excavating bias—may have caused the differences.

MATERIALS AND CONTEXT

The NSHS excavated the Village materials during its 1954 and 1955 field seasons. Proveniences of the materials were reestablished by personnel in the Smithsonian Institution Repatriation Office (Billeck et al. 2002) using Kivett and Jensen's (1976) published report, NSHS field survey notes, and excavation log. Those provenience determinations were employed here.

The Village remains were found scattered across the site (figure 7.1). This summary of the elements' contexts follows their spatial distribution, beginning with those remains found in the northern portion of the Village closest to the Bone Bed.

Human bones were recovered from a partially excavated lodge (Excavation J) located in the northern portion of the Village (figure 7.1, Exc J). Found in a pit inside a house, those remains consisted of a partially disarticulated skeleton, as mentioned above.

Additional elements were discovered in another location (Excavations D and E) close to the fortification ditch (figure 7.1, Exc D and Exc E). Near the south end of the ditch, these elements included a partial postcranium in a pit near an older, inner fortification ditch (Feature 101); a few cranial and postcranial fragments from postholes near and in the inner ditch (Feature 120); a cranial fragment from a house floor (Feature 102); an innominate in a pit inside a house (Feature 116); and a femur and cranial remains in pits outside other houses (Features 110, 142 and 119/104A).

The Initial Coalescent elements most distant from the Bone Bed consisted of cranial remains near the south end of the village (figure 7.1, Exc A). The context of the elements was somewhat uncertain, but they appeared to be associated with an Initial Coalescent house. A note with some of the curated elements indicated that the bones may have been found in a posthole.

In conclusion, the locations and contexts where the Village remains were recovered contradicted normal burial practices and disproved an attack focused only on one corner of the Village. The locations in the Village where bones were recovered spread across the much of the site. All major excavation units involving Initial Coalescent features uncovered human bones. The elements were scattered on house floors, in storage pits, and in postholes. The bodies were found in various degrees of disarticulation.

Methods

Examination of the Village human remains occurred in 1981 and again twenty years later, in 2001. Nearly all of the materials—and to some extent the questions—were the same, but the understanding of the materials and the processes differed.

The elements and the element portions present were identified. In addition, the sex and age of the remains were estimated to provide a demographic profile (Willey and Emerson 1993; Willey 1990). "Subadults" were individuals aged less than 18 years, "adolescents" a subset of subadults (12–18 years), and "adults" 18 years and older. Demographic parameters provided a context for perimortem and postmortem alterations of the elements.

The remains were examined for indications of sharp force, blunt force and thermal alterations. Sharp force alterations are produced by knives, blades, axes and other sharp objects and produce cuts, stabs or hacks (Galloway et al. 1999:5). Blunt force trauma is caused by round or flat objects striking tissues or the tissues striking the objects (Galloway et al. 1999:5). Blunt force usually produces larger areas of damage than those involved in sharp force. Thermal alteration occurs when tissues are heated (Fairgrieve 2008; Thompson 2009). The resulting changes to bones may be as slight as merely smoking or burning the element surfaces, thus blackening the bones but otherwise little modifying them. At the other extreme, thermally altered bones may be calcinated so that the elements display warping, extreme fragmentation, and white or light gray color. The Village remains were also examined for adhering pigments and scavenger activity. Puncture marks and splintering of bone ends indicated scavenger activity (Haglund 1997).

The second examination (2001) expanded, refined, and corrected the taphonomic and fresh-bone assessments of the earlier inspection. It refined the element and demographic assessments of the earlier examination, employing more recent studies and understandings.

Interpretations of the Village elements required comparisons with the Bone Bed elements.

Results, Comparisons, and Discussion

Discussion of the results begins with the basic demographic data and proceeds to the more specialized taphonomic analyses. Element inventory and minimum number of individuals, combined with age at death and sex, are offered first. Fresh-bone alterations, including those involving sharp force, blunt force, and scavenger modifications, are then detailed. Other alterations, such as thermal alterations and pigmentation, follow.

Elements and Minimum Number of Individuals

The Village bone fragments represented all major anatomical regions. The elements included cranial parts, some teeth, a few other axial elements, pectoral and pelvic girdle bones, pectoral and pelvic limb bones, and even a few tarsals and metatarsals (table 7.1).

Table 7.1. Element inventory of human skeletal remains from the Crow Creek Village Initial Coalescent component and the Crow Creek Bone Bed

	Village		Bone Bed[a]	
Element	Number	Percentage	Number	Percentage
Mandible	1	2.0	453	3.3
Vertebrae				
Cervicals	1	2.0	1608	11.8
Thoracics	10	19.6	3436	25.2
Lumbars	5	9.8	1671	12.3
Sacrum	1	2.0	405	3.0
Coccyx	0	0	46	0.3
Sternum	0	0	54	0.4
Scapula	3	5.9	509	3.7
Clavicle	4	7.8	228	1.7
Humerus	3	5.9	475	3.5
Radius	2	3.9	255	1.9
Ulna	2	3.9	268	2.0
Carpals	0	0	94	0.7
Metacarpals	0	0	52	0.4
Hand phalanges	0	0	44	0.3
Innominate	3	5.9	1155	8.5
Femur	3	5.9	906	6.6
Patella	1	2.0	40	0.3
Tibia	3	5.9	595	4.4
Fibula	4	7.8	477	3.5
Tarsals	2	3.9	558	4.1
Metatarsals	3	5.9	297	2.2
Foot phalanges	0	0	12	0.1
Total	51	100.1	13638	100.2

[a] Bone Bed counts modified from Willey 1990: 21, table 4. Rib and skull fragments are excluded from this inventory.

Comparisons with the Bone Bed element identifications were meaningful, although omission of the cranial and rib fragments was necessary for comparability between the two inventories. Many of the Village and the Bone Bed elements occurred in similar proportions, including mandibles, thoracics, lumbars, sacra, coccyxes, sterna, scapulae, humeri, radii, ulnae, carpals, metacarpals, hand and foot phalanges, innominates, femora, tibiae, and tarsals. However, Village elements showed proportionally more clavicles, patellae, fibulae, and metatarsals than the Bone Bed. In addition, the Village remains had proportionally fewer cervicals than the Bone Bed remains. It is possible that cervical underrepresentation among the Village remains resulted from decapitations and trophy taking by the raiders or collection for burial in the Bone Bed. The Village's small sample size, however, probably produced most of these differences.

The minimum number of individuals among the Village remains was derived from cranial material. Based on duplicated portions of adults and the presence of a probable subadult, at least three individuals were present. Considering the additional noncranial elements present and their widespread distribution across the site, this number must be considered an absolute minimum. With this probability in mind, the widespread materials are considered separately by accession throughout the rest of the analysis.

Demography

Age at Death

Both the Bone Bed and the Village remains included elements of adults and subadults. All but 2 of the 11 Village accessions represented adults or probable adults (82 percent adults).

The Village materials had proportionally more adults than the Bone Bed. The Bone Bed elements (Willey 1990:47, table 7.13) included 192 subadults (<20 years) and 145 adults—43 percent adults. A statistically significant difference occurred between the age categories of the Village materials and those from the Bone Bed ($X^2 = 6.50$, $df = 1$, $p < 0.025$). This underrepresentation of adults in the Bone Bed was unexpected: adult remains, being larger, should have been more easily discovered, gathered, and placed in the ditch than the smaller subadult remains. It is possible that after Village remains were gathered the subadult materials, being smaller and less dense, were more completely destroyed by taphonomic processes, such as scavengers, than the adult bones. It was also possible, although less probable, that subadult bones were more likely to be uncovered during the Village excavations.

Sex

Village remains consisted of three females (including one probable female) and three males (including two questionable or probable males). In addition to these individuals with sex estimations, five other sets of adult remains had undetermined sexes.

The Village sex ratio can be compared with the sex ratio derived from the Bone Bed remains. Employing more accurate innominates, the Bone Bed adult sex distribution approached a 1:1 ratio (99 males to 82 females; Willey 1990:48). No statistically significant difference between the sex distributions by Village or Bone Bed locations existed (Fisher's Exact = 1.000). This result suggested that both sexes were murdered and that the remains of each sex were equally gathered for placement in the Bone Bed.

Sharp Force Modifications

Scalping

Among the few Crow Creek Village remains, three frontals were present— the bone that most frequently displays cuts indicating scalping. Two of those three frontals showed cuts that may have been caused during scalping. One individual (Excavation D/E, Feature 104A/F119, young adult male) had a shallow cut (10.6 mm long) on the superior portion of the frontal. Another (Excavation D, Feature 142, possible subadult) had two partial cuts on fragments of a right parietal. The third specimen, a nearly complete skull (Excavation D/E, Feature 104, adult female), showed no cuts.

Among the Bone Bed materials, approximately 90 percent of the frontals displayed cuts, suggesting scalping or at least scalping attempts (Willey 1990:106, table 32). In general, the Village materials showed similarities with what would be expected. The absence of cuts on a relatively complete Village skull (Feature 104) was surprising and may have indicated its inaccessibility, to both the raiders and recoverers alike.

Decapitation and Dismemberment

Many of the Bone Bed elements displayed cuts suggesting decapitation. Approximately 25 percent of the first cervical (atlas) vertebrae had cuts on the anterior surfaces; the adjacent occipital condyles and second cervicals (axis) vertebrae revealed similar, although less frequent, cuts (Willey 1990:106). However, neither the Village fragmentary second cervical (Excavation D, Feature 101, young adult) nor the cranium with occipital condyles (Excavation D/E, Feature 104, young adult female) had such modifications.

Despite the absence of cuts suggesting decapitations, the Crow Creek Village remains had numerous cuts on other postcranial elements, some of which suggest dismemberment. The most notable example of postcranial cuts among the Village remains was an adolescent skeleton found in a lodge near the Bone Bed (Excavation J, Feature 185)—the one that Kivett and Jensen (1976:27) interpreted as possibly an unimportant village member or a member of another tribe. It had at least fifteen cuts on the distal right humerus (figure 7.2A1 and A2), the longest being 5.9 mm. Such cuts were consistent with attempts to disjoint the right elbow and remove the forearm from the upper arm—possibly a successful effort, because the right forearm and hand were absent. Both innominates displayed at least one cut on the ilium, perhaps indicating attempts to remove the thigh from the hip.

Some of the Bone Bed postcranial elements had similar cuts (Willey 1990:123–125, table 41), although the frequency of the Bone Bed cuts was much less than in the Village materials. Of the 2,427 limb bones in the Bone Bed, only 19 (0.8 percent) presented cuts (Willey 1990:16, table 2).

In addition to the greater frequency of cuts, the Village materials also showed some forms of sharp force that were absent in the Bone Bed elements. One form consisted of cuts on bone shafts distant from joints and apparently not associated with dismemberment. The unfortunate adolescent (Excavation J, Feature 185) mentioned above was the prime example. This individual suffered cuts on the posterior surfaces of two left ribs (longest cut 9.2 mm, figure 7.2B); a deep cut (11.25 mm long) on the lateral midshaft of the right humerus near the deltoid tuberosity (figure 7.2C); two cuts on the right tibia: a shallow cut (14.1 mm long, figure 7.2D) on the proximal medial tibia shaft and a deep cut (8.4 mm long, figure 7.2E) on the medial tibia distal shaft; and a deep cut on the proximal posterior right fibula shaft (5.3 mm long, figure 7.2F). Although it is possible that all of these cuts represented dismemberment, they would indicate relatively ineffective butchering attempts, which would not be expected of people familiar with butchering large game. Perhaps these deep cuts indicated more extensive mutilation of corpses located within easy reach of the raiders but not so easily recovered for burial.

An additional form of cutting was observed on another Crow Creek Village specimen. It had many cuts in a single anatomical location. A right

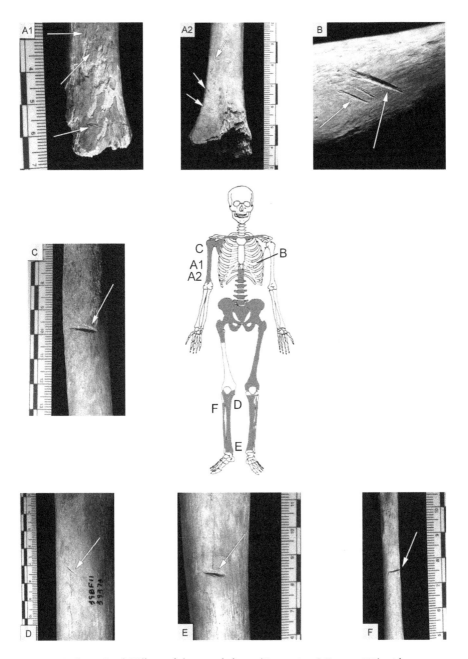

Figure 7.2. Crow Creek Village adolescent skeleton (Excavation J, Feature 185) with cuts on postcranial elements. The remains were recovered from a pit in a lodge near the Bone Bed. Shaded bones are present (ribs and vertebrae omitted from this inventory sketch). Scales in centimeters. Arrows indicate cutmarks. (*A1*) Shallow cuts, anterior distal humerus; (*A2*) Shallow cuts, posterior distal humerus; (*B*) Shallow cuts, posterior external rib surface; (*C*) Deep cut, lateral humerus midshaft; (*D*) Shallow cut, proximal medial tibia shaft; (*E*) Deep cut, medial distal tibia shaft; (*F*) Deep cut, proximal posterior fibula shaft.

maxilla with four teeth, zygomatic, and a portion of the palate (Excavation A, Feature 2, young adult male?) displayed extensive, concentrated cutmarks. Along the maxilla's infraorbital margin at least five shallow cuts occurred (longest 7.2 mm). The external surface of the zygomatic suffered at least eleven shallow cuts (longest 10.3 mm), and the external alveolar surface had six cuts (longest 9 mm).

Such defacing probably indicated extensive processing, not haphazard butchering or even casual mutilation. In other Northern Plains skeletal series, similar alterations have been identified as mortuary processing associated with secondary burial (Olson and Shipman 1994). In the case of some Northern Plains secondary burials, remains were defleshed with sharp tools, often leaving "short, fine cutmarks . . . similar to filleting marks" (Olson and Shipman 1994:380–381).

Intentions other than preparation for burial are also likely in the case of the Crow Creek Village remains. Because no indications of burial or mortuary intention emerged, the most likely purpose of the concentrated shallow cuts was to remove soft tissue from the bones and those processed parts retained as "trophies" or mementos, perhaps by the Crow Creek villagers themselves before the raid. Additional apparent trophies have been described from other sites on the Plains (Owsley et al. 1994:368–369). It is also possible, however, that the successful raiders made the cuts, although this scenario would require that the victors occupied the Village for a considerable period (a point discussed later).

Among the Bone Bed materials, in contrast, such extensive processing of remains was unusual. The major exception to this generalization consisted of possible skull bowls from the Bone Bed. Two of those four human bone artifacts displayed grooving around the neurocranium, snapping along the groove, then smoothing the broken rough edge (Willey 1990:141–142). Such manufacturing steps required considerable attention and time.

Pigmentation

Two of the Crow Creek Village elements exhibited red pigment on their surfaces. One was an adult mandibular horizontal ramus with four teeth (Excavation D, Feature 120), and the other was an adult right parietal fragment (Excavation A, Feature 2A). Although chemical analyses were not performed, the pigment was consistent with red ochre or another iron oxide.

Similar to the facial skeleton with extensive cutting, the pigmented mandible and parietal demonstrated processing of elements, specifically portions of the faces and cranial vaults. This processing may have been performed before the massacre by the Crow Creek Villagers themselves, keeping parts of friends, foes, or both as trophies or mementos; or it may have happened following the massacre, performed by the victors, processing some of the corpses. This second interpretation would require occupation of the site by the victors for a relatively long period rather than a tactic of hit, conquer, and depart. It is also possible that survivors who returned to scour the village following the massacre performed the processing. Few—if any—of the Bone Bed remains had such adhering pigments.

Blunt Force Modifications

Cranial Fractures

The Crow Creek Village materials included four crania with indications of blunt force trauma. The first one (Excavation A, Feature 2) had a possible right-to-left fracture through the maxilla's frontal process; the probable aboriginal "curation" of the specimen is notable; and the possibility of careless handling or processing must be considered as likely a cause as perimortem forces. The second specimen (Excavation D, Feature 120) consisted of an occipital and right parietal fragment with an internal fracture. No fracture showed on the external surface—a classic example of bone failing first on the tension side and not breaking on the compression side. The most likely direction of force was from posterior or posterior-lateral toward the anterior. The third specimen (Excavation D/E, Feature 104) had a possible fracture of the right zygomatic, although this assessment remained questionable. The fourth specimen (Excavation D/E, Feature 119/104A; figure 7.3) was the anterior portion of a cranium, which displayed two fresh-bone fractures. One of those fractures passed through the coronal suture into the frontal (figure 7.3A); the other was a possible perimortem break through the left zygomatic and adjacent portions of the maxilla (figure 7.3B).

Depressed or linear fractures were found on 40 percent of the more complete Bone Bed crania (Willey 1990:114). The Village and Bone Bed materials had similar frequencies.

Postcranial Fractures

Some elements of the Village postcranial remains exhibited modifications that may have been caused by blunt force. All of these postcranial modifications occurred in a single skeleton—a hapless young adult (Excavation D, Feature 101; figure 7.4). That individual's proximal right humerus, both

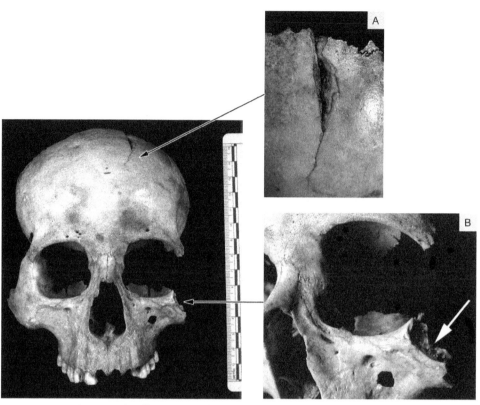

Figure 7.3. Crow Creek Village young adult male anterior cranium (Excavation D/E, Feature 119/104A, 39BF11-39349) with fresh bone fractures. Scale in centimeters. (*A*) Break near coronal suture; (*B*) Possible fresh-bone break (*white arrow*) near left zygomatic arch.

proximal and distal ends of both radii (figures 7.4A1 and 7.4A2), both proximal and distal ends of both ulnae (figure 7.4A1), the distal end of the left, and both ends of both fibulae (figure 7.4B) were splintered. Although these may have been caused by blunt force, as suggested here, another possibility is that they resulted from scavenger chewing. But none of the elements had the puncture or scraping marks diagnostic of scavenging (Lynn Snyder, personal communication, 2001). Apparently similar alterations were present in one of the Fay Tolton specimens; those fractured forearms were interpreted as having been broken to aid removal of the hands (Holliman and Owsley 1994:348). A similar process may explain the modifications to the Crow Creek Village forearm bones.

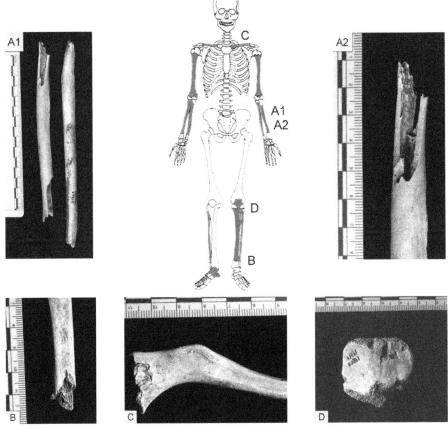

Figure 7.4. Crow Creek Village young adult partial skeleton (Excavation D, Feature 101) with fresh-bone breaks and chewing. (*A1*) Left radius and ulna with fresh-bone fractures; (*A2*) Close-up proximal end of left radius with fresh-bone fracture; (*B*) Left distal fibula with fresh-bone fractures; (*C*) Left lateral clavicle inferior surface with chewing; (*D*) Left patella articular surface with chewing.

Evulsions

Several Crow Creek Village dentitions showed evulsions, the forcible removal of teeth and/or the adjacent alveolar process. A young adult female's (Excavation D/E, Feature 104) right maxillary canine had a possible evulsion. A right maxilla and zygomatic (Excavation A, Feature 2) had a maxillary right first premolar and second molar with modifications possibly caused by force, although this damage may have been caused by heat (see below). And a young adult male's facial skeleton (Excavation D/E, Feature

119/104A) had a left maxillary second incisor and possibly a right maxillary canine that were evulsed.

Approximately 25 percent of the Bone Bed dentitions had indications of evulsions (Willey 1990:106, table 32). The Village and Bone Bed dentitions were generally similar in this regard.

Thermal Alterations

Several Crow Creek Village specimens demonstrated alterations consistent with singeing. The dental arcade of the young adult male mentioned above (shallow cuts and possible blunt force trauma; Excavation A, Feature 2) may also have shown thermal alteration. In addition, a parietal fragment of a probable subadult (Excavation D, Feature 142) had smoking or light burning on both internal and external surfaces. The frontal of a young adult female (Excavation D/E, Feature 104) had possible light smoking on the surface.

Few indications of light burning or smoking occurred among the Bone Bed materials; none was calcined (M. Swegle in Zimmerman et al. 1981:182–186). Generally the Bone Bed thermal alterations were similar to those of the Village remains. These results were surprising. Remains found in the Village, often in burned and collapsed lodges, should have been more frequently and extensively burned than those that had been gathered and placed in the fortification ditch.

It is possible that burning of the Village and Bone Bed elements was comparable because the lodge burnings were incomplete and allowed access to the burned remains inside lodges and their recovery for burial in the Bone Bed. It is also possible that the thermal alterations were not an accidental result of the lodge burnings but were performed purposefully as a part of mutilating the corpses. In that case whether or not the lodges were burned would have had little effect on the frequency of burning of the bones.

Scavenger Chewing

Some Crow Creek Village elements displayed scavenger chewing. Generally found in locations similar to those in the Bone Bed, the alterations typically occurred at or near the ends of long bones, such as those of the young adult in Excavation D (Feature 101). Its clavicles' lateral ends (figure 7.4C), the distal left humerus, possibly the right ulna, and the distal left tibia had punctures and splintering. It is also possible that its radii and ulnae were scavenged, although those alterations were more likely caused by blunt force trauma (see above). Some short bones also displayed punctures, such as the left patella (figure 7.4D) and right calcaneous. The anterior superior iliac spine of another individual (Excavation E, Feature 116) showed similar punctures.

The Bone Bed remains displayed chewing on as many as 25 percent of the specimens, depending on the element and portion of element. In both the Bone Bed and Village assemblages, the most exposed and distal portions were most frequently scavenged. The other characteristics of scavenging appeared to be comparable as well.

Conclusions and Summary

The earlier misidentification of violence based on those remains was not unexpected, considering the few and fragmentary elements recovered from the village excavations, a confounding of earlier and later occupational components, and the equivocal nature of the evidence for warfare. In part, however, the incorrect interpretations resulted from influences other than simple small sample size and element fragmentation.

The progress in osteological techniques and interpretations in the decades since the recovery of the Bone Bed remains has been remarkable. Strides in techniques and interpreting fresh-bone alterations permit more precise and reliable interpretations, specifically those related to sharp force, blunt force, scavenging, chewing, and burning in the present instance.

Some Village remains indicated alterations in keeping with what had been described among the Bone Bed remains. However, other alterations of Village elements suggested more elaborate actions. As an example, the adolescent excavated from a pit inside a lodge had numerous cuts on the thorax, arm, and leg, some of which were deep. No comparable frequency or depth of cutting occurred on any of the Bone Bed specimens. The time required to make these cuts, together with the possibility of processing skulls as trophies, suggests the possibility that the raiders occupied the village for a while, not as a simple attack-conquer-and-run tactic.

Burning the bodies and lodges likely marked the end of corpse mutilation and the raiders' occupation of the village. Both element burning and scavenging seem to have occurred with approximately the same frequency and severity in both the Bone Bed and Village elements.

Gathering body parts, placing them in the fortification ditch, and covering them (thus forming the Bone Bed) were presumed to have been done by surviving village members, family member and allies from other villages, or some combination of those people. The conquering raiders would not be likely to provide such respect or expend the energy required. If the raiders occupied the village for a long period, however, such a possibility is more likely (see Komar 2008).

The gathered (Bone Bed) and omitted (Village) elements should have been complementary, but the two sets of specimens were generally comparable. This indicated relatively random collection of Village elements and burial. The exceptions to this generalization were the more frequent superior body portions and subadult remains in the Bone Bed. The Village elements included proportionally more inferior body and adult remains—the denser elements. This distribution may have reflected the taphonomic effects of scavenging and weathering after the gathering. Denser bones more frequently survive than less dense elements (Willey et al. 1997).

It is unfortunate that these approaches and understandings were not available decades ago when the Bone Bed materials were being analyzed. The Bone Bed remains were delivered to the Crow Creek Sioux Tribe in May 1979 and buried in August 1981. It is also unfortunate that the improvements of the decades to come will not be applied to the Crow Creek Village remains, which are slated for return to the Plains and reburial in the near future.

Analyzing the Village osteological materials has added insights into the Crow Creek massacre and the subsequent events. Their spatial distribution elaborated what was suggested by the Bone Bed elements. Violence occurred at many Crow Creek Village locations, spread across the site and not limited to the northwestern part of the site adjacent to the Bone Bed. This widespread distribution and the staggering body count indicate a general devastation of the village in the massacre. Because of this wholesale engagement, the probability rises that additional remains were left scattered across the unexcavated portions of the village. It is even possible that an additional bone bed (or beds) exists in the Village or other parts of the fortification ditch.

Although this chapter has emphasized that indications of violence have been overlooked in previous analyses of the site, the point should not be overstated. Villages circled by fortification ditches, burned lodges, or scattered human remains found on house floors do not necessarily prove that a successful raid occurred. Similarly, remains that were burned or showed cuts or fresh bone breaks do not always indicate interpersonal violence. To commit the reverse error—incorrectly identifying violence where none occurred—would be a grievous mistake (see Milner et al. 2000 for such a revision concerning a site in the U.S. Southeast).

ACKNOWLEDGMENTS

Larry Zimmerman, then at the University of South Dakota, served as principal investigator, overseeing the fieldwork and laboratory analysis of the Crow Creek Bone Bed. Thomas Emerson functioned as field director, guiding the excavations of the Bone Bed. The Corps of Engineers, Omaha District, funded the work (Purchase Order DACW45-78-C-0018).

Gayle Carlson and Marvin Kivett, Nebraska State Historical Society (NSHS), provided permission to examine the Crow Creek Village materials in 1981. And the NSHS kindly gave permission to reproduce the Crow Creek Site map (figure 7.1). Steve Ousley and Bill Bellick of the Smithsonian Institution's Repatriation Program provided space and permission to examine the Village materials again in 2001. Elizabeth V. Eubanks of Smithsonian Institution's Repatriation Program provided a draft of her report on the context and affiliations of the Crow Creek materials. Lynn Snyder examined the modified radii and ulnae of Excavation D, Feature 101.

Shannah Miilu, an intern with Chico State's Technology and Learning Program, executed the layout of the photographs. Judy Stolen, my long-suffering wife, drew the regional site map (map 7.1) and modified the NSHS map (figure 7.1).

Abbreviated versions of this paper were presented in a symposium organized by William Belcher and John Byrd at the Society for American Archaeology Annual Meeting, New Orleans, 2001, as well as a symposium organized by Debra Martin and Cheryl Anderson at the American Association of Physical Anthropology, Atlanta, 2016. William Belcher and John Byrd read and edited an earlier version of this chapter and kindly gave permission to publish it in this volume.

NOTE

1. Massacre: a brief, purposeful, violent event that results in the homicide of a substantial portion of a group. In addition to typical combatant deaths, casualties usually include relatively helpless non-fighters among the fatalities.

REFERENCES

Bamforth, D. B. 1994. Indigenous People, Indigenous Violence: Precontact Warfare on the North American Great Plains. *Man*, new series 29(1):95–115.

Bamforth, D. B., and C. Nepstad-Thornberry. 2007. Reconsidering the Occupational History of the Crow Creek Site (39BF11). *Plains Anthropologist* 52(202):153–173.

Bass, W. M., and H. E. Berryman. 1976. Physical Analysis. In *Fay Tolton and the Initial Middle Missouri Variant*, edited by W. R. Wood, pp. 29–31. Research Series, No. 13. Missouri Archaeological Society, Columbia.

Billeck, W. T., E. Eubanks, A. Lockard, and P. Cash. 2002. Inventory and Assessment of Human Remains Potentially Affiliated with the Arikara in the National Museum of Natural History, Smithsonian Institution. Unpublished report, Smithsonian Institution Repatriation Program, Washington, DC.

Butler, W. B. 1976. Human Skeletal Remains. In *Fay Tolton and the Initial Middle Missouri Variant*, edited by W. R. Wood, pp. 27–29. Research Series, No. 13. Missouri Archaeological Society, Columbia.

Caldwell, W. W. 1964. Fortified Villages in the Northern Plains. *Plains Anthropologist* 9(23):1–7.

Fairgrieve, S. I. 2008. *Forensic Cremation: Recovery and Analysis*. CRC Press, Boca Raton, FL.

Galloway, A., S. A. Symes, W. D. Haglund, and D. L. France. 1999. The Role of Forensic Anthropology in Trauma Analysis. In *Broken Bones*, edited by A. Galloway, pp. 5–31. C. C. Thomas Press, Springfield.

Haglund, W. D. 1997. Dogs and Coyotes: Postmortem Involvement with Human Remains. In *Forensic Taphonomy: The Postmortem Fate of Human Remains*, edited by W. D. Haglund and M. H. Sorg, pp. 367–382. CRC Press, Boca Raton, FL.

Holliman, S. E., and D. W. Owsley. 1994. Osteology of the Fay Tolton Site: Implications for Warfare during the Initial Middle Missouri Variant. In *Skeletal Biology in the Great Plains*, edited by D. W. Owsley and R. L. Jantz, pp. 345–354. Smithsonian Institution Press, Washington, DC.

Johnson, C. M. 2007. *A Chronology of Middle Missouri Plains Village Sites*. Smithsonian Contributions to Anthropology, no. 47. Smithsonian Institution Press, Washington, DC.

Kendell, A. E. 2016. Examining Skeletal Trauma on the North American Great Plains: Applications of Coded Osteological Data from the Smithsonian Repatriation Database. PhD dissertation, Anthropology Department, Michigan State University.

Kivett, M. F., and R. E. Jensen. 1976. *Archaeological Excavations at the Crow Creek Site (39BF11), Ft. Randall Reservoir Area, South Dakota*. Publications in Anthropology No. 7. Nebraska State Historical Society, Lincoln.

Komar, D. 2008. Patterns of Mortuary Practice Associated with Genocide: Implications for Archaeological Research. *Current Anthropology* 49(1):123–133.

Krause, R. A. 2001. Plains Village Tradition: Coalescent. In *Handbook of North American Indians, Vol. 13*, edited by R. J. DeMallie, pp. 196–206. W. C. Sturtevant, general editor. Smithsonian Institution Press, Washington, DC.

Lehmer, D. J. 1971. *Introduction to Middle Missouri Archaeology*. National Park Service, Anthropological Papers 1. Department of the Interior, Washington, DC.

Milner, G. R., C. S. Larsen, D. L. Hutchinson, M. A. Williamson, and D. A. Humpf. 2000. Conquistadors, Excavators or Rodents: What Damaged the King Site Skeletons? *American Antiquity* 65(2):355–363.

Olson, S., and P. Shipman. 1994. Cutmarks and Perimortem Treatment of Skeletal Remains on the Northern Plains. In *Skeletal Biology in the Great Plains*, edited by D. W. Owsley and R. L. Jantz, pp. 377–387. Smithsonian Institution Press, Washington, DC.

Owsley, D. W. 1994. Warfare in Coalescent Tradition Populations of the Northern Plains. In *Skeletal Biology in the Great Plains: Migration, Warfare, Health, and Subsistence*, edited by D. W. Owsley and R. L. Jantz, pp. 333–344. Smithsonian Institution Press, Washington, DC.

Owsley, D. W., H. E. Berryman, and W. M. Bass. 1977. Demographic and Osteological Evidence of Warfare at the Larson Site, South Dakota. *Plains Anthropologist* 22(78):119–131.

Owsley, D. W., R. W. Mann, and T. G. Braugh. 1994. Culturally Modified Human Bones from the Edwards I Sites. In *Skeletal Biology in the Great Plains: Migration, Warfare, Health, and Subsistence*, edited by D. W. Owsley and R. L. Jantz, pp. 363–375. Smithsonian Institution Press, Washington, DC.

Pringle, H. 1998. Crow Creek's Revenge. *Science* 279:2039.

Thompson, T. 2009. Burned Human Remains. In *Handbook of Forensic Anthropology and Archaeology*, edited by S. Blau and D. H. Ubelaker, pp. 295–303. Left Coast Press, Walnut Creek, CA.

Wedel, W. R. 2001. Plains Village Tradition: Central. In *Handbook of North American Indians, Vol. 13*, edited by R. J. DeMallie, pp. 173–185. W. C. Sturtevant, general editor. Smithsonian Institution Press, Washington, DC.

Willey, P., and T. E. Emerson. 1993. The Osteology and Archaeology of the Crow Creek Massacre. *Plains Anthropologist* 38(145):227–269.

Willey, P., A. Galloway, and L. Snyder. 1997. Bone Mineral Density and Survival of Elements and Element Portions in the Bones of the Crow Creek Massacre Victims. *American Journal of Physical Anthropology* 104:513–528.

Willey, P. S. 1990. *Prehistoric Warfare on the Great Plains: Skeletal Analysis of the Crow Creek Massacre Victims*. Garland Publishing, New York.

Wood, W. R. (editor). 1976. *Fay Tolton and the Initial Middle Missouri Variant*. Research Series, No. 13. Missouri Archaeological Society, Columbia.

Zimmerman, L. J. 1997. The Crow Creek Massacre: Archaeology and Prehistoric Plains Warfare in Contemporary Contexts. In *Material Harm*, edited by J. Carman, pp. 75–94. Cruithne Press, Glasgow, Scotland.

Zimmerman, L. J., T. E. Emerson, P. Willey, M. Swegle, J. B. Gregg, P. Gregg, E. White, C. Smith, T. Haberman, and M. P. Bumstead. 1981. The Crow Creek Site (39BF11) Massacre: A Preliminary Report. Prepared by the University of South Dakota Archaeology Laboratory for the Omaha District, U.S. Army Corp of Engineers.

8

Khmer Rouge Regime Massacres

Skeletal Evidence of Violent Trauma in Cambodia

JULIE M. FLEISCHMAN, SONNARA PRAK, VUTHY VOEUN,
AND SOPHEARAVY ROS

The Khmer Rouge (KR) was a totalitarian regime directed by Pol Pot and his Communist Party of Kampuchea (CPK). In March 1976, one year after seizing control of Cambodia, the CPK established the new state of Democratic Kampuchea (DK) (Chandler 2000). Inspired by Mao Zedong's revolutionary Great Leap Forward in China, and an extreme focus on Cambodia's national pride, the Khmer Rouge established policies idealizing the peasantry and creating a complete agrarian economy (Kiernan 2006). The Khmer Rouge emptied nearly every city of its residents: all Cambodians were forcibly relocated to rural collective communities where they participated in agricultural and development projects for DK. Living conditions deteriorated rapidly, and disease and death were common.

The Khmer Rouge saw enemies—either real or imagined, within and outside of its own ranks, and regardless of age and sex—throughout Cambodia. In order to suppress these enemies, security centers were established to imprison, interrogate, torture, and often execute enemies and their families (Ea 2005). In conjunction with the systematic violence taking place at these security centers, historians estimate that approximately 1.7 to 2 million people (one-quarter of the Cambodian population at the time) died from mistreatment, overwork, disease, and malnutrition (Kiernan 2008).

In January 1979 the Vietnamese army, with support from Cambodians who managed to escape DK, overwhelmed the KR forces in Phnom Penh, ending the three years, eight months, and twenty days of DK. The

KR, however, retreated into the northern regions of Cambodia, where they remained a powerful guerrilla force for the next decade (Slocomb 2003). In the early years after the KR retreated, the newly established, Vietnamese-supported People's Republic of Kampuchea (PRK) government implemented initiatives to reveal the violence committed by the KR.

In 1980 the Khmer Rouge's central-level security center in Phnom Penh, referred to by the KR as S-21, was converted from a torture/execution center into the Tuol Sleng Genocide Museum (Hughes 2003; map 8.1). Additionally, the PRK tried Pol Pot and Ieng Sary (CPK's deputy prime minister for foreign affairs) in absentia for genocide, established a Genocide Research Committee to conduct exhumations of mass graves, and created a museum/memorial at the mass gravesite of Choeung Ek, today known as the Choeung Ek Genocidal Center (see below and map 8.1; Hughes 2003). The Choeung Ek Genocidal Center and the Tuol Sleng Genocide Museum are perhaps the most visible remnants of the PRK government.

As Hinton (2013) and Ledgerwood (1997) argue, the PRK codified and perpetuated KR violence to establish its legitimacy. Ultimately this representation of the KR period became the official state narrative of the past. The national narrative defined the KR regime as synonymous with death, brutality, and destruction, and all measures were to be taken to prevent the return of Pol Pot and his regime. The Tuol Sleng and Choeung Ek museums, as well as other memorials throughout the country containing human remains, were evidence or proof of the violence and death committed by the KR (Hinton 2013). For example, as Vietnamese general Mai Lam, the designer of the Tuol Sleng Genocide Museum, said, it is important for Cambodians to preserve the bones from the KR period because "it's the proof" (Ledgerwood 1997:89). This national discourse was perpetuated when a 2001 circular on the preservation of remains, signed by the current prime minister Hun Sen, stated that the mass graves and human remains throughout Cambodia stand as "evidence" and "physical testimony" of the KR regime's crimes (RGC 2001). Documenting and displaying KR violence is therefore a well-established practice.

This state-level narrative of KR brutality is an ingrained component of Cambodian history that persists as a culturally relevant ideology today. This chapter discusses how the discourse of KR violence is deployed as the impetus for conservation and memorialization of human skeletal remains throughout the county. The site of the Choeung Ek Genocidal Center is used as an illustration. The site's importance in Cambodian history

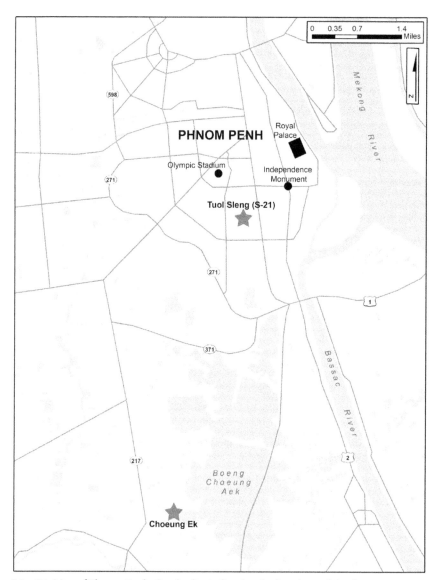

Map 8.1. Map of Phnom Penh, Cambodia, indicating the locations of the former security center Tuol Sleng (S-21) and the Choeung Ek Genocidal Center. (Created by Julie M. Fleischman.)

is detailed first, followed by a discussion of the recent project to conserve the human remains disinterred from mass graves. Finally, a case study documenting skeletal evidence of massacre—in this case, the intentional execution of thousands of individuals in one clandestine location—at the Choeung Ek Genocidal Center is presented.

Understanding Khmer Rouge Violence through Skeletal Analysis

The study of human skeletal remains resulting from fatal mass violence or genocide is imperative for numerous reasons. First, an analysis of remains can provide information that might not otherwise be available. In Cambodia, for example, KR survivors have described the brutal treatment of individuals, indicating that executions would often be carried out by a blow to the victim's head and/or neck (ECCC 2016c, 2016e, 2016f). Examining the remains from Cambodian mass graves can provide scientific evidentiary support for these accounts, while also providing evidence for additional mechanisms of execution not previously reported or documented.

Second, evidence of physical violence and victims' demographics (such as age at death and sex) are important for legal justice. If leaders of violent regimes are held accountable in a court of law, evidence from the human remains can help quantify and explain the patterns of violence that occurred. For example, the senior leaders of the KR have been on trial at the Extraordinary Chambers in the Courts of Cambodia (ECCC) or Khmer Rouge Tribunal, and the court requested the final reports from the skeletal analysis completed at the Choeung Ek Genocidal Center (discussed below).

Third, analyzing human remains can provide healing for families and nations. The information provided by anthropologists can help to identify victims in some cases, resulting in the return of remains to family members, although this can be controversial (see Crossland and Joyce 2015; Rosenblatt 2015; Stefatos and Kovras 2015). While identifying a victim of fatal mass violence is never a joyous occasion,[1] this knowledge can assist a family in finding closure and permits the victim to receive culturally appropriate death rituals.

Therefore, it is vital to understand all we can about past atrocities for historical and future knowledge, and skeletal analysis is one method for achieving this comprehensive understanding. Many of the twentieth-century genocides have received this type of detailed forensic/skeletal assessment, but until recently the KR victims had not. In Cambodia skeletal analyses are urgent as the bones have deteriorated with time and will continue to do so, resulting in a loss of physical/scientific evidence. As this chapter shows, analysis and preservation of the human skeletal remains from the KR period is under way in Cambodia, and a great deal of pertinent information is being collected.

History of the Choeung Ek Site

The modern Choeung Ek Genocidal Center, colloquially known by foreigners as the "Killing Fields," sits approximately 15 km southwest of the center of Phnom Penh in Choeung Ek Commune, Dangkor District (map 8.1). Today it is the location of at least 129 KR-period mass graves. Prior to the KR, however, this region had a rich and significant history.

From the sixth to twelfth centuries CE (pre-Angkorian and Angkorian eras), the region was known as ចុងច្រមុះ (*jong jrmoh*, "tip of the nose": Choeung Ek Genocidal Center staff, personal communication 2015). Recent archaeological work has uncovered architecture, statuary, inscriptions, and pottery dating from the fifth to the tenth centuries, indicating that initial settlement of this region occurred during prehistoric times (Phon 2011). An early site with sixty-one kilns was discovered in the region of Choeung Ek, suggesting that this was one of the largest pottery production locations in Cambodia (Phon et al. 2013).

Unfortunately, little is known about the Choeung Ek region from the post-Angkorian era until the mid-twentieth century. Documentation begins to reappear when discussing the use of the region by the Chinese-Khmer community. Beginning in the 1960s, this community used the land as a cemetery. According to Phon (2011), Chinese or ethnically Chinese residents of the region would repurpose ancient mounds and possibly ancient kilns for the construction of tombs. This location was chosen for a cemetery because it encompassed features considered positive or lucky in Chinese funerary traditions, such as a body of water east of the tomb— Lake Choeung Ek (transliterated as Boeng Cheoung Aek on map 8.1) is directly east (Phon 2011). At least sixteen graves have been identified in what remains of this former Chinese cemetery (Narrowcasters 2011). Still visible today at the Choeung Ek Genocidal Center are a few Chinese gravestones and a cement kiosk that was used for Chinese funeral services. Today this kiosk is used for national-level ceremonies held at Choeung Ek.

In addition to the Chinese cemetery, in the mid-1960s, this region was well known for its glass factory (រោងចក្រកែវ) where glass bottles were produced for beer (Choeung Ek Genocidal Center staff, personal communication, 2015). This factory was equipped with electricity that later became important for the KR's activities at Choeung Ek.

After the initial seizure of Phnom Penh in 1975, KR work groups were sent to the region of Choeung Ek for agricultural production. These work groups were responsible for growing rice and hemp and harvesting palm juice to make palm sugar (ECCC 2016d; Choeung Ek Genocidal Center staff, personal communication, 2015). Farming, however, would not remain the only activity in this region. Between 1976 and mid-1977, Duch (the chairman of S-21), his deputy Hor, and Son Sen (Duch's superior) determined that a new execution and burial location for S-21 prisoners was needed (ECCC 2016e).[2] In his testimony before the ECCC, Duch stated that the decision to bury victims farther away from S-21, and thus the reason for the establishment of Choeung Ek, was that the number of corpses at S-21 was posing a risk of disease epidemics (ECCC 2016e). The staff members at the Choeung Ek Genocidal Center (personal communication, 2015) suggest instead that the KR deemed this location acceptable because it was far from the city center, had numerous large trees for privacy, and was already a cemetery.

Upon determining that this site was to be the new execution and burial grounds, a fence with five rows of barbed wire was built around the former Chinese cemetery. Electricity from the aforementioned glass factory was brought in to power only a few lights and a loudspeaker playing Khmer Rouge revolutionary propaganda (Choeung Ek Genocidal Center staff, personal communication, 2015). The propaganda from the loudspeaker is said to have dampened the sounds of victim's screams, a practice reported at execution sites throughout Cambodia. Although many Khmer Rouge cadres were working in the vicinity, the purpose of Choeung Ek was a closely guarded secret. According to her interviews with local farmers, Bennett (2015) states that Choeung Ek was known to be a KR facility. Trucks were seen driving in and out, but they thought it was a training ground for the army. No one was permitted to enter the site unless they worked within.

After the Khmer Rouge

While it is still unknown how many individuals were killed and buried at this site between 1977 and 1979, its location and purpose were revealed shortly after the KR were overthrown. However, accounts of the discovery of Choeung Ek and the exhumation of the graves vary. Chandler (1999) and Hughes (2006) state that Choeung Ek was not discovered until 1980—one year after the KR abandoned the site in January 1979. Conversely, Jarvis (2015) states that Choeung Ek was opened as a memorial in 1980, suggesting that it had already been discovered, and the remains exhumed, before that year.

Accounts of Cambodians interviewed by Caroline Bennett and the first author during their respective fieldwork are in line with Jarvis's chronology.

After the KR were disbanded, villagers began returning to their homes. Those who returned to their villages near Choeung Ek stumbled into the site seeking anything of value. They began to unearth the graves searching for gold, equipment, and other valuables (Bennett 2015). One Choeung Ek staff member said that he arrived at the site only two days after the KR had abandoned it. He and other villagers took chemicals and tools left by the KR to sell at a local market;[3] other villagers dismantled the buildings at Choeung Ek, using the wood to build new homes. He said that the Vietnamese/PRK had been informed about Choeung Ek but were initially more concerned with preserving and documenting S-21 (Choeung Ek Genocidal Center staff, personal communication, 2015). Thus Choeung Ek and its physical evidence of massacre was known, although perhaps not well documented, prior to 1980.

In late 1979 or early 1980 formal exhumations of the mass graves at Choeung Ek began. Of the estimated 129 mass graves covering more than two hectares of land, 86 graves were excavated by government officials.[4] The exhumed skeletal remains were placed along the edges of each grave, the crania were counted by the Department of Culture and Information of Kandal Province, and a plaque was placed next to each grave indicating the number of individuals that had been disinterred (figure 8.1; Choeung Ek Genocidal Center staff, personal communication, 2015). The Department of Culture and Information officially counted and recorded a total of 8,985 exhumed crania.

After the formal exhumations, the PRK established the Choeung Ek Killing Center (មណ្ឌលពិឃាតជើងឯក) in 1981. Despite the formal establishment of this center, for numerous years the bones remained at the edges of the graves, and local villagers continued to search through the graves to find valuables and clothing. At some point in the early 1980s the PRK put an end to the grave looting by assigning guards to Choueng Ek (Choeung Ek Genocidal Center staff, personal communication, 2015). An open-walled, wooden memorial was constructed at that time and the human remains were placed inside (figure 8.2). In 1986 Choeung Ek officially became the responsibility of the Department of Culture and Information of Kandal Province.

When the provincial boundaries shifted in 1988, the Choeung Ek Killing Center fell within the province of Phnom Penh instead of Kandal. As such, the responsibility for the center was transferred to the Phnom Penh Municipality and the name was changed to the Choeung Ek Genocidal Center (មជ្ឈមណ្ឌលប្រល័យពូជសាសន៍ជើងឯក) (Choeung Ek Genocidal Center

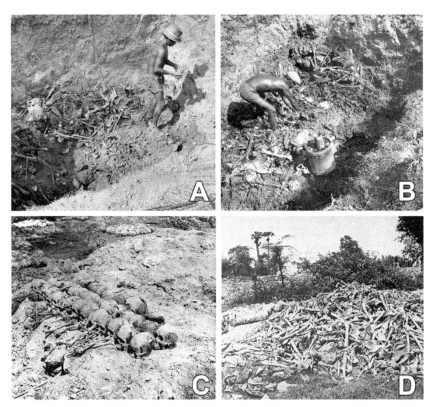

Figure 8.1. Photographs from the formal exhumation of the mass graves at Choeung Ek. Images *A* and *B* depict workers within the graves removing skeletal elements. Images *C* and *D* depict the remains placed on the edges of the mass graves after removal. In some cases the remains (primarily the crania) were neatly ordered, as in image *C*, while the remainder of the skeletal elements were commingled in piles, as seen in image *D*. (Photos courtesy of the Tuol Sleng Genocide Museum's photography archive.)

staff, personal communication, 2016). At this time the Phnom Penh Municipality's Department of Culture commissioned a scientific study of the remains by a Vietnamese team from Ho Chi Minh University. Directed by Professor Quang Quyen and Dr. Tran Hung, the team cleaned approximately 4,000 crania with water and lye, evaluated the crania for age, sex, and cause of death, and wrote identification numbers on them (Fawthrop and Jarvis 2004; Choeung Ek Genocidal Center staff, personal communication, 2015). In this same year, under the direction of Vietnamese general Mai Lam, the government had a large concrete *stupa* (Buddhist shrine) erected on the site to more effectively house and memorialize the remains. The Choeung Ek Genocidal Center was also officially opened to tourists,

Figure 8.2. Photographs of the original wooden memorial at Choeung Ek. The date of these images is unknown, but they were likely taken in the early to mid-1980s. The middle image shows a sign hanging in the memorial describing the mass graves and the number of victims. Translated from Khmer it reads: "The total number of graves: 129. The total number of graves excavated: 86. The total number of corpses: 8,985 people. The victims were killed by Pol Pot." (Photos courtesy of the Tuol Sleng Genocide Museum's photography archive; translation by Julie M. Fleischman.)

although international visitors and journalists had been brought regularly to Choeung Ek since 1980, as Bennett (2015) notes. With the public opening of the site, it came to serve as the national memorial to the victims of the Khmer Rouge and as an educational center (Bennett 2015; ECCC 2016a). In addition to memorialization, the *stupa*, with its visceral and confronting display of human remains, situates the site as a location for evidence of the KR's crimes. "Choeung Ek," as Hughes (2006:98) states, "serves to illustrate 'typical evidence' of mass political violence." Jarvis (2015) argues that the human bones displayed at Choeung Ek, as well as the artifacts and photographs at S-21, have become iconic images representing Cambodia and the legacy of the KR. The Choeung Ek Genocidal Center therefore plays a central role in memorializing Cambodia's past and reinforcing the place of KR violence in the country's national historic discourse.

In order to advance the conservation of the site and protect the human remains, in 2005 the Phnom Penh Municipality agreed to a 30-year contract in which the Choeung Ek Genocidal Center will be managed by the JC Royal Company, Ltd. (Bennett 2015; ECCC 2016a). Since this contract was signed, extensive improvements have been made to the center. A new museum and parking lot were built in 2008, the memorial *stupa* was renovated, and the audio guide by Narrowcasters was first offered in 2011 (today it is available in fifteen languages). In 2015 vertical blinds were installed within the *stupa* to protect the human remains from direct sunlight, and vast stretches of wooden walkways were built to keep visitors off of the ground, where bones and clothing continue to erode (Choeung Ek Genocidal Center staff, personal communication, 2015). In addition to all of these site works, the Choeung Ek Genocidal Center initiated the first systematic analysis of the human skeletal remains from the Khmer Rouge period.

Analyzing Human Remains in Cambodia

The Choeung Ek Genocidal Center Project

In 2012 Cambodia's prime minister, Hun Sen, instructed that the Ministry of Culture and Fine Arts should conserve Choeung Ek's *stupa* and the remains within to maintain them as evidence of KR violence (ECCC 2016a). A committee of officials representing the ministry, the Phnom Penh Municipality, and the Choeung Ek Genocidal Center was established, and the

Choeung Ek Conservation of Victims at the Killing Fields project was initiated (Beavan 2015; ECCC 2016a).

The goals of the project were to preserve and curate the human bones, tools/weapons, and textiles found at Choeung Ek. Analysis and inventory of the human remains were not part of the original project contract, but Voeun Vuthy, the project's conservation director, believed that it was important to properly document and record information about the remains for posterity. Thus in late 2013 he and his exclusively Cambodian team began the first comprehensive scientific analysis and preservation of human remains from a Khmer Rouge period mass gravesite in Cambodia.[5]

Within the *stupa* are seventeen levels containing human remains including crania, mandibles, long bones, and other skeletal elements (sacra, os coxae, scapulae, and so forth). The lowest level in the *stupa* holds remnants of clothing exhumed from the mass graves as well as replicas of tools/weapons found at Choeung Ek after it was abandoned by the KR. Over the subsequent two and a half years the team systematically removed, cleaned, analyzed, and preserved the contents within the *stupa*.

The skeletal conservation and analytical protocols developed for this project can be summarized as follows: the human remains were removed from the *stupa* and were photographed prior to cleaning. Each cranium was labeled with a new Choeung Ek identification number and an inventory/analysis sheet was started for that individual. Next the remains were cleaned with water, soaked in insecticide and fungicide, and then dried and placed in a dehumidifying chamber. Attempts were made to reassociate disarticulated cranial bones with their respective cranium; if a match was found, the loose bone was glued back into place (Beavan 2015).

Each cranium was then analyzed. The following data were recorded: the date of analysis, the estimated age-at-death and sex of the decedent using international anthropological standards, the weight of the cranium, the length and width of the cranium, the percentage of bone preservation, and what type(s) of traumatic injuries were present (Beavan 2015). The injuries were described in detail, then the cranium was photographed again to show that no damage had occurred during the cleaning and analytical phases. Finally, the remains were returned to the dehumidifying chambers, where they were coated with polymers to strengthen the bones and further seal them against humidity. After the completion of analysis and preservation, the remains were returned to the *stupa*. A note was made on the inventory form as to where each cranium was placed within the *stupa* in case it should need to be located in the future (Beavan 2015). The same processes were undertaken for the other bones of the body, but scientific analyses were not conducted.

The Choeung Ek conservation project was completed in December 2015. In less than three years Voeun Vuthy and his team preserved nearly 70,000 human bones, representing more than 7,000 individuals (ECCC 2016b). This is an extraordinary achievement that has yet to be replicated on such a grand scale. As documentation of the completed project, the inventory/analytical forms for each cranium have been published in a 32-volume Khmer-language set retained by the Choeung Ek Genocidal Center, the Cambodian Ministry of Culture and Fine Arts, the Phnom Penh Municipality, and the ECCC.

Cooperative Research at the Choeung Ek Genocidal Center

The first author had the privilege to work at the Choeung Ek Genocidal Center to conduct her doctoral research. The following case study is a small portion of this research, presented here to highlight the skeletal evidence of KR massacres. For this study, 50 unidentified crania were randomly selected from a larger sample. All crania were of skeletally mature or nearly mature adult individuals. Skeletal maturation typically occurs in the late teens or early twenties when all bones have completed fusion; remains of children (with unfused cranial elements) were not examined. The majority of the crania were complete. Each cranium was assessed by the first author, using morphoscopic anthropological methods (Buikstra and Ubelaker 1994) to estimate age-at-death, sex, ancestry, and traumatic injuries.

Each traumatic injury was evaluated to determine the timing (antemortem, perimortem, or postmortem), location (specific bone and region of the cranium affected), and force (sharp force, blunt force, or projectile force) of the injury. Data were recorded on skeletal analysis forms and later entered into an Excel spreadsheet and tabulated. The first author photographed all crania, and some were also radiographed.

Demographic Results

Males were more common in this sample than females: 46 individuals (92 percent) were morphologically assessed to be male or probable male and only 4 were assessed to be female or probable female. This was not unexpected because at S-21 the KR targeted individuals of high responsibility and those in command of military units, who were often males, as Chandler (1999) hypothesizes. The demographics of detainees and those who were tortured and executed depended on numerous factors, however, including the level (district, regional, zone, or central-level) of the security center/prison. Chandler (1999) states that high-ranking prisoner's wives, children, and family members were imprisoned, held for a short time, and then executed. Thus, while all ages and sexes were targeted for imprisonment and execution, those at S-21 were more likely to be male than female, although further research is needed on this topic.

Of those individuals whose ancestral origin could be assessed (88 percent), all were Asian. Using Buikstra and Ubelaker's (1994) age categories, the majority of individuals (96 percent) were young to middle-aged adults (20–50 years old). The total age estimations for this sample are as follows: 2 individuals were adolescents (12–19 years old), 33 were young adults (20–35 years old), and 15 were middle-aged adults (36–50 years old). This sample, however, is not representative of all individuals at Choeung Ek, as children were not included.

Evidence of Massacre

Of the crania sampled, 2 had healed antemortem trauma, 29 (58 percent) had perimortem trauma, and all 50 had evidence of postmortem damage. When they were divided by sex, only 1 female had evidence of perimortem trauma; thus males (including those classified as probable males) were nearly 5 times more likely to have evidence of trauma than females (odds ratio = 4.7). However, the low number of females in this study indicates the need for a larger sample and further analysis to clarify whether there is truly a relationship between trauma and sex (see Fleischman 2017 for further clarification).

Some individuals had more than one injury/impact to their cranium; the 29 individuals with perimortem trauma had a total of 49 injuries (figure 8.3). Of the individuals with injuries, 18 had 1 injury, 5 had 2 injuries, and 6 had 3 or more (figure 8.4). In this study an individual was 61 percent (Relative Risk = 0.61) more likely to have *only* one injury compared to more than one injury.

According to historical and eyewitness accounts of KR executions (Hinton 2013:156–157),[6] blunt force injuries were hypothesized to be the most common mechanism of skeletal trauma in this study. This hypothesis could not be rejected; blunt force trauma represented 80 percent of the cranial injuries in this study. This was statistically significant ($p < 0.0001$) compared to the other traumatic injuries. There was only a single sharp force injury (2 percent) and no gunshot/projectile injuries. The remaining injuries (18 percent) were of an indeterminate mechanism.

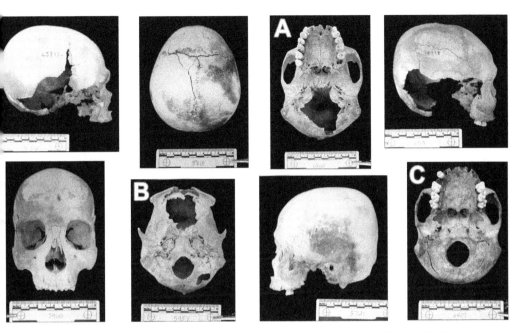

Figure 8.3. Examples of traumatic injuries from this sample. The lettered images (*A*, *B*, and *C*) are examples of trauma to the basicranium, the most common region of injury. (Photos by Julie M. Fleischman.)

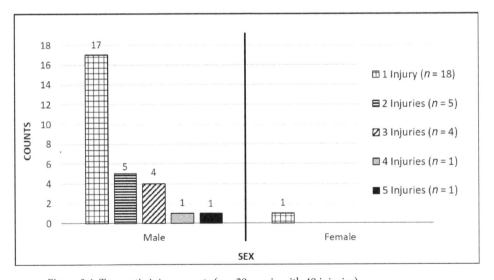

Figure 8.4. Traumatic injury counts (*n* = 29 crania with 49 injuries).

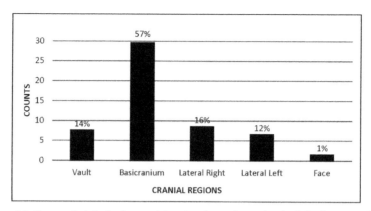

Figure 8.5. Traumatic injuries by cranial region ($n = 51$): 2 individuals had injuries that spanned both the right and left lateral sides, resulting in more than 49 total injuries, as seen in figure 8.4.

Injuries were also assessed by their location, specifically the region of the cranium that was affected. For the purposes of this study, cranial regions were defined as: vault (frontal and parietal bones), basicranium (occipital and inferior sphenoid), right and left lateral (temporal bones and greater wings of the sphenoid), and face (bones of the face excluding the frontal and mandible). When assessed by cranial region, trauma to the basicranium was the most common (57 percent). Injuries to the basicranium were nearly twice as likely when compared to all other regions of the cranium, although this difference was not statistically significant ($p = 0.23$) (figure 8.5; see also figure 8.3, lettered images).

Trauma, particularly blunt trauma, to the basicranium was expected since eyewitness accounts of Khmer Rouge executions frequently describe victims sitting or kneeling at the edge of a grave pit and being struck on the base of the head or neck with a heavy object. For example, according to Him Huy, a KR soldier who was a guard at S-21 and later assigned to transport prisoners from S-21 to Choeung Ek for execution, the tools used for killing people at Choeung Ek were oxcart axles and knives. In his testimony at the ECCC he stated that victims "were clubbed, then they—their throats would be slashed" (ECCC 2016e:22). Tay Teng, a guard at S-21 under the direction of Him Huy and later a guard at Choeung Ek, stated during an interview with the Office of the Co-Investigating Judges of the ECCC: "First, [the prisoners] sat about one meter from the edge of the pit. They had two or three sit beside one another and they used a water pipe to strike the base of their necks. When the prisoners fell over, they removed the handcuffs, then they used the knives to finish killing them" (ECCC 2016c:107). Tay Teng later testified that the KR "used iron bars to beat people to death" and that the iron bars "were iron axles the width of a knife handle and about half a meter long" (ECCC 2016d:9). Additionally, Him Huy was quoted as having said that his superiors, Duch and Hor, taught their subordinates how to kill. They instructed Huy to have prisoners "kneel, then strike at the base of the neck, then cut the throat" (ECCC 2016c:110). Thus the available skeletal evidence of trauma from this study is consistent with the historical accounts of what transpired at Choeung Ek during the KR regime.

Discussion and Conclusion

While much has been written about the history of KR violence, the work undertaken by the Cambodian research team at Choeung Ek was the first large-scale effort to analyze and preserve the millions of human remains that serve as a visceral reminder of these massacres. The task of documenting KR violence in Cambodia, preserving the physical remains of such violence and disseminating the subsequent information, is an exceptional accomplishment. The skeletal analytical research by the Choeung Ek team, as well as the research by the first author, is an effort to record what no other national or international entity has undertaken in over thirty years—including the ECCC in its preparations for the trials of the top KR leaders.

It must be acknowledged that this research, and the impetus for the Choeung Ek Conservation of Victims at the Killing Fields project, fits comfortably within the deeply rooted national discourse of KR violence. Despite this state-level narrative of Cambodian history, the accounts, memories, and evidence of massacre represented at the Tuol Sleng Museum and the Choeung Ek Genocidal Center are not necessarily hegemonic and may not represent the experiences of all survivors (Hinton 2013; Williams 2004). In fact, the very "evidence" of the KR violence (the human remains) has been the center of debate both in the past and today. Contrary to the state discourse of "preservation of evidence," some Cambodians, including the late King Norodom Sihanouk, have argued that the remains should be cremated to promote familial and national healing (Chy 2016; Cougill; Ledgerwood 1997). Nonetheless, Choeung Ek and Tuol Sleng persist as institutions founded on the national discourse of KR violence that serve to remind both locals and foreigners about this period in Cambodian history.

When evaluating the specific skeletal evidence, as presented in the case study above, the hypotheses regarding the traumatic injuries could not be rejected. Blunt force trauma was significantly more common than any other injury and trauma to the posterior and/or inferior region of the head was the most common. These results corroborate eyewitness accounts indicating that victims at Choeung Ek were often struck on the back of the head or neck with a heavy implement. This case study has an extremely small sample size, however, so additional analytical and statistical assessments must be conducted to determine if these patterns of trauma are representative at Choeung Ek. Additional cultural research (to assess the concept of human remains as evidence) is also necessary at Choeung Ek and other sites in Cambodia. The first author has completed these additional research tasks and will soon publish the interpretations of these data.

With the completion of the Choeung Ek conservation project and four additional projects to preserve and analyze human remains from the KR period, the members of the Choeung Ek team have demonstrated their competency and dedication to this effort. The authors argue that scientifically analyzing and preserving human remains from violent massacres or other human rights atrocities is not sufficient. The sociocultural context in which the remains reside must be understood; comprehension of the social, political, and even religious ideologies that shape how the remains are exhumed (or not exhumed), regarded, analyzed, and memorialized is indispensable. As this chapter has described, human remains from a violent event of this magnitude do not reside in a vacuum. The massacres committed by the KR are ensconced in Cambodia's national historical narrative, which is reflected in the treatment of the human remains in both the past and present.

Acknowledgments

The authors would like to recognize the support received from the following institutions and individuals: the Choeung Ek Genocidal Center staff, the Cambodian Ministry of Culture and Fine Arts, the Phnom Penh Municipality, Neang Si, Heang Sreang, Heng Mesa, Ry Sovannarith, Phat Phina, Cheun Navun, Sam An Sopheaktra, and Kim Keo.

The first author would like to thank the following organizations for funding her research: the Fulbright IIE Student Program, Graduate Women in Science, the Kussy Endowment, and Michigan State University's Foreign Language and Areas Studies Program. Many thanks to the first author's doctoral committee: Dr. Lynne Goldstein, Dr. Joseph Hefner, Dr. Elizabeth

Drexler, Dr. Laura Fulginiti, and Dr. Charles Keith. Thank you as well to Dr. Helen Jarvis, Youk Chhang, and Phon Kaseka for assistance in reviewing this manuscript and providing historical information.

NOTES

1. In this case, mass violence refers to intentional and often clandestine killings of individuals in large numbers (e.g., Rwanda, Bosnia, Kosovo, Argentina, Peru, Colombia, Guatemala, Spain, Timor Leste, and others), typically sanctioned by governments or groups in power.

2. Prior to the establishment of Choeung Ek, executions occurred at S-21. The bodies were buried on the grounds or nearby. However, important prisoners were still executed and buried at S-21 even after Choeung Ek was in use (Chandler 1999; ECCC 2016d).

3. Chemicals such as DDT and អង់ត្រីន (angtrein) were found at Choeung Ek by returning villagers. It is speculated that the chemicals were placed on top of the bodies in the grave to prevent animal scavenging and to accelerate the decomposition of the bodies (Choeung Ek Genocidal Center staff, personal communication, 2015).

4. Hughes (2006) states that 89 graves were excavated. The number 86, for the count of exhumed graves, is supported by posted signs at the Choeung Ek Genocidal Center, the audio tour (Narrowcasters 2011), and a document submitted to the ECCC (2016a).

5. Skeletal analyses have been conducted since the exhumation of the remains in the 1980s, but none have assessed the remains in their entirety. For examples, see Berg (2008a, 2008b, 2015), Pollanen (2002), and Ta'ala et al. (2006, 2008).

6. This is merely one example describing a mechanism of execution. There are many more documented descriptions of victims being beaten on the edge of mass graves.

REFERENCES

Beavan, N. R. 2015. *Evaluation of the Choeung Ek Conservation of Victims at Killing Fields Project*. Choeung Ek Genocidal Center, Phnom Penh.

Bennett, C. 2015. To Live amongst the Dead: An Ethnographic Exploration of Mass Graves in Cambodia. PhD dissertation, School of Anthropology and Conservation, University of Kent, Canterbury, Kent, UK.

Berg, G. E. 2008a. Biological Affinity and Sex Determination Using Morphometric and Morphoscopic Variables from the Human Mandible. PhD dissertation, University of Tennessee, Knoxville.

———. 2008b. Case Report 6.1: Probable Machete Trauma from the Cambodian Killing Fields. In *Identification of Traumatic Skeletal Injuries Resulting from Human Rights Abuses and Armed Conflicts*, edited by E. H. Kimmerle and J. P. Baraybar, pp. 314–320. Taylor and Francis Group, New York.

———. 2015. Biological Affinity and Sex from the Mandible Utilizing Multiple World Populations. In *Biological Affinity in Forensic Identification of Human Skeletal Remains: Beyond Black and White*, edited by G. E. Berg and S. C. Ta'ala, pp. 43–82. CRC Press, Boca Raton, FL.

Buikstra, J. E., and D. H. Ubelaker (editors). 1994. *Standards for Data Collection from Human Skeletal Remains: Proceedings of a Seminar at the Field Museum of Natural History.* Research Series, No. 44. Arkansas Archaeological Survey, Fayetteville.

Chandler, D. 1999. *Voices from S-21: Terror and History in Pol Pot's Secret Prison.* University of California Press, Berkeley.

———. 2000. *A History of Cambodia.* 3rd ed. Silkworm Books, Chiang Mai, Thailand.

Chy, T. 2016. One Last Measure for the Wandering Souls of Cambodia, edited by The Asia Foundation. *In Asia.* http://asiafoundation.org/2016/06/29/one-last-measure-wandering-souls-cambodia/.

Cougill, W. *Buddhist Cremation Traditions for the Dead and the Need to Preserve Forensic Evidence in Cambodia.* Documentation Center of Cambodia, Phnom Penh. http://www.d.dccam.org/Projects/Maps/Buddhist_Cremation_Traditions.htm.

Crossland, Z., and R. A. Joyce (editors). 2015. *Disturbing Bodies: Perspectives on Forensic Anthropology.* School for Advanced Research, Santa Fe, NM.

Ea, M.-T. 2005. *The Chain of Terror: The Khmer Rouge Southwest Zone Security System.* Documentation Center of Cambodia, Phnom Penh.

Extraordinary Chambers in the Courts of Cambodia (ECCC). 2016a. *Cheung Ek Genocidal Center: The Inventory of the Skeletons of the Victims, Preface.* Trial Chamber, Case 002/02. Doc. number: E404/2.1.3. ECCC, Phnom Penh.

———. 2016b. *Co-Prosecutors' Rule 87(4) Submission Regarding Choeung Ek Project Documents.* Trial Chamber, Case 002/02. Doc. number: E404/1. ECCC, Phnom Penh.

———. 2016c. *Transcript of Hearing on the Substance in Case 002/02–21 April 2016.* Trial Chamber, Case 002/02. Doc. number: E1/420.1. ECCC, Phnom Penh.

———. 2016d. *Transcript of Hearing on the Substance in Case 002/02–25 April 2016.* Trial Chamber, Case 002/02. Doc. number: E1/421.1. ECCC, Phnom Penh.

———. 2016e. *Transcript of Hearing on the Substance in Case 002/02–04 May 2016.* Trial Chamber, Case 002/02. Doc. number: E1/427.1. ECCC, Phnom Penh.

———. 2016f. *Transcript of Hearing on the Substance in Case 002/02–05 May 2016.* Trial Chamber, Case 002/02. Doc. number: E1/428.1. ECCC, Phnom Penh.

Fawthrop, T., and H. Jarvis. 2004. *Getting Away with Genocide? Elusive Justice and the Khmer Rouge Tribunal.* Pluto Press, London.

Fleischman, J. M. 2017. Remains of Khmer Rouge Violence: The Materiality of Bones as Scientific Evidence and Affective Agents of Memory. PhD dissertation, Michigan State University.

Hinton, A. L. 2013. Genocide and the Politics of Memory in Cambodia. In *Hidden Genocides: Power, Knowledge, Memory,* edited by A. L. Hinton, T. L. Pointe, and D. Irvin-Erickson, pp. 149–169. Rutgers University Press, New Brunswick, NJ.

Hughes, R. B. 2003. Nationalism and Memory at the Tuol Sleng Museum of Genocide Crimes, Phnom Penh, Cambodia. In *Contested Pasts: The Politics of Memory,* edited by K. Hodgkin and S. Radstone, pp. 175–192. Routledge, London.

———. 2006. Fielding Genocide: Post-1979 Cambodia and the Geopolitics of Memory. PhD dissertation, Faculty of Arts, University of Melbourne, Melbourne, Australia.

Jarvis, H. 2015. Powerful Remains: The Continuing Presence of Victims of the Khmer Rouge Regime in Today's Cambodia. *Human Remains and Violence* 1(2):1–20.

Kiernan, B. 2006. External and Indigenous Sources of Khmer Rouge Ideology. In *The Third Indochina War: Conflict between China, Vietnam and Cambodia, 1972–79*, edited by O. A. Westad and S. Quinn-Judge, pp. 187–206. Routledge, London.

———. 2008. The Demography of Genocide in Southeast Asia: The Death Tolls in Cambodia, 1975–79, and East Timor, 1975–80. In *Genocide and Resistance in Southeast Asia: Documentation, Denial & Justice in Cambodia & East Timor*, pp. 269–282. Transaction Publishers, New Brunswick, NJ.

Ledgerwood, J. 1997. The Cambodian Tuol Sleng Museum of Genocidal Crimes: National Narrative. *Museum Anthropology* 21(1):82–98.

Narrowcasters. 2011. *Choeung Ek Genocidal Center Audio Tour*, Phnom Penh.

Phon, K. 2011. Archaeology and Cultural Resource Management South of Phnom Penh, Cambodia. In *Rethinking Cultural Management in Southeast Asia: Preservation, Development, and Neglect*, edited by J. N. Miksic, G. Y. Goh, and S. O'Connor, pp. 123–142. Anthem Press, New York.

Phon, K., R. Chay, V. Voeun, V. Chhum, S. Khin, and M. Dega. 2013. *The Ceramic Production Center of Cheung Ek*. Royal Academy of Cambodia: Institute of Culture and Fine Arts, Phnom Penh.

Pollanen, M. S. 2002. *Mission Report: Forensic Survey of Three Memorial Sites Containing Human Skeletal Remains in the Kingdom of Cambodia*. Documentation Center of Cambodia, Phnom Penh.

Rosenblatt, A. 2015. *Digging for the Disappeared: Forensic Science after Atrocity*. Stanford Studies in Human Rights. Stanford University Press, Stanford, CA.

Royal Government of Cambodia (RGC). 2001. *Circular on Preservation of Remains of the Victims of the Genocide Committed during the Regime of Democratic Kampuchea (1975–1978), and Preparation of Anlong Veng to Become a Region for Historical Tourism*. http://www.d.dccam.org/Projects/Maps/Victim_Memorials.htm. Royal Government of Cambodia, Phnom Penh.

Slocomb, M. 2003. *The People's Republic of Kampuchea, 1979–1989: The Revolution after Pol Pot*. Silkworm Books, Chiang Mai, Thailand.

Stefatos, K., and I. Kovras. 2015. Buried Silences of the Greek Civil War. In *Necropolitics: Mass Graves and Exhumations in the Age of Human Rights*, edited by F. Ferrándiz and A.C.G. M. Robben, pp. 161–184. Pennsylvania Studies in Human Rights. University of Pennsylvania Press, Philadelphia.

Ta'ala, S. C., G. E. Berg, and K. Haden. 2006. Blunt Force Cranial Trauma in the Cambodian Killing Fields. *Journal of Forensic Sciences* 51(5):996–1001.

———. 2008. Case Report 4.2: A Khmer Rouge Execution Method: Evidence from Choeung Ek. In *Identification of Traumatic Skeletal Injuries Resulting from Human Rights Abuses and Armed Conflicts*, edited by E. H. Kimmerle and J. P. Baraybar, pp. 196–200. Taylor and Francis Group, New York.

Williams, P. 2004. Witnessing Genocide: Vigilance and Remembrance at Tuol Sleng and Choeung Ek. *Holocaust and Genocide Studies* 18(2):234–254.

9

Sowing the Dead

Massacres and the Missing in Northern Uganda

TRICIA REDEKER HEPNER, DAWNIE WOLFE STEADMAN,
AND JULIA R. HANEBRINK

The Acholi people of northern Uganda have a serious problem with bones. During the 1986–2006 war between the Lord's Resistance Army (LRA) and the government of Uganda, tens of thousands of people were abducted and killed by rebels, sometimes far from their homes. Marauding bands of LRA rebels often attacked villages, killing civilians and leaving stricken survivors to bury the victims hastily. In the name of repressing the rebellion, the National Resistance Army (NRA; later known as the Ugandan People's Defense Forces: UPDF) also committed atrocities against Acholi individuals and communities that it accused or suspected of sympathizing with the LRA. Both the army and LRA often deposited bodies of civilians or soldiers in pit latrines or mass graves in school or churchyards. Other victims were simply left exposed in the bush, where their remains decayed in the open and were scavenged by animals.

In 2006 a cease-fire between the rebels and government ushered in an uneasy peace. People gradually began returning to their villages and fields from displacement camps, urban refuges, and even abroad. Those who were able to recover their land or resettle in new areas soon discovered—or realized with horror—the vast and sinister cemetery that the region had become. Acholiland remains riddled with partially buried or exposed remains, mass graves containing victims both known and unknown to survivors, and tens of thousands buried in former displacement camps where disease and violence were rampant. Whole portions of land were abandoned where graves were known or discovered. Bones encountered in the bush were hastily covered, perhaps only with *olwede* leaves in a ritual act of respect. Formerly displaced people pined for deceased loved ones whose remains were left behind in the camp, while those who owned the land where camps were located worried about how to avoid graves whose external features were rapidly swallowed by the encroaching vegetation. Government development projects such as road construction also disturbed or threatened graves, retraumatizing both survivors and the remains of the deceased (see Jahn 2016).

Additionally, soon after the cease-fire and return of displaced persons to their villages, survivors began experiencing strange and terrible things. They described how mental or physical illness sometimes descended on those who encountered bones or lived in proximity to them. They reported that apparitions frequently haunted survivors at night, appearing in dreams or knocking at doors, often asking relatives to find their remains and bring them home for proper burial. In one village ghostly fires and cacophonous voices could be seen and heard from a distance around a mass grave of NRA soldiers. In another, young children ran screaming from school where a pit latrine had been used as a grave, complaining of spirits beating them about the head. At a site where NRA soldiers had been buried en masse, a borehole could be observed pumping water, or sometimes blood, by itself at dusk. People walking along the road at night might even pass a ghost or see uncanny white-skinned babies perched in trees.

These experiences illustrate how the dead are not vacated in Acholiland but retain a presence and an agency among the living (Baines 2010; Ellison and Jessee 2012; Kembel 2015; Meinert and Whyte 2013; Seebach 2016; Victor and Porter 2014). Their remains are omnipresent: the spirits of those who died violently and without proper burial persistently impinge on survivors of the war.[1] These spiritual impingements also have economic and social dimensions, leading people to puzzle over how to address the problem of bones in a period characterized by both the formal and informal processes of reconciliation, economic recovery, and psychosocial healing. While the living and dead seem to share a demand for acknowledgment of atrocities, survivors require concrete material assistance in conducting reburials and/or rituals that would cleanse the land and restore cosmological balance. Is there a role for forensic investigation in this context—and if so, for what purposes? What specific challenges does ethnographic inquiry highlight for such a potential investigation in northern Uganda?

This chapter addresses the manner in which rebels, the army, and survivors went about "sowing the dead" and the various meanings attached to improperly buried human remains in the postwar period. Drawing on original ethnographic data, including focus groups, individual interviews with survivors, and burial site documentation, collected throughout the Acholiland region since 2012, we focus here on one widespread type of massacre-related burial—a shallow grave containing multiple unknown victims—to examine more broadly the cultural and political landscape of massacres in northern Uganda.[2] We also address how the perceived agency of the dead impacts the living and their evolving perspectives on the serious problem of bones in the aftermath of war. While forensic investigation of war-related graves in Acholiland may possibly contribute to broader goals for recovery, reconciliation, and justice among living and dead alike, a careful consideration of its potential application illustrates how massacres in northern Uganda were not simply atrocious events punctuating the trajectory of war. We argue that this is an attribute of mass violence more generally: massacres-as-events emerge from longer and deeper political processes and have left legacies that endure in material and nonmaterial ways. While massacres may be dramatic moments in the exercise and experience of violence, they are made meaningful by their historical contexts and future consequences. Therefore, improper burials in Acholiland are tethered to conflicting memories and differing perceptions and claims among survivors, from the modus operandi and identity of the perpetrators to the identities of the victims, their spiritual agency, and the implications of the presence of physical remains. These factors in turn create various possibilities for how the living should respond. Considering whether and how a forensic investigation might proceed—and for what purposes—helps unravel these threads and reveals the underlying patterns of both physical and structural violence from which they are spun.

Patterns of Violence in Acholiland

A large, bright yellow roadside billboard announces in bold letters: "Peace, Stability, and Security" (figure 9.1). It features the familiar visage of President Yoweri K. Museveni, who came to power in 1986 as leader of the National Resistance Movement (NRM) and National Resistance Army (NRA). The message elaborates: "28 rebel groups have been defeated since 1986. Uganda is now secure and peaceful for takeoff. Enjoy your peace and make it work for you!" And finally, "Vote NRM, Vote Yoweri K. Museveni" (RLP 2014:2).

Figure 9.1. NRM billboard. (Photo by Anand Sandesara.)

Uganda is no stranger to violent political conflict. An estimated 125 distinct conflicts, most of them armed, have occurred since independence from Britain in 1961 (RLP 2014:3). The current NRM-dominated government itself emerged as a victorious rebel movement in 1986. Some rebel groups are well known—perhaps none so much as the infamous Lord's Resistance Army and its leader, Joseph Kony. But many more are "neither well-defined nor well-described" (RLP 2014:2). Perhaps most importantly, the role of the current government and national military in exacerbating conflict and committing atrocities in various regions of the country, often in the name of protecting civilians and the nation from armed rebel groups, has been "effectively silenced by the broader narrative of Uganda's post-1986 'renaissance'" under Museveni (RLP 2014:2). Within this narrative, the repression of the LRA war in the north has been cast as a heroic crusade against anomic religiously inspired terrorism, stifling a more politicized discussion of the historic marginalization and systematic underdevelopment of the northern region itself (Branch 2010).

Thus the dramatic and visible nature of political violence such as massacres, disappearances, or child abductions by rebels can obscure other forms of violence that underpin and often give rise to those violent expressions (Scheper-Hughes and Bourgois 2003). Structural violence precedes and continues after periods of physical violence in the form of ethno-regional discrimination against northerners as backward and violent, poor infrastructural development, land grabs by elites and outsiders, and, in the postwar period, the government's failure to heed survivors' demands for recognition of atrocities and compensation for losses of life, land, labor, and livestock—a constellation that Dolan (2011) has described as "social torture."

As Acholiland today recovers from more than twenty years of violent conflict between the LRA and the NRA/UPDF, several features are especially salient. One is a keen effort led by local nongovernmental and research and advocacy organizations to document massacres and other atrocities and to help mobilize survivors to articulate their past and present experiences in ways that facilitate reconciliation while making specific political and legal demands on the government. This is particularly vital as Uganda looks to adopt and implement a National Transitional Justice Policy intended to address the "lack of awareness of the numerous conflict related traumas, tensions and reconciliation needs which linger in diverse corners of the country" (RLP 2014:3). A second salient feature is an increasing consciousness and voice among Acholi survivors in regard to NRA/UPDF participation in extreme violence against civilians. Although the image of the LRA war is one "in which Joseph Kony's dreadlocked warriors are depicted as the sole perpetrators of atrocities, while the Ugandan army tirelessly defended its civilian population against their brutality" (Ellison and Jessee 2012), survivors increasingly reveal—if not without fear and hesitation—how many equally brutal atrocities were committed by the NRA/UPDF.

As these same survivors puzzle over the serious problem of bones, all of these features (and more) become dynamically engaged. In the following section we describe and analyze a particularly troublesome and yet common form of massacre-related grave for what it reveals about patterns of past and current violence. Finally, we examine how a careful consideration of the possibility of forensic investigation of such graves throws these complex issues into starker relief.

A Burned Hut, Unknown Bones, and Voices at Night

"I don't know what happened to the skulls," the young man told us quietly. "There were three in the dry season, in April, when I found these bones and covered them again. It has since grown very bushy." We were standing around a massacre site in Nwoya District on a July afternoon—two anthropologists, one colleague from Justice and Reconciliation Project, an Acholi friend acting as an interpreter, and four men of varying ages from the nearby homestead and village. The thick underbrush that had grown up during the recent rains was now whacked flat with machetes and stomped down by foot (figure 9.2). The foundations of a large circular building were clearly visible amid the crushed grasses and saplings. Large, half-buried storage pots marked its perimeter, some nearly whole and others charred black and broken in bits. The earth had been scratched and hacked by the men with hoes.

Visible among the whitish, traumatized roots of trees were several pale and degraded long bones, some of them newly cracked by the impact of the tools. A scrap of clothing and a zipper were also visible. "You asked about the bones, so now we are showing you," one of the leaders of a survivor's association told us. "Now you can tell others what you saw here."

Working quietly and quickly, we improvised to document the now destroyed site with photographs and measurements as the men collectively

Figure 9.2. Path from homestead to massacre site. (Photo by Julia R. Hanebrink.)

tried to reconstruct from memory what had happened (figure 9.3). The incident had been recorded by the survivors' association as an LRA attack in 1996. Six people hiding in the hut were shot inside. The wall of the hut was then pushed down, collapsing the roof on the victims, and the whole structure was set on fire (figure 9.4). While these details were agreed upon, some of the men disagreed that it was in fact the LRA that committed the massacre. According to the senior male resident of the compound who led us to the site, the massacre had actually been committed by the NRA. As for the victims, they were unknown to the local residents and were not from the area. Perhaps they had been abducted by rebels and had escaped, the man suggested, hiding in the hut when the area was swept by the NRA. But who was to tell? During such moments all was chaos and fear—and rebels and government forces wore the same uniforms and carried the same weapons.

In the intervening years, after the local residents had been forced into displacement camps, the area had returned to wilderness. Now back at their former homestead, residents abandoned this portion of land where the massacre occurred. The remains had been covered by vegetation, but periodically—especially during the dry seasons—the bones would re-emerge on the surface. The young man who had seen the remains several

Figure 9.3. Stone covering exposed long bone, with tiny cross and leaves placed by residents as sign of respect and apology to the dead for disturbing their remains. (Photo by Julia R. Hanebrink.)

Figure 9.4. Site of collapsed hut and shallow mass grave, overgrown with trees and brush in the Acholi sub-region. (Photo by Julia R. Hanebrink.)

months earlier had collected the visible bones himself and buried them again in a shallow pit. His older brother would have liked to use this land for farming or building, but the presence of the bones renders the land unusable. Moreover, their elderly mother is especially affected by spiritual disturbances. At night she hears voices, often calling her by name, but she cannot find where they are. The youngest child has also been persistently ill. Could these troubles be caused by the spirits of those who died here, whose remains are left in such an abominable and abandoned state, following such a horrific death? But who were they? And if cleansing rituals should be performed to appease them, who should take responsibility for it, and where will the money come from to purchase the necessary ceremonial items? If government forces committed this massacre, shouldn't the government compensate the residents for the loss of this land and provide resources to hold rituals? But why would the government admit to such things? Even more importantly, if we anthropologists knew something about bones, couldn't we use our machines to find out who these people were and send them back to their families for proper burial?

Many other sites in the same village were also said to contain the remains of the physically, though perhaps not spiritually, dead. On the carefully handwritten document created for us by the survivor's association, 12 distinct massacres by the LRA were reported by survivors in this one subcounty of Nwoya District alone, representing at least 224 victims, many of them abducted from elsewhere but killed here. The association had also documented 16 massacres committed by the NRA, with an estimated 325 victims. Just across the street from the site where we stood, for example, was a pit latrine containing at least 25 people, only a few of whom were known to be from the village.

Scenarios like the one described above are common throughout Acholiland (map 9.1). Like virtually everywhere in the Acholi subregion, Nwoya District was profoundly impacted by the war. Villages and homesteads were attacked by groups of LRA rebels, children and young people were abducted, and food and livestock were looted. The NRA/UPDF likewise moved through the area seeking to repress the rebels and, after 1997, to enforce the government's policy of encampment. Those who resisted going to the camps or were discovered on their own land were often accused of collaborating with the rebels, with deadly consequences. In a broader sense, however, all Acholi were suspect; the very ethnic identification itself led them to be labeled "LRA" or, even worse, "Kony."

While more than 4,500 attacks by the LRA have been recorded by the research and advocacy organization Refugee Law Project since it began its "massacre scoping" project in 2010, hundreds more have since been identified, many of them attributed by survivors and eyewitnesses to NRA/UPDF attacks (RLP 2014; Ellison and Jessee 2012). As early as 1988 the new NRM government was already ordering villagers to vacate areas where rebel activity was known. Survivors relate how "NRA soldiers committed atrocities including the widespread rape of men (*tek gungu*), defecating in food and drinking water, burning houses in villages under the pretext of clearing fighting ground, mass arrests of civilian suspects, [and] killings and massacres" (RLP 2014:139). Yet clearly identifying the NRA/UPDF as perpetrators is difficult, not just because the modus operandi of the killings committed

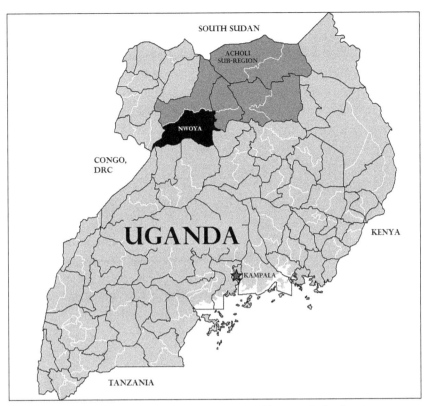

Map 9.1. Map of Uganda indicating Nwoya District and larger Acholi subregion. (Created by Julia R. Hanebrink.)

by rebels and soldiers was so similar, but because the government and military responsible remains in power today. The enduring political and economic vulnerability of survivors is palpable, as is the suffering etched on bodies and minds. Mental illness and addiction to cheap "sacket" alcohol (sold for about 25 cents in small plastic bags) is omnipresent in places like Nwoya District; the physical and emotional trauma is exacerbated for survivors by the knowledge that "we can't be sure who killed us" (Hopwood 2011). The spiritual disturbances likewise associated with massacre-related burials are often inscrutable insofar as the identities and origins of so many victims—and perpetrators—remain unknown. Who, then, can appease these spirits? How can they go home when no one knows who they are or where they came from? If perpetrators should make amends with the living and the dead, who exactly are the perpetrators in the context of such a war?

Dilemmas with the Dead in the Postconflict Period

Even a cursory grasp of the sheer scale and complexity of improper burials in northern Uganda should give the most seasoned forensic anthropologists pause. Yet shallow mass burials are only one type of troublesome deposition context. The living also contend with mass graves of known and unknown victims as well as graves of soldiers and rebels and burials on former IDP camp lands. Following massacre events, the immediate survivors often hastily buried the victims in mass graves. Their locations may still be known today, but they have "spoiled the land," as one landowner told us. Following battles between rebels and soldiers, graves were either constructed by the victorious group or dug by villagers themselves, sometimes at gunpoint. Individual graves in former displacement camps are scattered throughout the land that has now been returned to its owners or reclaimed by new occupants, presenting considerable problems for agricultural recovery and development (Jahn 2016; Jahn and Wilhelm-Solomon 2015; Meinert and Whyte 2013). While spiritual disturbances are associated with many of these graves, the ability of the living to address them through ritual means, or by exhumations and reburials in instances where the deceased are known, is extremely limited by the lack of resources, including funds to purchase sacrificial animals, cement, and coffins or burial wraps and to host and feed kin and community. In addition, ritual specialists may need to be paid for their services, labor and transport are required, and rituals must be performed at both exhumation and at reburial (see Seebach 2016).

As the government ramps up investment, development, and infrastructure efforts in northern Uganda, "bones literally come to the surface" (Jahn 2016:33). The disruptions associated with disinterment in such contexts produce or aggravate acute cosmological imbalances among the living and dead. As a result, some development organizations, such as the Northern Uganda Transitional Initiative (NUTI), have funded rituals intended to appease the spirits and reconcile the living and dead. Partners in development projects with the government, such as the Japanese International Cooperation Agency (JICA), have facilitated exhumations and reburials from former IDP camps (Jahn 2016) in cases where graves are in the path of road or building construction. The scale of the problem far outpaces the ability of any individuals or entities to deal with it comprehensively, however, and the impact of past interventions on survivors has been mixed. Some survivors reported to us that cleansings facilitated by NUTI did not always "work," while Jahn (2016:34) documented how "many of the affected families experienced these [development-driven] reburials as a forceful violation of their cosmological imaginations, with unsettling consequences."[3]

The specific case examined in this chapter, a shallow mass burial of unknown victims in Nwoya District, illustrates a number of important concerns facing the Acholi people: the problems of mass graves and the patterns of violence in Northern Uganda. First, survivors disagreed on the identity of the perpetrators due to bias, memory, or absence at the time of the massacre. The modus operandi could fit either the LRA or the Ugandan military. While many survivors desire accountability for atrocities, this desire is often overshadowed by fear and cynicism that meaningful justice can actually be achieved in the current political environment. For example, Pham et al. (2007) found that only 3 percent of nearly 3,000 Acholi surveyed listed justice as a top priority; however, 95 percent stated that a written historical record of atrocities should be prepared and over 90 percent supported the establishment of a truth-seeking process. Despite the fear, hopelessness, and uncertainty surrounding accountability, the desire for resolution of issues related to the unhappy dead continues. As one victim's support group member in Nwoya explained:

> Atrocities were committed on both sides by LRA and NRA. The former LRA are trying to reintegrate; the healing process is easier in this respect because they are actively engaging in the process. The government is not acknowledging or apologizing for NRA atrocities. . . . The process of healing is complicated by bodies that are buried throughout the community. People fear and avoid those areas. . . . If people see the remains they feel shock and fear; it reminds them of the atrocities and the pain comes back. . . . The community is puzzled about what to do about grave sites, but they know they must do something to get rid of bad spirits so they don't have to fear.

Another concern expressed is that massacre victims buried or left within a particular village were often not local but rather were abducted from distant villages before being killed and hence are unknown to the current residents, hampering identification efforts. A resident of Nwoya described this concern:

> Sometimes people were killed, but they came from elsewhere so we can't know who they are. All we can do is perform rituals to rebury them. . . . The challenge is to separate the bodies in the mass graves and make them individuals. . . . The challenge is the bones. If

there was a way to understand which bone belongs to which body, it would be good to exhume these graves and put the bodies back together. . . . Some people [were] killed very far away, so they are not connected to these bones here. So we don't know if it will help them heal. And something may already have been done far away to help the dead heal. So the connection is not clear. But it can help the people living nearby the bones because the voices and the disturbances will stop. That's why people were appeasing hills. They can grow crops again and be at peace.

In sum, survivors and homestead residents reported considerable distress and hardship associated with the shallow mass grave. Portions of land are unusable, and spiritual disturbances affect those living in proximity. Available ritual remedies (ceremonies, cleansings, reburials) are largely inaccessible due to prohibitive costs and/or perceived to be limited in effectiveness. Additionally, exhumations, reburials, and local cosmologies are entangled with development projects, land disputes, political agendas, and postconflict reconstruction efforts (see, for example, Jahn 2016; Jahn and Wilhelm-Solomon 2015). Despite these challenges, the need for resolution through exhumation, identification, reburial, and ritual persists, not only in order to appease the dead but also to assist the living. An elder in Nwoya summed up this desire: "The whole world and Uganda knows there was war in northern Uganda. Our problem is to end the suffering of the living, and the only way to save the community is to perform rituals."

The Potential and Challenges for Forensic Investigation

Given these considerations, what role can forensic investigation play in northern Uganda? And for whom and what purposes? The answers to this question remain unclear. The broad purpose of forensic human rights investigations is to utilize the physical evidence of human remains and the grave context to create an objective historical record of the event(s). The basic steps of a forensic investigation are to (1) conduct historical research to determine where graves are located and who may have been buried within each; (2) apply archaeological methods systematically to locate and excavate human remains within each grave; (3) enumerate and identify the victims using appropriate scientific methods; (4) document and interpret trauma; and (5) generate reports that are accessible to families, communities, and medicolegal personnel (Doretti and Snow 2009; Gassiot and

Steadman 2008; Haglund et al. 2001). Despite the variation in burial contexts in Acholiland, this basic approach remains patent (Fondebrider 2015). The use of archaeological and molecular technologies renders possible the recovery and identification of the Acholi victims, yet the context at Nwoya and the national political environment—as well as the religious and cultural considerations—demonstrate the significant challenges at each step in the process.

The combined efforts of researchers and transitional justice advocates—our team included—have not only exposed the variation in perceptions of the dead among survivors and landowners but also provided a preliminary set of data concerning the location of surface scatter sites and burials and the potential identities of those believed to be buried in specific graves. These sites and known victims, however, are often contested among survivors, and comparatively little independent historical documentation is available to verify the information. Our current efforts, expanded in 2016, are exploring ethnographically the various meanings of burial contexts for survivors and, increasingly, documenting known and suspected clandestine surface and burial sites and IDP burials, using geographic information systems (GIS) technology and other spatial mapping techniques. There is literally no time to lose. As this case study of Nyowa acutely demonstrates, evidence of burial and site formation is quickly becoming destroyed by site disturbance, hidden by environmental recovery, and forgotten as memories fade or are lost with the passing of witnesses. As recollection dims, it is imperative to locate, verify, and scientifically document clandestine mortuary sites across the landscape as well as accumulate lists of potential victim names or at least notions of whether the dead were local or nonlocal victims. Such documentation also can support and supplement the oral testimony of witnesses and survivors, such as in the "massacre scoping" efforts conducted by Komakech Deo of the Refugee Law Project (see Ellison and Jessee 2012). The application of GIS will allow highly accurate spatial mapping of sites that also enables graves to be tied to each other, to specific massacre sites and IDP camps, and—when identifications are made—to the victims themselves and their surviving kin and communities. Thus, in addition to ongoing ethnographic analysis, one major and immediate goal of this research is to conduct further gravesite mapping and to train Ugandan colleagues in these techniques.

As indicated in the case of Nwoya, victims killed in one village were often from far-flung locations and unrelated clans, meaning that they represent an open population, such that investigators do not have a clear indication of the number and identity of the missing.[4] Moreover, few to no medical or dental records exist, making traditional methods of identification impossible. These operational facts, as well as the large scale of the missing throughout this region, make the formation of a DNA database integral to the process of scientific identification, such as that developed by the International Committee of Missing Persons (ICMP) for the former Yugoslavia (Hanson 2015; ICMP 2016). This is a Herculean effort on the part of scientists, nongovernmental organizations, and the communities to educate families about the science and potential of DNA while also faithfully conveying the limitations of the science, not to mention the large-scale collection, cataloguing, and sequencing of DNA in a fast-changing technological landscape. While our ethnographic research to date has uncovered little family opposition to the notion of DNA sample collection, the scientific community within Uganda is unprepared to create and maintain a DNA database, meaning that international assistance will be essential. Moreover, most survivors are unfamiliar with scientific techniques used in professional excavations and identification of remains and therefore cannot yet consider it seriously as an option. One immediate goal of this ongoing project is to train Ugandan colleagues in the methods of forensic investigation and its limitations and to design and implement together a public education and sensitization campaign among survivor communities. An important part of such a campaign is to understand the articulations (and conflicts) among cultural, religious, and scientific approaches to remedying the dilemmas with the dead.

Another major obstacle in northern Uganda is the lack of clarity about which government agencies will facilitate and oversee any future forensic investigations in Acholiland, including those atrocities committed by the NRA, some of whose personnel still maintain seats of power in the military or government. As demonstrated most recently in Spain, the success of independent forensic investigations is strongly tied to the political will and structural integrity of national governments, especially the judicial bodies (Gassiot and Steadman 2008; Rios and Etxeberria 2017). In 2013 the government of Uganda published a Draft Transitional Justice Policy, which, among other concepts, proposed a loose framework for reparations, truth telling, and local-based transitional justice mechanisms (e.g., *mato oput*, an Acholi ceremony of atonement and social justice). However, there has been no further crafting or action on the draft since its publication three years ago. Moreover, the draft policy does not directly address a legal mechanism to recover, identify, and repatriate the dead or provide reparations to families.

CONCLUSION

In many postconflict contexts, the ability of survivors to cope with the aftermath of violence is tethered to the fate of the dead and the missing (see Crossland 2009, 2013; Rosenblatt 2015; Wagner 2008). Such shared fates are even more acute in cultural contexts where the dead retain active agency among the living, as in northern Uganda. This chapter has drawn on our own ethnographic research in Acholiland and related studies as well as knowledge developed in forensic human rights investigations elsewhere to examine the political, legal, and spiritual significance of improper burials in northern Uganda and assess what role forensic analysis may play.

The dilemmas facing Acholi survivors are many: spiritual disturbances, uncertainty regarding the identities of the dead and those who killed them, lack of resources for necessary rituals, disagreement about the type and efficacy of rituals required, continued structural violence impeding reconciliation, and hasty ceremonies spawned by development projects, land disputes, political agendas, and postconflict reconstruction efforts. Several challenges for potential forensic investigations also exist: contested details over massacres, unknown numbers and identities of the missing, site disturbances, destruction of evidence, fading memories, scarce medical and dental records, lack of knowledge and resources to establish and maintain a DNA database, and difficult physical, cultural, and political terrains. Nevertheless, considerable potential exists for culturally sensitive forensic investigations to acknowledge the agency of both the living and the dead and to develop community sensitization materials and programs that will inform survivors of the potentials/limitations of forensic analysis, build capacity by training Ugandan colleagues in the techniques of forensic investigation, and establish a body of physical evidence that will contribute powerfully to accurate historical records of atrocities.

ACKNOWLEDGMENTS

The research for this chapter has informed the development of larger team project and is influenced by the ongoing participation of researchers Jaymelee Kim, Hugh Tuller, and Wilfred Komakech, with assistance from Joshua Oballim Jr., Jeffrey Opiyo, and Godfrey Okot. Special thanks to Jeffrey Opiyo and Lindsay McClain Opiyo for their contributions and assistance during the period of fieldwork on which this chapter is primarily based. We are also grateful to our colleagues at the Refugee Law Project and the Justice and Reconciliation Project, as well as the local survivors association. Funding for this research was generously provided by the University of Tennessee and NIH/NIMHD Grant #T37MD001378. We are grateful for further support from the Wenner-Gren Foundation, Grant #9075.

NOTES

1. Improper burial in Acholi includes any or all of the following elements: multiple bodies in a grave; burials conducted in a hurried fashion without collective gatherings of family and community; not performing rituals, often including sacrifice of goats, sheep, or chickens; burying the body away from the home village and homestead; and leaving the grave unmarked or untended. Importantly, Acholi also view the spirit of the dead person as a stranger and possible enemy after death; the spirit must therefore be appeased, tamed, and brought back into the fold of the kin group to avoid misfortune, which is itself an ongoing process or relationship. See Seebach 2016 for a detailed analysis of death rites in Acholi.

2. Since 2012 we have conducted ethnographic research among Acholi survivors in collaboration with Ugandan transitional justice organizations (specifically, Justice and Reconciliation Project and Refugee Law Project). Team members have conducted site visits to burial locations, examined existing data on massacre events, engaged in focus groups with elders and community leaders, and conducted approximately fifty semistructured interviews with other survivors. We present a case study of a homestead in Nwoya District as an example of this work.

3. Whether and how cleansing or other rituals to appease the dead actually "work" is a matter of debate among survivors (see, for example, Neuner et al. 2012; Victor and Porter 2014). In summer 2016 members of our research team observed a cleansing ritual sponsored by Refugee Law Project in a local village that had been the site of mass atrocity; afterward, the chief (*rwot*) and elders discussed the potential for its failure. If the spiritual disturbances (nightmares, voices, strange visions, illness) did not cease then this would be the major sign the ritual failed; however, the failure could be due to numerous factors, including the small number of people who attended, the absence of close kin of the victims, and the fact that the ritual had not been exclusively organized and funded by the survivors of the incident.

4. In contrast, a closed population refers to a situation where the number and identities of victims are known, such as from a plane crash and the flight manifest.

References

Baines, E. 2010. Spirits and Social Reconstruction after Mass Violence: Rethinking Transitional Justice. *African Affairs* 109(436):409–430.

Branch, A. 2010. Exploring the Roots of LRA Violence. In *The Lord's Resistance Army: Myth and Reality*, edited by T. Allen and K. Vlassenroot, pp. 25–44. Zed Books, London.

Crossland, Z. 2009. Of Clues and Signs: The Dead Body and Its Evidential Traces. *American Anthropologist* 111(1):69–80.

———. 2013. Evidential Regimes of Forensic Archaeology. *Annual Review of Anthropology* 42:121–137.

Dolan, C. 2011. *Social Torture: The Case of Northern Uganda, 1986–2006*. Berghahn Books, New York.

Doretti, M., and C. Snow. 2009. Forensic Anthropology and Human Rights. In *Hard Evidence: Case Studies in Forensic Anthropology*, edited by D. Steadman, pp. 305–322. 2nd ed. Prentice Hall, Upper Saddle River, NJ.

Ellison, M., and E. Jessee. 2012. Mapping Uganda's Massacres. *Al-Jazeera Online Magazine.* http://marcellison.com/aj/Mapping%20Uganda's%20massacres.pdf.

Fondebrider, L. 2015. Forensic Anthropology and the Investigation of Political Violence. In *Necropolitics: Mass Graves and Exhumations in the Age of Human Rights*, edited by F. Fernandiz and A.C.G. M. Robben, pp. 41–52. University of Pennsylvania, Philadelphia.

Gassiot, E., and D. W. Steadman. 2008. The Political, Social and Scientific Contexts of Archaeological Investigations of Mass Graves in Spain. *Archaeologies: Journal of the World Archaeological Congress* 4(3):429–444.

Haglund, W. D., M. Connor, and D. D. Scott. 2001. The Archaeology of Contemporary Mass Graves. *Historical Archaeology* 35(1):57–69.

Hanson, I. 2015. Forensic Archaeology and the International Commission on Missing Persons: Setting Standards in an Integrated Process. In *Forensic Archaeology: A Global Perspective*, edited by J. M. Groen, N. Marquez-Grant, and J. Robert C, pp. 415–426. Wiley-Blackwell, West Sussex, UK.

Hopwood, J. 2011. *We Can't Be Sure Who Killed Us: Memory and Memorialization in Post-Conflict Northern Uganda*. International Center for Transitional Justice and Justice and Reconciliation Project, New York and Gulu.

International Commission on Missing Persons (ICMP). 2016. Databases and Data Processing System. http://www.icmp.int/.

Jahn, I. R. 2016. Post-war Development and Camp-site Graves: The Politics of Reburials in Former Pabbo IDP Camp, Acholiland. *Journal of Peace and Security Studies (JPSS)* 2(1):33–44.

Jahn, I. R., and M. Wilhelm-Solomon. 2015. Bones in the Wrong Soil: Reburial, Belonging, and Disinterred Cosmologies in Post-conflict Northern Uganda. *Critical African Studies* 7(2):182–201.

Kembel, A. 2015. When the Dead Are Not Silent: The Investigation of Cultural Perspectives Concerning Improper Burials in Northern Uganda. Master's thesis, Department of Anthropology, University of Tennessee.

Meinert, L., and S. R. Whyte. 2013. Creating the New Times: Reburials after War in Northern Uganda. In *Taming Time, Timing Death: Social Technologies and Ritual*, edited by D. R. Christensen and R. Willerslev, pp. 175–193. Ashgate Publishing Group, Abingdon, Oxon, UK.

Neuner, F., A. Pfeiffer, E. Schauer-Kaiser, M. Odenwald, T. Elbert, and V. Ertl. 2012. Haunted by Ghosts: Prevalence, Predictors and Outcomes of Spirit Possession Experiences among Former Child Soldiers and War-Affected Civilians in Northern Uganda. *Social Science & Medicine* 75:548–554.

Pham, P., P. Vinck, E. Stover, A. Moss, M. Wierda, and R. Bailey. 2007. *When the War Ends: A New Population-Based Survey on Attitudes about Peace, Justice, and Social Reconstruction in Northern Uganda*. Human Rights Center: University of California, Berkeley.

Refugee Law Project (RLP). 2014. *Compendium of Conflicts in Uganda*. Makerere University Faculty of Law, Kampala.

Rios, L., and F. Etxeberria. 2017. The Spanish Civil War Forensic Labyrinth. In *Legacies of Violence in Contemporary Spain: Exhuming the Past, Understanding the Present*, edited by O. Ferran and L. Hilbink, pp. 44–64. Routledge, New York.

Rosenblatt, A. 2015. *Digging for the Disappeared: Forensic Science after Atrocity*. Stanford Studies in Human Rights. Stanford University Press, Stanford, CA.

Scheper-Hughes, N., and P. Bourgois (editors). 2003. *Violence in War and Peace: An Anthology*. Blackwell Publishing, Malden.

Seebach, S. H. 2016. The Dead Are Not Dead: Intimate Governance of Transitions in Acholi. PhD dissertation, Aarhus University.

Victor, L., and H. Porter. 2014. Dirty Things: Spiritual and Psychological Distress and the Pursuit of Redress amongst Ex-Combatants of the Lord's Resistance Army, Northern Uganda. Paper presented at the African Studies Association United Kingdom Biannual Conference, University of Sussex, UK.

Wagner, S. E. 2008. *To Know Where He Lies: DNA Technology and the Search for Srebrenica's Missing*. University of California Press, Berkeley.

10

The Extended Massacre of Migrants

Exposure-Related Deaths in the Arizona Sonoran Desert

CATE E. BIRD

The desert is an isolating, unforgiving ecosystem where exposure-related deaths are agonizing end-of-life experiences. If thermoregulation is significantly disrupted, an individual's entire body stops functioning. When exposed to hot environments for prolonged periods, the body's heat-regulating mechanisms begin to fail. An individual experiences clinical signs of heat exhaustion: elevated core temperatures, excessive sweating, fatigue, increased heartbeat, rapid breathing, nausea, and/or vomiting (CDC 2017). If not properly treated, heatstroke (hyperthermia) can ensue: the body's temperature can rise above 103°F (39°C), as weakness, nausea, vomiting, syncope, and headaches set in. The body is unable to cool through perspiration, causing the skin to become hot and dry to the touch. The central nervous system exhibits greater disruptions: confusion, fainting, loss of control of body movements, seizures, and delirium. The heart rate dangerously increases. Hepatic transaminases elevate, indicating liver damage. Blood's ability to clot is impaired, resulting in coagulopathy (prolonged or excessive bleeding). Muscle fibers begin to die, releasing their contents into the bloodstream. Ultimately, the kidneys fail when they are unable to remove waste and concentrated urine from the body. Death occurs in hyperthermic patients if rapid cooling is not immediately administered (CDC 2017). These types of deaths are painful and solitary.

Hyperthermia occurs most frequently in hot, arid environments such as the Sonoran Desert in southern Arizona. Located between the Mohave and Chihuahuan Deserts, the Sonoran Desert sprawls across over 100,000 square miles of the southwestern United States and northwestern Mexico

Figure 10.1. The Arizona Sonoran Desert. (Courtesy of the PCOME.)

(National Park Service 2016). Temperatures frequently exceed 104°F (40°C) during summer months, often reaching highs of 118°F (48°C) or more. Winter temperatures are generally mild compared to higher-latitude areas of the United States, but high-elevation mountainous areas in the Sonoran Desert do receive dense snow cover with temperatures dropping below 32°F (0°C). Even in the driest biome, the Sonoran Desert supports diverse plant and animal species and is known for its characteristic succulents, such as agave, yucca, prickly pear, cholla, and saguaro cacti (figure 10.1).

While stunning, this ecological marvel can be treacherous to individuals exercising strenuously in it, especially when coupled with poor fluid intake. Migrants crossing this harsh desert terrain in the United States are particularly susceptible to high morbidity and mortality rates in this environment. Over 2,400 migrants have died within the last fifteen years while crossing the Sonoran Desert in Arizona.

According to a Pew Research Center study, the foreign-born population in the United States in 2014 totaled 43.6 million, with unauthorized immigrants representing only a quarter of the total number (Passel and Cohn 2016). The number of unauthorized immigration has changed over time, steadily increasing from 1990 (3.5 million) to 2007 (12.2 million), but leveling out and remaining stable since the end of the Great Recession from 2009 to 2014 (Passel and Cohn 2016). At the same time, the demographics of those entering the United States as undocumented migrants are also changing. While the number of unauthorized immigrants from Mexico has declined, those from Asia, Central America, and sub-Saharan Africa have increased from 2009 to 2014 (Passel and Cohn 2016). Unfortunately, in the last fifteen years, death of unauthorized immigrants along the U.S.-Mexico border has become part of the cultural landscape.

Violence in biological anthropology is frequently considered in terms of physical force of one agent against another, often indicated by traumatic injuries in osseous tissue (Kimmerle and Baraybar 2008; Lovell 1997, 2008; Passalacqua and Rainwater 2015; Wedel and Galloway 2014). However, violence can take other more subtle forms that are harder to observe in the archaeological and forensic records, such as symbolic, psychological, or structural forms (Hinton 2002). Structural violence refers to distress, suffering, and/or morbidity resulting from institutionalized or large-scale social forces of discrimination, such as racism, sexism, political violence, or poverty (Farmer 1996, 2004). Violence can also be discussed in terms of *massacres*, or episodes of violent behavior better described as processes, that are shaped by local patterned dynamics (Klusemann 2012; Martin and Harrod 2015). Klusemann (2012, 469) describes massacres as violent behaviors enacted as atrocities and shaped by "situational emotional dynamics." Massacres subjugate or eradicate individuals deemed to be "others" and frequently exhibit recurrent characteristics that are culturally and temporally specific (Martin and Harrod 2015). Notable massacres from North America are documented in prehistoric contexts, such the Crow Creek site in the Great Plains (Willey and Emerson 1993; Zimmerman and Bradley 1993) and the Orendorf (Steadman 2008) and Norris Farms sites in west-central Illinois (Milner et al. 1991; Santure et al. 1990).

Some researchers question whether the U.S. government's disregard for the effects of the harsh desert environment is a passive form of warfare, whereby noncitizens who attempt unauthorized entry into the United States are permitted to perish as a form of deterrence. This chapter investigates the circumstances of migrants who die in the Sonoran Desert and are subsequently examined at the Pima County Office of the Medical Examiner (PCOME). In particular it explores this large-scale, extended massacre in light of structural violence and the U.S. government's neglect to adequately address this humanitarian crisis.

MASSACRE CONTEXT

The Pima County Office of the Medical Examiner serves as the medical examiner for three counties in southern Arizona that border the U.S.-Mexico boundary and provides forensic pathology services for eight additional counties in Arizona as needed. Located in Tucson, the PCOME has encountered the migrant humanitarian crisis up close. Decedents suspected of being foreign nationals who die while attempting to cross the southern Arizona desert clandestinely are classified as Undocumented Border Crossers (UBCs) (Anderson and Parks 2008), an important categorization for determining the most prudent identification route for this unique population (Bird 2016).

Between the calendar years 2001 and 2015 the PCOME received the remains of 2,465 UBCs. Thinking that they had already experienced the worst of this humanitarian crisis, those who work to identify these decedents have been astounded by the number of migrant deaths since 2001. But every year migrants continually die in high numbers in the Sonoran Desert (figure 10.2).

The greatest number of UBCs occurred in 2010 (n = 223) and 2007 (n = 214), with an average of 171 UBC deaths every year over the last fifteen years (Pima County Office of the Medical Examiner 2015). However, the actual number of migrant deaths in this region is suspected to be much higher, as numerous bodies likely lie undiscovered on the desert floor.

Figure 10.2. Deceased migrant found under a tree during the summer months in the Sonoran Desert. (Courtesy of the PCOME.)

Individuals walking or hiking in hot environments who become dehydrated due to poor fluid intake are at the highest risk for suffering from hyperthermia. Those with severe heat stroke become confused and are often described as "intoxicated." These individuals are frequently discovered under the limited shade the open desert offers with their clothes stripped off (figures 10.3 and 10.4).

Figure 10.3. Deceased migrant found with his clothes stripped during the summer months in the Sonoran Desert. (Courtesy of the PCOME.)

Figure 10.4. Deceased migrant found wrapped in a garbage bag for warmth during the winter months in the Sonoran Desert. (Courtesy of the PCOME.)

Figure 10.5. Deceased migrant found covered with cactus spines. (Courtesy
of the PCOME.)

In addition to hyperthermic deaths, migrants crossing the Sonoran desert during winter months are also at risk of hypothermia (cold exposure),
when core body temperature falls below 95°F (35°C) due to inadequate
clothing and shelter.

Limited protection coupled with the harsh desert environment results
in migrants suffering a range of injuries, including blisters on the soles of
their feet and bodies covered with cactus spines (figure 10.5).

Exposure-related causes of death account for up to 28 percent of UBCs
between 2011 and 2015. But this percentage is misleadingly low. Due to the
nature of clandestine migration paths, decedents who die in remote desert
locations in southern Arizona may not be recovered for weeks, months, or
years. In the warmer months of the year bodies decompose at an advanced
rate and are subject to postmortem alterations by scavengers. For instance,
only 14 percent of the 138 UBCs recovered in 2015 showed minimal or no
signs of decomposition, while 86 percent were discovered decomposed,
mummified, or skeletonized. If they are not recovered immediately, many
of the identifying features of the deceased, as well as the ability to determine cause and manner of death, are lost. As a result of the advanced rate
of decomposition associated with the Sonoran Desert, the cause of death
in the majority of deceased migrants over the past five years is unknown.
However, it is believed that in most cases where the cause of death cannot

be determined due to decompositional changes the individuals likely died of exposure. Other causes of death associated with UBCs include cardiovascular disease, gunshot wounds, blunt force trauma, and drowning. Interpersonal violence represents a low percentage of UBC deaths. Evaluating manner of death in UBCs between 2006 and 2013, Bird and Soler (2015) found that homicide accounted for only 2.6 percent of UBC deaths, while accidents (41.9 percent) and undetermined (47.9 percent) manners of death were far more common. Data from southern Arizona are supported by research in other areas of the U.S.-Mexico border, which demonstrates that UBCs are overwhelmingly dying from causes other than homicide. In San Diego County, California, motor vehicle accidents and exposure to harsh environmental conditions were noted as the primary causes of death in UBCs between 1993 and 2004 (Hinkes 2008). In Imperial County, California, exposure and drowning represented the major causes of death from 1993 to 2004 (Hinkes 2008).

The migrants who died while crossing the Sonoran Desert during the last fifteen years are overwhelmingly young and middle-aged males. Between 2011 and 2015 males accounted for 76–86 percent of UBCs, while females accounted for only 8–11 percent. During this period, sex was not known in 3–13 percent of UBC cases (Pima County Office of the Medical Examiner 2011, 2012, 2013, 2014, 2015). The higher prevalence of males in this humanitarian crisis in southern Arizona is not completely unexpected, as the UBC sex profile closely mirrors that of U.S. Border Patrol apprehension data (Bird 2016).

Health disparities are also evident in deceased migrants from southern Arizona, manifested as high levels of physiological stress in skeletal remains. Comparing nonspecific indicators of stress between UBCs at the PCOME and known samples from collections of human remains in the United States, Beatrice and Soler (2016) found that porotic hyperostosis was 7.9 times more prevalent in UBCs than in U.S. samples, while enamel hypoplasias were 3 times more likely in UBCs. These findings likely reflect disparities in access to adequate nutrition and healthcare during childhood between U.S. citizens and foreign nationals primarily from Central America. The higher prevalence of stress markers in UBCs also implies that migrants crossing into the United States through southern Arizona may come from lower socioeconomic groups or marginalized communities in their home countries.

Death of undocumented migrants who die while crossing into southern Arizona from Mexico currently shows no signs of ceasing. From analysis of remains, these individuals are predominantly young to middle-aged males who die of exposure to the harsh Sonoran Desert environment. Many of these individuals exhibit signs of stress during childhood and possibly come from lower socioeconomic groups in their home countries. With over 2,400 known UBC deaths in the early twenty-first century, it is difficult not to view this humanitarian crisis as an extended massacre. But who shoulders the responsibility for these deaths? While the desert is certainly the cause, some researchers view the environment as merely a tool in the hands of human agents.

Discussion

Nongovernmental migrant advocacy organizations characterize the suffering and death of undocumented migrants along the U.S.-Mexico border as a humanitarian crisis. In their view, migrants who cross treacherous terrain often as a result of economic, political, or social pressures constitute refugees but are treated as criminals, whose lives are disposable. The characterization of foreign nationals who clandestinely enter the United States without the express permission of the government as "illegal entrants" is reflected in the response of policymakers and enforcers. Numerous researchers have discussed how the U.S. border militarization approach, particularly the "prevention through deterrence strategy," has resulted in increased death of undocumented migrants (Andreas 2000; Cornelius 2005; De León 2015; Dunn 1996, 2009; Martínez et al. 2013; Nevins 2010; Rubio-Goldsmith et al. 2006).

It is no coincidence that migrants crossing into the United States from Mexico traverse the most desolate paths. The location of these routes is the direct result of federal immigration control policies that have increased border security along some areas of the border, while leaving other areas open. The physical barriers that separate the U.S. from Mexican territories consist of a series of walls and fences. However, this defensive structure is not continuous: the U.S.-Mexico border is 1,989 miles long, while barriers are only present along approximately 580 miles of it (U.S. Customs and Border Protection 2016). Migrants do not scale these barriers: they move around them. Hence these intermittent barriers redistribute or funnel migrants into the most arid and isolated regions of the United States (Rubio-Goldsmith et al. 2006).

Researchers (Martínez et al. 2013; Rubio-Goldsmith et al. 2006) have described this "funnel effect" in relation to the increase in migrant deaths in Arizona. These researchers contend that U.S. immigration control policies initiated in the mid- to late 1990s intentionally redirected hundreds of thousands of unauthorized migrants away from crossing points in Texas and California toward the perilous landscape of southern Arizona. The underlying logic of this enforcement strategy reasons that migrants will discontinue their journey once they realize the danger of suffering and death in these uninhabitable desert regions. But this has not been the case. Martínez et al. (2013) recognize three distinct periods with increasing UBC deaths in southern Arizona from the PCOME: the "Pre-Funnel Effect" (FY 1990–1999) with a recorded 120 UBC deaths; the "Early Funnel Effect" (FY 2000–2005) with 804 UBC deaths; and the "Late Funnel Effect" (FY 2006–2012) with 1,314 UBC deaths. The U.S. government's strategy of enforcement through deterrence further increased from 2004 to 2012, with a surge in border security. During this period, resources were allocated to triple the size of the U.S. Border Patrol (Slack et al. 2016). Advocates of immigration reform contend that the increase in security and agents along the U.S.-Mexico boundary coupled with strategic defensive structures amounts to militarization of the border. However, despite the concerted effort by the U.S. government to curtail unauthorized immigration, Cornelius (2005) argues that the militarization of the border is a weak deterrent and that immigration control policies have failed, as migration steadily increased during the 1990s and mid-2000s.

Violence in current and past populations is often discussed in terms of osteological indicators of trauma resulting from individual or group conflict. Trauma of this nature is largely lacking in the migrant humanitarian crisis: individuals are felled over an extended period and vast swaths of space. This large-scale death event is only comprehensible through the aggregation of a series of individual deaths: over 2,400 bodies. It is even more difficult to categorize in terms of violence. However, Martin and Harrod (2015) have suggested that violence frequently defies generalizations due to its nuance and variability, especially when considered in relation to power and daily conflicts, like territorial protection and immigrants. These individual migrant deaths should be viewed within the larger social matrix in which they are embedded (Farmer 1996).

The migrant humanitarian crisis may be described as a relatively large-scale, low-intensity conflict (Bamforth 1994). Militarization of the border is extensive, but high mortality rates occur as a result of exposure to the environment rather than violent interpersonal encounters. In essence, the desert becomes an object of violence that can be wielded in order to deter, detain, and if necessary incapacitate "illegal" entrants. Death in this massacre context is more akin to deaths resulting from sieges rather than traditional warfare or interpersonal violence. The siege represents a military strategy: blockades surround enemy forces, cutting them off from essential resources with the aim of compelling surrender through attrition. Sieges are generally discussed in terms of cities and their surrounding spaces, where defensive structures originally meant as protective features can subsequently become a means of incarceration when residents cannot leave. Cut off from food, water, and other essential supplies, city inhabitants surrender or die of starvation, dehydration, or disease. While the U.S. Border Patrol, particularly in the Tucson Sector, attempts to mitigate migrant deaths through implementation of search and rescue teams and first responders, the intermittent defensive barriers along the U.S.-Mexico border that funnel migrants into remote, deadly desert areas serve an undeniable function: to weaken and debilitate an "enemy."

Given the current political climate in the United States, it is difficult to predict how immigration reform and border security will affect migrant deaths occurring in southern Arizona. The current U.S. authorities advocate completing a continuous, impassible barrier along the U.S.-Mexico border. The wish to construct this barrier appears to be driven by ideals rooted in nationalism, xenophobia, and fear rather than humanism. While announcing his bid for the presidency of the United States on June 16, 2015, candidate Donald Trump stated: "When Mexico sends its people, they're not sending their best. They're not sending you. They're not sending you. They're sending people that have lots of problems, and they're bringing those problems with us. They're bringing drugs. They're bringing crime. They're rapists. And some, I assume, are good people" (*Washington Post* 2016). The demonization of immigrants as "criminals" that characterized Trump's 2016 presidential campaign represents a wider expression of fear toward foreign nationals, which became palpable immediately following the 2016 presidential election. The Southern Poverty Law Center (SPLC) recorded 867 postelection incidents of harassment and intimidation in the ten days following Trump's win on November 8, 2016, 32 percent of which were anti-immigrant in nature (Miller and Werner-Winslow. 2016). The SPLC also noted a significant increase in overt expressions of verbal harassment, the use of slurs or derogatory language, and cultural symbols of hatred (such as swastikas, Nazi salutes, and Confederate flags) in K-12 schools directed toward marginalized students, including immigrants, in what has been called the "Trump Effect" (Costello 2016). In the United States today the exploitation of immigrant labor coupled with performances of hate toward migrants reveals a schizophrenic political and economic order characteristic of structural violence (Farmer 2004).

Death of migrants along the U.S.-Mexico border should be viewed within a broader, more nuanced anthropological framework (Martin and Harrod 2015). Deaths have occurred on a massive scale, yet they do not qualify as "violent" interactions as traditionally defined in biological anthropology. Neglect to acknowledge or ameliorate the humanitarian crisis of migrant deaths has become normalized in a cultural climate of inflammatory rhetoric and expressions of hatred toward immigrant communities. While this crisis includes extreme suffering, the fatal consequence exceeds traditional definitions of institutionalized racism associated with structural violence. These deaths appear to lie somewhere between structural and physical violence, a massacre with an invisible master.

It is unclear whether a defensive structure would prevent migrants from dying in remote desert areas of southern Arizona. Perhaps it could. Or it could result in funneling migrants into new, more dangerous regions or enterprises in order to cross into U.S. territory. The militarization of the U.S. borders will certainly not address the underlying fear and ethnic hostility that many U.S. citizens hold toward immigrant communities currently residing within the national boundaries. This militarization will also not address underlying causes of the migration of Central and South Americans, such as globalization, economic disparities, and political violence. Until the economic, political, and social problems of neighboring developing countries are improved, migration into the United States and the potential for a continued contemporary massacre on U.S. soil will exist.

References

Anderson, B. E., and B. O. Parks. 2008. Symposium on Border Crossing Deaths: Introduction. *Journal of Forensic Sciences* 53(1):6–7.

Andreas, P. 2000. *Border Games: Policing the US-Mexico Divide*. Cornell University Press, New York.

Bamforth, D. B. 1994. Indigenous People, Indigenous Violence: Precontact Warfare on the North American Great Plains. *Man*, new series 29(1):95–115.

Beatrice, J. S., and A. Soler. 2016. Skeletal Indicators of Stress: A Component of the Biocultural Profile of Undocumented Migrants in Southern Arizona. *Journal of Forensic Sciences* 61(5):1164–1172.

Bird, C. E. 2016. Population Bias and Its Advantages in Forensic Anthropological Casework. In *Proceedings of the 85th Annual Meeting of the American Association of Physical Anthropologists*, 97. American Association of Physical Anthropologists, Atlanta, GA.

Bird, C. E., and A. Soler. 2015. Interpersonal Violence in Undocumented Border Cross-ers from Southern Arizona between 2006 and 2013. *Proceedings of the 67th American Academy of Forensic Sciences Annual Scientific Meeting*. Orlando, FL.

Carman, J. 1997. Introduction: Approaches to Violence. In *Material Harm*, edited by J. Carman, pp. 1–23. Cruithne Press, Glasgow, Scotland.

Centers for Disease Control and Prevention (CDC). 2017. Warning Signs and Symptoms of Heat-Related Illness. https://www.cdc.gov/disasters/extremeheat/warning.html.

Cornelius, W. A. 2005. Controlling "Unwanted" Immigration: Lessons from the United States, 1993–2004. *Journal of Ethnic and Migration Studies* 31(4):775–794.

Costello, M. B. 2016. *The Trump Effect: The Impact of the 2016 Presidential Election on Our Nation's Schools*. Southern Poverty Law Center, Montgomery, AL.

De León, J. 2015. *The Land of Open Graves: Living and Dying on the Migrant Trail*. University of California Press, Oakland.

Dunn, T. J. 1996. *The Militarization of the U.S.-Mexico Border, 1978–1992: Low-Intensity Doctrine Conflict Comes Home*. University of Texas Press, Austin.

———. 2009. *Blockading the Border and Human Rights: The El Paso Operation That Re-made Immigration Enforcement*. University of Texas Press, Austin.

Farmer, P. 1996. On Suffering and Structural Violence: A View from Below. *Daedalus* 125(1):261–283.

———. 2004. An Anthropology of Structural Violence. *Current Anthropology* 45(3):305–325.

Hinkes, M. J. 2008. Migrant Deaths along the California-Mexico Border: An Anthropo-logical Perspective. *Journal of Forensic Sciences* 53(1):16–20.

Hinton, A. 2002. *Annihilating Difference: The Anthropology of Genocide*. University of Cali-fornia Press, Berkeley.

Keim, S. M. 2007. Heat Deaths among Undocumented US-Mexico Border Crossers in Pima County, Arizona. Master's thesis, University of Arizona.

Kimmerle, E. H., and J. P. Baraybar (editors). 2008. *Skeletal Trauma: Identification of In-juries Resulting from Human Remains Abuse and Armed Conflict*. CRC Press, Boca Raton, FL.

Klusemann, S. 2012. Massacres as Process: A Micro-sociological Theory of Internal Pat-terns of Mass Atrocities. *European Journal of Criminology* 9(5):468–480.

Lovell, N. C. 1997. Trauma Analysis in Paleopathology. *Yearbook of Physical Anthropology* 40:139–170.

———. 2008. Analysis and Interpretation of Skeletal Trauma. In *Biological Anthropology of the Human Skeleton*, edited by M. A. Katzenberg and S. R. Saunders, pp. 341–386. 2nd ed. John Wiley and Sons, Hoboken, NJ.

Martin, D. L., and D. W. Frayer. 1997. Introduction. In *Troubled Times: Violence and War-fare in the Past*, edited by D. L. Martin and D. W. Frayer, pp. xiii–xxi. CRC Press, Boca Raton, FL.

Martin, D. L., and R. P. Harrod. 2015. Bioarchaeological Contributions to the Study of Violence. *American Journal of Physical Anthropology* 156:116–145.

Martínez, D. E., R. C. Reineke, R. Rubio-Goldsmith, B. E. Anderson, G. L. Hess, and B. O. Parks. 2013. *A Continued Humanitarian Crisis at the Border: Undocumented Border*

Crosser Deaths Recorded by the Pima County Office of the Medical Examiner, 1990–2012. Binational Migration Institute: University of Arizona, Tucson.

Miller, C., and A. Werner-Winslow. 2016. *Ten Days After: Harassment and Intimidation in the Aftermath of the Election.* Southern Poverty Law Center, Montgomery, AL.

Milner, G. R., E. Anderson, and V. G. Smith. 1991. Warfare in Late Prehistoric West-Central Illinois. *American Antiquity* 56(4):581–603.

National Park Service. 2016. Sonoran Desert Ecosystem. http://science.nature.nps.gov/im/units/sodn/sonoran.cfm.

Nevins, J. 2010. *Operation Gatekeeper and Beyond: The War on "Illegals" and the Remaking of the US-Mexico Boundary.* Routledge, New York.

Passalacqua, N. V., and C. W. Rainwater (editors). 2015. *Skeletal Trauma Analysis: Case Studies in Context.* Wiley-Blackwell, Chichester, UK.

Passel, J., and D. Cohn. 2016. *Overall Number of U.S. Unauthorized Immigrants Hold Steady since 2009.* Pew Research Center. http://www.pewhispanic.org/2016/09/20/overall-number-of-u-s-unauthorized-immigrants-holds-steady-since-2009/.

Pima County Office of the Medical Examiner (Tucson). 2011. Annual Report.

———. 2012. Annual Report.

———. 2013. Annual Report.

———. 2014. Annual Report.

———. 2015. Annual Report.

Rubio-Goldsmith, R., M. McCormick, D. Martinez, and I. M. Duarte. 2006. *The "Funnel Effect" & Recovered Bodies of Unauthorized Migrants Processed by the Pima County Office of the Medical Examiner, 1990–2005.* Binational Migration Institute, Mexican American Studies and Research Center, University of Arizona Report, Tucson.

Santure, S. K., A. D. Harn, and D. Esarey (editors). 1990. *Archaeological Investigations at the Morton Village and Norris Farms 36 Cemetery.* Reports of Investigations, No. 45. Illinois State Museum, Springfield.

Slack, J., D. E. Martínez, A. E. Lee, and S. Whiteford. 2016. The Geography of Border Militarization: Violence, Death and Health in Mexico and the United States. *Journal of Latin American Geography* 15(1):7–32.

Steadman, D. W. 2008. Warfare Related Trauma at Orendorf, a Middle Mississippian Site in West-Central Illinois. *American Journal of Physical Anthropology* 136(1):51–64.

U.S. Customs and Border Protection. 2016. https://help.cbp.gov/app/answers/detail/a_id/578/~/border-in-miles (accessed December 13, 2016, no longer available).

Washington Post. 2016. Donald Trump Announces a Presidential Bid. *Washington Post,* June 16.

Wedel, V. L., and A. Galloway (editors). 2014. *Broken Bones: Anthropological Analysis of Blunt Force Trauma.* 2nd ed. Charles C. Thomas, Springfield, IL.

Willey, P., and T. E. Emerson. 1993. The Osteology and Archaeology of the Crow Creek Massacre. *Plains Anthropologist* 38(145):227–269.

Zimmerman, L. J., and L. E. Bradley. 1993. The Crow Creek Massacre: Initial Coalescent Warfare and Speculations about the Genesis of Extended Coalescent. *Plains Anthropologist* 38(145):215–226.

11

Migrant Death and Identification

Theory, Science, and Sociopolitics

KRISTA E. LATHAM, ALYSON O'DANIEL, AND JUSTIN MAIERS

Over the past decade tens of thousands of migrants have died crossing the border from Mexico to the United States. Historically, undocumented border crossers have entered by traveling the border terrains nearest California (Rose 2012). Changes in border policy and practice in the early 2000s, however, funneled would-be border-crossers into more treacherous landscapes of Arizona and, most recently, Texas borderlands. This shift has been catastrophic for migrants who find themselves in the far reaches of the desert with little, if any, resort to help when they are lost, dehydrated, injured, or otherwise victimized and endangered (De León 2015). As a result, known migrant deaths in these states have steadily risen to proportions of "mass disaster." These deaths are largely policy-driven and can therefore be viewed as an extended massacre occurring along the U.S. southern border (see Bird, chapter 10).

While Arizona has now had a decade to develop the infrastructure to address the large number of forensic investigations necessary to attend to this mass disaster scenario, the crisis in Texas has only recently reached such catastrophic proportions. As a result, the notion of migrant death as a crisis is still relatively new in the state and is therefore largely underfunded and underaddressed. In response, forensic investigators from a variety of organizations and institutions have been donating their time, materials, and expertise to aid in the recovery, identification, and repatriation of perished migrants found along migrant routes in Texas.

As volunteer forensic investigators quickly realized, challenges of migrant death were multifaceted. Many counties had buried the unidentified migrants discovered in their jurisdictions due to lack of funding to conduct the costly forensic investigations into their identity. Decisions to bury the unidentified individuals were made by each county, with designated areas of local cemeteries dedicated to these migrant burials. However, the detail of documentation (depth, orientation, marked burial, and so forth) varies from county to county and cemetery to cemetery. Under these challenging conditions, the work of exhumation, identification, and repatriation required cooperation among various entities, including among exhumation teams, local authorities, federal agents, university laboratories, human rights organizations, family members in Mexico, Central America, and South America, and various Latin American consulates. It also required basic knowledge of complicated sociocultural processes such as migration, international policy and practice, and locally situated responses to the challenges of unidentified migrant death. Simply put, the work of migrant identification has propelled forensic scientists into the heart of social landscapes thus far uncharted in relation to their purposes.

In this chapter we discuss the migrant death crisis in Brooks County, Texas, and explore the sociopolitical conditions shaping realities of and responses to this mass-death scenario. Within that, we broadly consider the importance of sociocultural theory for forensic science as practiced in this setting. Why has migrant death reached crisis proportions in Texas? What is the role of forensic science in this setting? How can attention to sociocultural theory and context better prepare forensic scientists to apply their work under conditions of mass death? This chapter considers these questions by tracing sociopolitical conditions and practical complexities of migrant death and identification in the Texas border region.

Anthropological Theory and Migrant Death and Identification

Political Economy

Making sense of migrant death and related forensic investigation in the South Texas context requires attention to broader conditions of culture, economy, and politics. In other words, as scientists we cannot properly understand the surge in migrant deaths, local conditions and response to migrant deaths, and therefore the tasks and activities of forensic scientists in this setting without knowing something about the historical, social, and economic processes giving rise to the crisis and our response as experts and volunteers. Similar contextual and theoretical grounding of scientific practice has already taken place among biological anthropologists working in "traditional" research settings aimed at producing knowledge of culture, society, and the human condition (see, for example, Goodman and Leatherman 2001; Hicks and Leonard 2014). They note the historical specificity of analytical models and argue that that the time has come for greater attention to links between local phenomena and global processes as well as the way biological anthropologists are situated in relation to their attention to these phenomena and the processes producing them. This work has constituted a critical and reflexive turn toward clarifying how systems-level inequalities shape human biology and the work of biological anthropologists. In the remainder of this chapter we propose that a similar critical reflexive turn is warranted in the forensic science of migrant death and assert that a political economy theoretical framework may help to shed light on key aspects of forensic scientific practice as applied to this humanitarian crisis.

A political economy theoretical framework takes into account major structural transformations in world history and traces interconnections among communities, regions, peoples, and nations (Wolf 1982). The perspective delineates processes of power producing inequality between nations and peoples and highlights how those processes are reproduced over time. For purposes of this chapter, the model is used to trace key moments in the material and ideological course of what is sometimes referred to as the "new global capitalism," to spotlight the role of the state in mediating inequalities related to migrant death, and to highlight how capitalist processes beyond individual control may be manifested, transformed, and resisted in the lives of affected populations (Wolf 1982:21; Roseberry 1988). In this framework, local communities are therefore seen as affected by and affecting wider, systems-level processes (Schneider 1995:9). Specifically, we examine effects of contemporary market-based strategies of governance across Latin America and the United States to highlight structural conditions of migrant death and identification in South Texas. Such an approach spotlights volunteer forensic scientists as a local "community" in dynamic relationship with contemporary political and economic conditions shaping migration events and realities.

The New Global Capitalism in Latin America: General Overview

The new global capitalism refers to both a moment along global capitalism's historical timeline and the unfolding of a far-reaching transformation in the guiding principles of the global economy. In the late 1970s and early 1980s global economic relations underwent a profound shift in management philosophy and policy. In the wake of World of War II, many nation-states focused in common on creating conditions for rebuilding and development by promoting state-driven strategies for economic growth, full employment, and the welfare of the citizenry. Latin American development and growth was heavily focused on creation of a strong manufacturing sector that was supported by aggressive government investment and subsidy, high tariffs designed to discourage manufactured imports, and funds borrowed from U.S. and European banks (Hershberg and Rosen 2007:4–6; Petras and Veltmeyer 2009). The state was seen in international economic policy as the reasonable arbiter of domestic market processes, including fiscal and monetary policies that protected domestic markets by discouraging foreign imports and investment. At the same time, international institutions such as the United Nations, the World Bank, and the International Monetary Fund regulated international trade relations and currency exchange rates. As Harvey (2005:11) explains, "market processes and entrepreneurial and corporate activities were [at this time] surrounded by a web of social and political constraints."

Slow economic growth, rising and historically driven inequality, U.S.-backed installment of authoritarian governance regimes, and oppositional counteroffensive action, however, ushered in civil wars and widespread state-sponsored repression and violence across Latin America, particularly in the Central American states of Guatemala, El Salvador, and Nicaragua (Esparza et al. 2013). Worldwide fiscal crises and the Organization of the Petroleum Exporting Countries (OPEC) oil embargo of 1973 also ushered in conditions of economic stagnation and intensified political tumult. A concurrent global decline of commodity prices and rising interest rates then further complicated many Latin American states' abilities to service external debt. When Mexico officially defaulted on its debt payments in 1982, the first wave of the global debt crisis began (Harvey 2005:94). It is this crisis and its reverberation throughout the world that formally ushered in the new style of international economic management and policy.

"Neoliberalism," as the new conditions of global capitalist expansion are often called, refers to a market-centered style of governance and an accompanying logic imposed around the world throughout the 1980s and the 1990s (Kotz 2002; Richland 2009). In its most basic sense, the term refers to a mode of governance wherein the state plays a role limited to the protection of private property and the facilitation of a "free market" economy. The logic of neoliberalism posits that state interference in economic markets hinders development and growth (Di Leonardo 2008:6; Harvey 2005) and that the state should therefore provide for the well-being of its citizens by dismantling programs, institutions, and policies that dampen or restrict foreign investment, exchange, and capital accumulation. Denationalization of industry via privatization, labor and commodities market deregulation, and disinvestment in government safety net programs have been key strategies characterizing neoliberal economic reform (Harvey 2005; Kim et al. 2000). The basic premise has been that "once government gets out of the way of [economic] 'opportunity,' . . . [social] progress will take care of itself" (Goode and Maskovsky 2001:9).

However, in Latin America economic growth via processes of neoliberalism has been far more complicated than the ideology suggests. Scholars highlight the destructive and sometimes violent consequences that structural reform has had for local workers and vulnerable populations more generally. These effects include persistent and widening poverty and social inequality (Kim et al. 2000); state-sponsored violence and diminishing citizen security (Sanchez 2006); and emboldened criminal cartels (Smith-Nonini 2000; Watt and Zepeda 2012). For example, the redistribution of wealth through criminal gang activity becomes an increasingly viable option for many of the poor to survive and support a family. This creates a situation of social stratification among nonelites where individuals deemed to be unnecessary to the gangs become disposable. Those that are not able to contribute financial resources, goods, or services to these organizations are often killed or forced to leave through threat of violence. Others form the disposable class of laborers for the capitalist class. Wages plummet as job security, benefits, and protections disappear. Workers have no choice but to work long hours for little or no pay. These laborers are easily replaced if hurt, sick, or disgruntled, leaving many with no means by which to support their families or guarantee their safety under the threat of exploitation (Harvey 2005; Paramo 2012). All of these conditions help to explain the acceleration of migration from Latin America in recent decades. As scholars suggest, migrants make the journey in an effort to escape poverty exacerbated by neoliberal economic reform, to flee growing violence and criminal cartels flourishing in the absence of strong state deterrence programs, and to seek lives other than those that may be available to them in their communities of origin (Hellman 2006). Migration in this way is an outcome of systems-level processes of capitalist expansion.

Politics of Death at the U.S.-Mexico Border

Unfortunately for too many migrants, the migration journey is fraught with the violence of capitalism as well. From exploitation en route (Vogt 2013) to the heightened vulnerabilities produced by restrictive immigration policies (Menjívar and Abrego 2012) and U.S. efforts to curtail undocumented border-crossing by a "prevention through deterrence" strategy (De León 2015), migrants fleeing conditions of poverty and violence in their home communities may fare little better in the liminal spaces of their journey (Vogt 2013). Brooks County, Texas, is one such liminal space. About 70 miles north of the Mexico border, it is not technically considered a border territory. Nevertheless, it has become an epicenter of migrant death as border crossers attempt to circumvent the local Border Patrol checkpoint on U.S. Highway 281. To avoid the checkpoint, migrants enter private ranch land and begin a trek that will likely take them through rough terrain and harsh environments for several days. Without proper footwear, clothing, and supplies, the walk through sandy soil and sharp sticker burrs is harrowing. Add to this the scorpions and snakes hiding in the brush and the scarcity of water and the trek becomes deadly. The flat landscape and lack of notable reference points often leave migrants lost and walking in circles in the heat and humidity. To complicate matters, large swaths of private ranch land are "dead zones" for cell phone reception. Even those able to call for help, however, may be unable to provide physical description of their location specific enough to help authorities to find them. As a result, hundreds of migrants die annually from exposure and heat exhaustion. Nearly five hundred unidentified migrants have been discovered in Brooks County since 2009 (Latham and Strand 2017). The question then becomes "Whose responsibility are the unidentified dead?"

Answering this question is no simple matter. The contemporary U.S. material and ideological landscape is heavily shaped by notions of personal responsibility and rugged individualism, both ideals that serve to reinforce the idea of migration as individual choice and migrant death as therefore nonpolitical. As in Latin America, neoliberal structural reforms in the United States severely curtailed access to safety net resources, deregulated markets, and privatized government-owned assets (Goode and Maskovsky 2001). End results are locally specific (as is the case across Latin America) but generally include deepening poverty across middle and lower strata of society and increased stress on local social support programs and charitable resources. Under these conditions, neoconservative values centering on cultural nationalism have continued a long-standing narrative that scapegoats migrants as external threats to U.S. prosperity and shared understandings of an American way of life (Flores 2003). Additionally, scholars have pointed out that in recent decades migrants have been inaccurately assumed to drain already diminishing safety net resources and to "steal" jobs from "ordinary" Americans (Chavez 2013). This notion is perpetuated by politicians and popular media coverage of migration, which fail to show how U.S. political and economic interests shape untenable conditions of violence and extreme deprivation in Latin America. Migrants, in this way, have been decontextualized and dehumanized; their deaths, in turn, have not been problematized as a concern of national significance. Such failures place the decision and burden to address the crisis (or not) squarely on the shoulders of individual community members and local officials in the towns where perished migrants are found.

PRACTICING FORENSIC ANTHROPOLOGY IN BROOKS COUNTY, TEXAS

Brooks County is a nonborder territory; however, it is home to the Falfurrias, Texas, Border Patrol Station. This checkpoint is located approximately 70 miles north of the border along U.S. Highway 281. Individuals encountering this station have already made it into the United States but are forced to enter the brush to circumvent this additional checkpoint. Brooks County thus occupies a challenging position within existing border policy and practice. While county officials find themselves in the midst of a border crisis, their physical distance from the actual U.S.-Mexico border means that they have less state-sponsored funding for border-related issues. Law enforcement authorities in Brooks County report being financially, physically, and emotionally overwhelmed as they stretch meager resources to search for living individuals in distress and properly attend to the recovered bodies of the deceased.

Managing bodies of the unidentified dead is a multistep process that requires logistical administration and financial resources. For example, once a body is recovered, county officials are required to send the remains to the nearest available medical examiner (ME). Not every county in Texas has its own Office of the Medical Examiner, however. To date, Texas has only thirteen medical examiners for the entire state (Emerson 2006). Brooks County is one such county without its own ME. It is thus often the case that the nearest available ME is several counties away. The transporting county is then required to pay costs of transport *and* examination, which run approximately $1,500 per individual. They must additionally coordinate and pay for the use of other identification tools, including forensic anthropology and DNA analysis. Currently, forensic anthropologists are volunteering their services, and DNA profiles are being generated in a lab that is federally funded. However, the cost of these services would run well over a thousand dollars per individual if not covered by grants. When an identification is made, the transporting county continues to coordinate the repatriation process. If the deceased is a foreign national, the county will work very closely with the consular office to return the remains to the family. To complicate an already challenging situation, Brooks County, like other South Texas counties, has undergone recent budget cuts and a related reduction in the number of law enforcement officials (Saslow 2014). Given the escalating number of migrant deaths, diminishing available resources, and the logistical challenges of ushering remains through the identification process, local authorities decided to bury the remains in a local cemetery until the time comes when additional funding and personnel will enable costly forensic analyses. This decision was viewed as more respectful of the dead than leaving them in funeral home and mortuary freezers around the county. The unidentified migrant burials are located in three main areas at the Sacred Heart Burial Park in Falfurrias, Texas. Most burials date from 2009 to 2013, with over one hundred individuals being exhumed to date (exhumations are ongoing). An exact number of burials is unknown, as surface markers indicating burial locations have been damaged, removed, or misplaced.

Since 2013 teams of volunteer forensic scientists have been traveling to Brooks County to assist the Brooks County Sheriff Department with the exhumation of the unidentified migrants from Sacred Heart Cemetery, one of the known locations where unidentified migrants have been buried. The large-scale volunteer effort was launched by Baylor University in response to the lack of funding and resources facing local authorities. While armed with a body of knowledge and experience in forensic investigation, the teams quickly found themselves in situations quite different from the traditional forensic anthropology work to which they had become accustomed.

Practical Realities of Humanitarian Forensic Science: Exhumation

Despite some of the inconsistencies in burial practice, the excavation of plots in the cemetery proceeded in the controlled and systemic approach characteristic of archeological technique. We established a datum and set up an excavation grid; we cleaned off all surface debris from our target area; we systematically excavated the area and thoroughly documented the process using notes, drawings, maps, and photographs; we collected the remains and personal effects; and we cleaned up the area once our excavation was complete. At the same time, however, the nature and scope of the situation created a reality where improvisation was needed. For example, the number of exhumations required coordination of a large number of workers. While some were credentialed professionals and graduate students trained in forensic archeology with forensic experience in contexts of the criminal justice system, many more of the volunteer excavators were inexperienced undergraduate students taking a summer class through Baylor University on Crime Scene Recovery. These students needed rapid, on-the-spot training and close supervision. This ultimately meant that the experienced archaeologists had to spend more time teaching basic excavation skills and technique than conducting the work themselves. Traditional archaeological field schools often last six to eight weeks to allow for proper training and to accommodate the slow pace of new practitioners, but the excavations were limited to ten days in Brooks County. This means that teachable moments were essentially crash courses in nontraditional archaeological techniques aimed at a timely excavation rather than teachable moments intended to impart a full and lasting understanding of archaeological theory. The practical applications were emphasized at the expense of building theoretical knowledge of why each step in the excavation process was appropriate and necessary. For example, the students were instructed on the proper use of a trowel to excavate layers of soil but an in-depth discussion of soils and stratigraphy was not possible. Ultimately, our crash-course strategy and concomitant emphasis on practicality reflected broader sociopolitical conditions of state disinvestment in social welfare and humanitarian programming. In the absence of state-sponsored funding, resources, and time, this humanitarian crisis was addressed using improvisational technique and perhaps unusual conditions of volunteer labor. The archaeological recovery of migrant remains is in this way socially and technically shaped by a broader political and economic climate not amenable to optimal crisis response.

The media attention surrounding exhumation also created challenges and opportunities unique to the settings of unidentified migrant exhumation. Media attention is an expected part of forensic field recoveries. In more traditional death-scene settings news coverage often reflects the community's desire to know more about a local issue. However, the fieldwork at a crime scene is frequently shielded from the media by the coroner's office or local law enforcement to protect the details of the investigation and the privacy of the decedents and their families. This was not the case at Sacred Heart, where media interest revolved mostly around the currently hot and politically charged issue of immigration. There were few days when the teams were not being filmed, photographed, or questioned. Many questions were technically outside the scope of archaeological knowledge at that time: What are the exact laws governing burials in Texas? Who are the legally responsible parties for each step from recovery to repatriation of the migrants? How do the families feel about their loved ones being buried here? Other questions were ethically inappropriate for the archaeology team to answer: How do you feel about helping criminals? Can you open the body bags for us to photograph? Is there any evidence of trauma to the bodies? Are these deaths due to drug cartels or human trafficking and sex trade? This was not only a distraction, especially for the unexperienced workers, but also quickly led to sensationalizing and potentially exploiting the situation by enabling media outlets to profit from stories based on half-truths, fear, and morbidity. Many news outlets asked to photograph the deceased and their personal effects as a way to gain viewers and followers based on shock value. We denied their requests not only out of respect for the dead and their families but also in recognition that these were open forensic cases that needed to be treated like every other consultation that we handled through our laboratory. Others attracted attention by claiming that large numbers of minors and victims of violent crime were buried in Sacred Heart, allegations that cannot be supported by forensic analyses.

The volunteer archaeologists in the field thus had to adjust their approach to shield human remains from cameras. In many cases seasoned volunteers developed ways to educate the media so as to bring awareness to the situation while protecting the dignity of the dead. For example, a few reporters and freelance writers spent days with us in the field to better understand forensic archeology, what we were doing, and why we were doing it. They also took the time to learn about the identification process and what would happen to the individuals after exhumation. The ability to interact with these interested parties required that we modify our excavation strategies on the days when they were with us. This entailed excavating more slowly, not only to allow for demonstrations and explanations but also because one member of the team was usually dedicated to interaction with the writers and not directly participating in the fieldwork. This educated and thoughtful approach was clear in their publications, as they intertwined information about the scientific process with the details of the exhumations in Brooks County. While we may have worked slower on the days when these particular writers were with us, our approach ultimately helped to provide the public with information of the current events in Sacred Heart, an education in forensic analysis, and an introduction to the volunteers and local authorities tackling these issues.

Practical Realities of Humanitarian Forensic Science: Identification

Once the migrants were exhumed forensic volunteers could begin the process of identification. Identification of a large number of foreign nationals is already a challenging situation due to lack of comparison standards for Latin American populations (Kimmerle 2014), but the need for family reference samples (Spradley 2013) and lack of communication across national boundaries (Anderson and Parks 2008) present additional challenges. The lack of a clear set of best practices or investigative protocol resulted in a fragmented approach to the analyses in terms of timeliness and methodological approach.

The pace of analysis varied across institutions and correlated with the motivation of the analysts as well as their available time and resources to devote to analyses. Standard forensic osteological analyses (determination of ancestry and sex, estimation of age and stature, documentation of dentition, pathological conditions and trauma) and the documentation of personal effects are being conducted on all the unidentified migrants. However, some of the unidentified migrants had a forensic anthropology analysis and sample submitted for DNA profiling within months of exhumation. Others are still awaiting analysis. That translates into an approximately three-year difference in the submission of samples for DNA profiling that could lead to identification.

The lack of appropriate reference samples and experience doing skeletal analyses within the medicolegal system can also have real ramifications on the possibility for identification. For example, Latin Americans are on average smaller than individuals who come from families that have lived in the United States for several generations. Because many of the techniques used to determine the sex of an individual rely on size, smaller Latin American males may be mistakenly classified as females if the analysts are relying on reference populations from the United States for their analyses. The social history of Latin America has created a population with admixtures in varying amounts from indigenous Latin American populations, Europeans, and Africans. The reality of human biological variation and lack of appropriate reference samples leaves analysts with the task of placing the skeletal remains into broad ancestral categories based on metric and discrete skeletal analyses. It is expected that these individuals may fall into more than one broad category based on their unique evolutionary history. A report may say, for example, that the analyst is unable to distinguish between Hispanic and African ancestry. Decisions on how to word reports and how to enter decedent information into databases is based on experience. Writing "probable male" in the report would suggest some hesitancy, so the database should say "sex unknown" until confirmed by genetic tests. This prevents the individual from being ruled out of missing persons considerations based on the wrong sex determination. Similarly, the analyst should consider how Latin Americans view themselves when entering ancestry information. Would using categories like "Native American," "Asian," or "Black" create a situation in which family members or database searches would skip these cases because of the way the ancestral affiliations are worded?

Additionally, samples are being collected from each individual to send for DNA profile generation. All cases are being added to the National Missing and Unidentified Persons System (NamUs: http://www.namus.gov/). However, additional specialized tests are being conducted to contribute to identification, based on the available resources of the laboratory conducted the forensic analyses. Some individuals have had histological samples taken to aid in age estimation, others have had samples taken for elemental and isotopic analyses to aid in the determination of geographic origin, and still others have been evaluated for skeletal markers of stress, among other things. While there is no set of required analytical techniques or time limit on analyses, this does create disparities in time-to-identification based on where remains were analyzed. This can be especially problematic in the context of identifying migrant refugees, where other family members are often moving and migrating as well. The ability to obtain family reference samples or repatriate remains relies on the ability to contact family members. Collection of reference samples may be more likely for cases that get processed in a timely manner versus those that wait years in the line.

Social Considerations

In addition to the methodological realities of forensic work in humanitarian crisis, the social realities differ from those of forensic science practiced in other settings. Stated simply, the neutrality characteristic of forensic science may be problematic or difficult to achieve in the context of mass disaster and migrant death. For example, forensic scientists are typically accustomed to doing their job in isolation from larger social and political contexts, allowing them to focus solely on execution of the scientific method. The ability to make a positive identification of a decedent is based on testing various identification hypotheses. The observations and data necessary to test the identification hypotheses must be collected in an objective and unbiased way. Forensic anthropologists cannot assume that an individual is male based on the type of personal items associated with the body upon discovery. Making such assumptions would lead them to question and potentially change their skeletal analyses to match preconceived expectations. The individual may have been female but have been wearing masculine items perceived as advantageous on the long, arduous journey. In this case the bias of the scientists would obscure identification. This is similar to the way bias can come to play in a court of law if it appears that the scientific expert is favoring a particular council (government or defense) or sympathizing with a particular side. These feelings can introduce bias and complicate scientific interpretations. Therefore, forensic scientists must practice scientific neutrality.

However, the realities of forensic science within a humanitarian crisis place the scientists in a politically and perhaps emotionally charged environment that requires them to balance neutrality and activism in novel ways. For example, forensic anthropologists working along the U.S.-Mexico border have worked not only on the identification aspect of the crisis but also on bringing awareness to the situation along the border. Many of these forensic scientists volunteer their time out of a moral obligation in a time of crisis. They have a very specific skill set that can be employed during the identification and repatriation process. As anthropologists, many are knowledgeable regarding various social justice issues, such as the marginalization of impoverished populations under conditions of global neoliberalism. Some see this work as an avenue to express political opinion regarding social discriminations and to take a stance against such injustices. As an expert, they have a platform from which to speak about the crisis and bring awareness to the struggle for life and, in death, identification.

Awareness is a potential way to garner resources to assist with the analyses and reduce the number of deaths, the human toll, of this crisis. Additionally, forensic scientists can work to change the way many perceive the border crisis. By speaking for the dead they humanize the migrants and urge a sympathetic response to the migrant plight. The forensic work is helping to put names and faces on the dead and to make people realize that these are dead family members who have parents, siblings, or children searching for them. Their personal effects tell a story of desperation for a better life with photos, letters, and lists of dreams intertwined with a real misunderstanding of the dangers of walking through South Texas. Inadequate clothing, food, water, and basic medical supplies suggest they were uninformed as to the realities of the journey. The migrants themselves can't tell these tales, but perhaps the forensic scientists can. Is this activism? Or is it an economic strategy to enable humanitarian assistance?

The Forensic Science of Migrant Death: Future Directions

Given the social and political specificities of migrant death and identification, the volunteer forensic investigation of this humanitarian crisis in the Texas borderlands may be best understood within the theoretical framework of political economy. Even if forensic scientists were to make conscious decisions to forgo playing an overtly activist role on behalf of the unidentified dead, their involvement as volunteer scientists in the process of humanitarian aid along the border positions them as actors operating within and on the frameworks and processes of global capitalism and neoliberal ideology. As such, volunteer forensic scientists find themselves imbricated with the sociopolitical system producing conditions of migration and death. Their work responds to shifting conditions of violence and deprivation in Latin America and the migration patterns that they create. This response shapes meanings and realities of contemporary global capitalism insofar as it intervenes in the ideological and material landscape to humanize migrants, tell the stories of their death, and garner what is needed to address the problem.

Through the lens of migrant death and identification in South Texas, it becomes clearer that forensic science practiced under conditions of humanitarian crisis is contextually specific and socially meaningful in ways not often openly discussed in the field. Examining the work within a political economy framework allows us to consider in new ways that there is "no natural division between science and activism or science and human rights" (Goodman and Leatherman 2001: 25). Our best route forward is thus to make conscious critical decisions that protect the integrity of our practice while balancing the very real social and political role that we play in mediating outcomes of this pressing humanitarian crisis.

References

Anderson, B. E., and B. O. Parks. 2008. Symposium on Border Crossing Deaths: Introduction. *Journal of Forensic Sciences* 53(1):6–7.

Chavez, L. 2013. *The Latino Threat: Constructing Immigrants, Citizens, and the Nation.* Stanford University Press, Stanford, CA.

De León, J. 2015. *The Land of Open Graves: Living and Dying on the Migrant Trail.* University of California Press, Oakland.

Di Leonardo, M. 2008. Introduction: New Global and American Landscapes of Inequality. In *New Landscapes of Inequality: Neoliberalism and the Erosion of Democracy in America,* pp. 3–20. School for Advanced Research Press, Santa Fe, NM.

Emerson, P. 2006. Texas Association of Counties. In Autopsy Costs in Various Counties. County Information Project. https://www.county.org/about-texas-counties/county-data/Documents/MedicalExaminer.pdf.

Esparza, M., H. R. Huttenbach, and D. Feierstein (editors). 2013. *State Violence and Genocide in Latin America: The Cold War Years.* Routledge, New York.

Flores, L. A. 2003. Constructing Rhetorical Borders: Peons, Illegal Aliens, and Competing Narratives of Immigration. *Critical Studies in Media Communication* 20(4):362–387.

Goode, J. G., and J. Maskovsky (editors). 2001. *The New Poverty Studies: The Ethnography of Power, Politics and Impoverished People in the United States (No. 9460).* New York University Press, New York.

Goodman, A. H., and T. L. Leatherman. 2001. Traversing the Chasm between Biology and Culture: An Introduction. In *Building a New Biocultural Synthesis: Political-Economic Perspectives on Human Biology,* edited by A. H. Goodman and T. L. Leatherman, pp. 3–42. University of Michigan Press, Ann Arbor.

Harvey, D. 2005. *A Brief History of Neoliberalism.* Oxford University Press, Oxford.

Hellman, J. A. 2006. Give or Take Ten Million: The Paradoxes of Migration to the United States. In *Latin America after Neoliberalism: Turning the Die in the 21st Century?,* pp. 213–231. New Press, New York.

Hershberg, E., and F. Rosen (editors). 2007. *Latin America after Neoliberalism: Turning the Tide in the 21st Century?* New Press, New York.

Hicks, K., and W. R. Leonard. 2014. Developmental Systems and Inequality: Linking Evolutionary and Political-Economic Theory in Biological Anthropology. *Current Anthropology* 55(5):523–550.

Kim, J. Y., J. V. Millen, A. Irwin, and J. Gershman. 2000. *Dying for Growth: Global Inequalities and the Health of the Poor.* Common Courage Press, Monroe, ME.

Kimmerle, E. H. 2014. Practicing Forensic Anthropology: A Human Rights Approach to the Global Problem of Missing and Unidentified Persons. *Annals of Anthropological Practice* 38(1):1–6.

Kotz, D. M. 2002. Globalization and Neoliberalism. *Rethinking Marxism* 14(2):64–79.

Latham, K. E., and R. M. Strand. 2017. Digging, Dollars, and Drama: Economics of Forensic Archaeology and Migrant Exhumation. In *Sociopolitics of Migrant Death and Repatriation: Perspectives from Forensic Science,* edited by K. E. Latham and A. O'Daniel, pp. 99–113. Springer, Cham, Switzerland.

Menjivar, Cecilia, and Leisy Abrego. 2012. Legal Violence: Immigration Laws and the Lives of Central Americans. *American Journal of Sociology* 117(5):1380–1421.

Paramo, A. 2012. *Looking for Esperanza*. Benu Press, Hopkins, MN.

Petras, J., and H. Veltmeyer. 2009. Neoliberalism and the Dynamics of Capitalist Development in Latin America. Globalresearch.org.

Richland, J. B. 2009. On Neoliberalism and Other Social Diseases: The 2008 Sociocultural Anthropology Year in Review. *American Anthropologist* 111(2):170–176.

Rose, A. 2012. *Showdown in the Sonoran Desert: Religion, Law, and the Immigration Controversy*. Oxford University Press, Oxford.

Roseberry, W. 1988. Political Economy. *Annual Review of Anthropology* 17:161–185.

Sanchez, M. 2006. Insecurity and Violence as a New Power Relation in Latin America. *Annals of the American Academy of Political and Social Science* 606(1):178–195.

Saslow, E. 2014. In Poorest County in Texas, at Center of US Border Crisis, Brooks County Sheriff's Deputies Go It Alone. *Monitor*, http://www.themonitor.com/news/local/in -poorest-county-in-texas-at-center-of-us-border/article_f0b3bfc2-25a0-11e4-8644 -0017a43b2370.html.

Schneider, J. 1995. *Articulating Hidden Histories: Exploring the Influence of Eric R. Wolf*. University of California Press, Berkeley.

Smith-Nonini, S. 2000. Dying for Growth: Global Inequality and the Health of the Poor. In *The Smoke and Mirrors of Health Reform in El Salvador: Community Health NGOs and the Not-So-Neoliberal State*, pp. 359–381. Common Courage Press, Monroe, ME.

Spradley, M. K. 2013. *Project IDENTIFICATION: Developing Accurate Identification Criteria for Hispanics*. U.S. Department of Justice, Washington, DC.

Vogt, W. A. 2013. Crossing Mexico: Structural Violence and the Commodification of Undocumented Central American Migrants. *American Ethnologist* 40(4):764–780.

Watt, P., and R. Zepeda. 2012. *Drug War Mexico: Politics, Neoliberalism and Violence in the New Narcoeconomy*. Zed Books, New York.

Wolf, E. R. 1982. *Europe and the People without History*. University of California Press, Berkeley.

Wolf, E. R., and T. H. Eriksen. 2010. *Europe and the People without History*. University of California Press, Berkeley.

12

Conclusion

What Bioarchaeology and Forensic Anthropology Reveal about Massacres

RYAN P. HARROD

The word "massacre" often invokes images of bloodshed and a profound awareness of the loss of human life. Sémelin (2007:9) states that it often "evokes the sheer barbarity human beings are capable of: blood spewing everywhere, unthinkable atrocities, bodies torn asunder." This word did not always invoke this type of reaction and in fact used to be a rather benign concept. According to Greengrass (1999:69), the massacre gained its current status in the mid-1500s. The word "massacre," originally used to describe what happens on a butcher's block (knife = *massacreur*), was coopted to describe a historic event in medieval Europe. In France during the twelfth century a group known as the Poor of Lyons was led by Peter Waldo. Audisio (1999:8–9) identifies him as Vaudès, "equivalent to an accusation of sorcery" (Monastier 1859:60), as in the pamphlet written by Jean Crespin in 1556. This Christian group, known as the Waldensians or Vaudois (Audisio 1999:77), and the followers of Martin Luther were considered to be in opposition to the Roman Catholic Church. On November 18, 1540, the Mérindol decree was passed, which allowed the village to be targeted as heretics instead of just individuals (Audisio 1999:191). While the punishment for the crime of heresy was delayed, in 1545 this village and others in the area were attacked. The people were killed. According to Greengrass (1999), the systematic cleansing of the Christian followers was so heinous the attacks were described as a massacre, something that might be done to an animal on a butcher's block (Crespin 1556).

Parquoy maintenant tous Chrestiens doyuent autrement estre in-
formez des Vaudois, & les tenir pour gens de bien & imitateurs du
fainct Euangile, pour lequel ils ont esté de nostre temps si cruellement
maffacrez & mis à fac, à Cabrieres & Merindol.

[Now, therefore, all Christians think otherwise of being informed
of the Vaudois, and of keeping them for good men and imitators of
the holy Gospel, for which they have been so cruelly *massacred* and
sacked at Cabrieres and Merindol.] (Crespin 1556:ix)

After the massacre the word "Vaudois" took on an alternative meaning.
Aside from being associated with heretics, it was used to describe sorcerers
or witches (Audisio 1999:74). Later it was used interchangeably with other
words to describe things like lustfulness or sodomy as well as murderers,
thieves, and whores (Audisio 1999:76). As in many of the chapters in this
volume, the word "massacre" was first used against people who were seen as
the other, who were purposefully dehumanized and identified as the cause
of everyone else's problems.

The association with butchery is also very appropriate. Massacres often
involve not only the death of multiple individuals but also the processing of
their remains. Butchers are exceptional at the process and thus provide an
ideal source for us to reference. Osterholtz (chapter 6) provides a poignant
example of how destruction and processing of the body is a part of the
creation of a burial sample that creates what we call a massacre.

In the introduction to this book Anderson and Martin cite Dwyer and
Ryan (2012:xv), who define massacres as violence against another group
not necessarily based on who they are or predicated on any specific motive.
Anderson and Martin use this definition to highlight that what we might
identify as massacre events do not necessarily have a specific pattern but
instead include a number of different encounters that result in the loss of
human life. Using the term "mass violence," which includes mass killing or
massacre events and genocide, Staub (2016) provides a definition of what
this type of violence includes. He states that mass violence, also known as
collective or group violence, can be motivated by a number of different
factors. Regardless of the proximate cause, however, it is generally characterized as "violence between groups, most often part of the same country"
(Staub 2016:205). One limitation of Staub's definition of violence is that it is
focused on extant populations with modern socially and politically defined
boundaries. Looking at past societies, the term "country" may not be applicable. Instead we might argue that we are looking at violence that involves

people within the same cultural group inhabiting a particular region. The human skeletal remains that we analyze to reveal instances of past violence often lack written records and are assigned to groups based on material remains, subsistence strategies, residence patterns, and other archaeologically based patterns. Researchers use these characteristics to suggest the presence of distinct cultural identities, which can range from something as broad as ethnicity and religion to something as narrow as kinship group and clan.

BIOARCHAEOLOGICAL AND FORENSIC APPROACHES TO UNDERSTANDING MASSACRES

The goal of this book is to bring together researchers in biological anthropology with perspectives from the subdisciplines of bioarchaeology or osteoarchaeology and forensic anthropology to explore the complexity of violent encounters that we should recognize as massacres. Looking at both recent and past societies with evidence of violence involving multiple individuals, the researchers hope to expand our understanding of this human behavior. Having read all of the chapters, I think that this book and its contributors have succeeded in their goal.

As many of the chapters illustrate, the violence may target anyone regardless of age and biological sex and affect large groups of people or small isolated portions of the population. De Vore, Jacobi, and Dye (chapter 2) do an excellent job articulating this point when discussing the notion of massacres in the precontact Middle Tennessee River Valley. They suggest that we need to rethink how we define a massacre and challenge us to think about how we use basic osteological methods like the minimum number of individuals (MNI). I found myself realizing that there is no magic number that defines when lethal violence can or cannot be defined as a massacre.

Staub (2016:205), looking at modern-day mass violence, suggests that the events that involve numerous members of the community constitute genocide, while smaller episodes of violence might be called mass killings. While he distinguishes between these two types of mass violence, it is important to note that he believes that the same factors lead to both (Staub 2016:206). I want to define the two terms in the reverse order, because I think the second part of the definition of genocide is especially relevant for this volume. In an earlier publication Staub (1989:8) describes mass killing as "killing members of a group without the intention to eliminate the whole group or killing large numbers of people without a precise definition of group membership." He defines "genocide" as an event where "a government or some group acts to eliminate a whole group or people, whether by directly killing them or creating conditions that lead to their deaths or inability to reproduce" (Staub 2011:100). Acknowledging that obvious violence is not necessary for genocide to occur is crucial, because structural violence (Farmer 2004; Galtung 1969; Galtung and Höivik 1971; Winter and Leighton 2001) plays a role in what we define as mass violence. Several of the chapters discuss structural violence. For example, Bird (chapter 10) provides an excellent example of how death not typically attributed to violence, like exposure to a harsh climate, is ultimately related to a structural system that places people at risk. This chapter is intriguing because it questions whether people who succumbed to the extreme conditions of the desert needed to die. I doubt that any crime-tracking database (ViCap, Interpol, and others) would ever record these deaths as anything other than accidents due to exposure, but Bird makes an excellent argument that these deaths along the Arizona border were violent. While exposure may not invoke the butcher block notion of a massacre (Greengrass 1999), the targeting of certain people (Undocumented Border Crossers) seen as the other and their subsequent dehumanization are mechanisms for allowing for the systematic mass killing of a particular group. Latham, O'Daniel, and Maiers (chapter 11) show how this same process of structural violence is also happening along the border in Texas. This chapter highlights the difficulties of understanding the whole story of what happens to immigrants crossing the U.S.-Mexico border.

Chapter 11 also discusses the problems with our biases when we conduct our analysis. Many biological anthropologists working on these sites with massacres are working with populations that differ from the teaching and research collections on which our methods were established and tested (Bass 1971; El-Najjar and McWilliams 1978; Krogman 1962;; McKern and Stewart 1957; Thieme 1957; Todd 1920). Chapter 11 suggests that this is a rather considerable problem when working with the human remains of individuals from Mexico and Central America.

Looking specifically at a population that I have analyzed, researchers fairly early on realized that standard methods for sex and ancestry estimation did not work well (Birkby 1966). The importance of this realization is that researchers can and should attempt to use as many biological markers as possible when constructing their osteobiography (Saul 1972). Toyne (chapter 4) does an excellent job of identifying the biological sex of the victims of the massacre in the Andes community, showing that men are at higher risk of death and that women and some children may have been captured and not killed during the raids. This selectivity differs drastically from what Osterholtz (chapter 6) found at the Sacred Ridge site in southwestern Colorado, where men, women, and children were all targeted. Willey (chapter 7) found a similar pattern at the Crow Creek Village site, where the perpetrators did not discriminate by age or sex.

The chapters all show that violence and more specifically massacres are variable in nature and culturally driven. Unlike massacre events that may only involve one or two individuals, mass violence in the form of genocide is anything but subtle. These large-scale massacres offer insight into the nature of mass violence because they clearly show how entire groups can systematically target and exterminate other groups without much hesitation. Unlike a small massacre or the processes that lead to the systematic death of people through structural violence, these events are hard to deny. Fleischman, Prak, Voeun, and Ros (chapter 8) take a critical look at the violence that the Khmer Rouge perpetrated throughout Cambodia. Looking specifically at the "killing fields" with over a hundred mass graves of the victims of Pol Pot and his followers, they explore the process of locating and identifying the dead and how and why it was turned into a tourist destination. Cultural memory is very important in ensuring that violence is never forgotten and never repeated. Colwell-Chanthaphonh (2007) discusses the importance of remembering these traumatic events as a means of reconciliation when discussing what happened at Fort Apache and the actions that the White Mountain Apache took when they restored the fort. Hepner, Steadman, and Hanebrink (chapter 9) also discuss the importance of reconciliation for communities in their discussion of genocide in Uganda. Their chapter explores the delicate nature of achieving reconciliation when a community does not necessarily trust that justice is a possibility. Our work as anthropologists, while important, also comes with serious responsibility to the community or descendants that we work with. This is especially true when we work on human skeletal remains associated with an event involving mass violence like a massacre or genocide.

Finally, an important contribution of this volume is that it challenges researchers to reexamine the data that have been collected on violence to see whether we can see more evidence of these mass killing events. The number of individuals involved is relative, of course, in terms of the population size of the group we are studying. Pilloud and Schwitalla (chapter 3) and Kendell (chapter 5) illustrate the value of systematically recording and storing data collected from human skeletal remains so that future researchers can ask different questions. Having analyzed data collected by researchers on human remains that were subsequently repatriated, I realize the challenges associated with this type of endeavor. However, both chapters clearly show that massacres were present in these precontact societies. We have historic accounts of massacres shortly after contact (Addis 2005; Hearne and Mc-Googan 2007; Roberts 2004). In the past people have argued that these societies were often at peace and that the violence was a result of major culture change (Kent 1980; LeBlanc and Register 2003). The presence of a massacre or even several in a region, however, does not inherently mean that people are violent. Willey ends chapter 7 by cautioning researchers to avoid making such statements that normalize violence and paint a picture of savagery in the past. People in the past like people today are very capable of violence.

Other researchers have argued that the world today is more peaceful than it was in the past, often citing things like enlightenment or civilization as a reason for this more peaceful behavior (Eisner 2003, 2009; Pinker 2011; Rousseau 2008 [1762]). However, the reality is that violence is low in societies where egalitarian ideals are strongest (Ferguson 2013; Fry 2013). In other societies it declines (or at least obvious forms are less apparent) when systems are in place to control the expression of violence and enact strict consequences when these controlling mechanisms are violated (Forsberg 2001; Janowitz 1975; Ross 1901).

The existence of one or even more than a dozen massacre events in a region over time obviously cannot be used to suggest that a particular people is "naturally" more violent or peaceful. Violence like any other behavior is situational. Unfortunately, a deep exploration of the cultural context of the violence often is not possible because of a lack of records (archaeological case studies) or even opposition by the aggressors (genocide case studies). For example, much of my own research has been in the precontact U.S. Southwest, where there are a number of very prominent examples of massacres. The case study discussed by Osterholtz (chapter 6) is only one of a number of sites (see, for example, Billman et al. 2000; Brooks 2016; Kuckelman et al. 2002; Turner and Morris 1970). While the presence of massacre events is not in dispute, the cause of the violence is controversial. Looking at one variable like the environment might suggest that it was a natural reaction. However, in a past publication (Harrod and Martin 2014), Martin and I argued that the reality is that these events are sporadic and associated with many other factors. To understand why they occur we need to look at the social and political context and consider environmental factors along with regional interaction (Alvarez 2016; Hamburg 2010).

Conclusion

The combination of bioarchaeological and forensic data contributes to expanding our understanding of mass violence, by providing a temporal and spatial view of these violent events. While no two events are the same, they often do share some features. Staub (2011:15) suggests that there are both material and psychological motives for violence. In reality these two categories are not really exclusive of one another. People kill for a number of reasons, some of which are beyond logic. Regardless of the motivation (or lack of a clear motivation), however, the end result is the death of innocent people. While some people may argue that Undocumented Border Crossers were committing a crime and hence cannot be considered "innocent," the reality is that these people are reacting to a structural system that leaves few other alternatives. Instead of setting up fences and redirecting desperate migrants through areas where their chance of survival is slim to none, our response should be to attempt to fix the broken systems that are motivating people to embark on the risky journey.

Going back to the Christian followers of Peter Waldo mentioned earlier, we can not only deconstruct why these people died but, more importantly, identify how it could have been prevented. In fear of losing more followers the Roman Catholic Church pushed to suppress the religious reformations taking place in Germany and France. The passage of the Mérindol decree in 1540 could have served to illustrate that there was something inherently dangerous about switching from prosecuting individuals on a case-by-case basis to identifying communities as targets. When we judge an entire group instead of assessing individuals based on their own actions, it is easy to move away from systems of punishment and embrace acts of mass violence like massacres and genocide. While the heresy laws of the time were undoubtedly flawed, the situation only got worse when they applied the judgment to all individuals who had any association with these so-called heretics. What happened in France in the mid-1500s was significant enough to warrant a new word that sticks with us even today. However, it was not the first time that this type of thing happened and unfortunately will not be the last. My hope is that the chapters in this volume will help to illustrate the importance of understanding why massacres and genocide happen, provide methods for identifying these events, and enable us to learn from our past and avoid endorsing movements that support the use of mass violence in the future.

REFERENCES

Addis, C. 2005. The Whitman Massacre: Religion and Manifest Destiny on the Columbia Plateau, 1809–1858. *Journal of the Early Republic* 25(2):221–258.

Alvarez, A. 2016. Borderlands, Climate Change, and the Genocidal Impulse. *Genocide Studies International* 10(1):27–36. DOI:10.3138/gsi.10.1.03.

Audisio, G. 1999. *The Waldensian Dissent: Persecution and Survival, c. 1170–c. 1570.* Translated by C. Davison. Cambridge University Press, Cambridge.

Bass, W. M. 1971. *Human Osteology: A Laboratory and Field Manual.* Missouri Archaeological Society, Columbia.

Billman, B. R., P. M. Lambert, and B. L. Leonard. 2000. Cannibalism, Warfare, and Drought in the Mesa Verde Region in the Twelfth Century AD. *American Antiquity* 65:1–34.

Birkby, W. H. 1966. An Evaluation of Race and Sex Identification from Cranial Measurements. *American Journal of Physical Anthropology* 24(1):21–27.

Brooks, J. F. 2016. *Mesa of Sorrows: A History of the Awat'ovi Massacre.* W. W. Norton and Company, New York.

Colwell-Chanthaphonh, C. 2007. History, Justice, and Reconciliation. In *Archaeology as a Tool of Civic Engagement*, edited by B. J. Little and P. A. Shackel, 23–46. AltaMira Press, Lanham, MD.

Crespin, J. 1556. *Histoire mémorable de la persécution et saccagement du peuple de Mérindol et Cabrières et autres circonvoisins, appelez Vaudois.* Jean Crespin, Geneva, Switzerland.

Dwyer, P. G., and L. Ryan. 2012. Introduction: the Massacre and History. In *Theatres of Violence: Massacres, Mass Killings and Atrocity throughout History*, edited by P. G. Dwyer and L. Ryan, pp. xi–xxv. Berghahn Books, New York.

Eisner, M. 2003. Long-Term Historical Trends in Violent Crime. *Crime and Justice* 30:83–143.

———. 2009. The Uses of Violence: An Examination of Some Cross-cutting Issues. *International Journal of Conflict and Violence* 3(1):40–59.

El-Najjar, M. Y., and K. R. McWilliams. 1978. *Forensic Anthropology: The Structure, Morphology, and Variation of Human Bone and Dentition.* Thomas, Springfield, IL.

Farmer, P. 2004. An Anthropology of Structural Violence. *Current Anthropology* 45(3):305–325.

Ferguson, R. B. 2013. Pinker's List: Exaggerating Prehistoric War Mortality. In *War, Peace, and Human Nature: The Convergence of Evolutionary and Cultural Views*, edited by D. P. Fry, pp. 112–131. Oxford University Press, Oxford.

Forsberg, R. C. 2001. Socially-Sanctioned and Non-Sanctioned Violence: On the Role of Moral Beliefs in Causing and Preventing War and Other Forms of Large-Group Violence. In *Gewalt und Konflikt in einer Globalisierten Welt: Festschrift für Ulrich Albrecht*, edited by R. Stanely, pp. 201–230. Westdeutscher Verlag, Wiesbaden, Germany.

Fry, D. P. (editor). 2013. *War, Peace, and Human Nature: The Convergence of Evolutionary and Cultural Views*. Oxford University Press, Oxford.

Galtung, J. 1969. Violence, Peace and Peace Research. *Journal of Peace Research* 6:167–191.

Galtung, J., and T. Höivik. 1971. Structural and Direct Violence: A Note on Operationalization. *Journal of Peace Research* 8(1):73–76.

Greengrass, M. 1999. Hidden Transcripts: Secret Histories and Personal Testimonies of Religious Violence in the French Wars of Religion. In *The Massacre in History*, edited by M. Levene and P. Roberts, pp. 69–88. Berghahn Books, New York.

Hamburg, D. A. 2010. *Preventing Genocide: Practical Steps towards Early Detection and Effective Action*. Paradigm, Boulder, CO.

Harrod, R. P., and D. L. Martin. 2014. *Bioarchaeology of Climate Change and Violence: Ethical Considerations*. Springer, New York.

Hearne, S., and K. McGoogan. 2007. *A Journey to the Northern Ocean: The Adventures of Samuel Hearne*. Previously published as *A Journey from Prince of Wales's Fort in Hudson Bay to the Northern Ocean, in the Years 1769, 1770, 1771, and 1772*. TouchWood Editions, Surrey, BC, Canada.

Janowitz, M. 1975. Theory and Social Control. *American Journal of Sociology* 81(1):82–108.

Kent, S. 1980. Pacifism: A Myth of the Plateau. *Northwest Anthropological Research Notes (NARN)* 14(2):125–134.

Krogman, W. M. 1962. *The Human Skeleton in Forensic Medicine*. C. C. Thomas, Springfield, IL.

Kuckelman, K. A., R. R. Lightfoot, and D. L. Martin. 2002. The Bioarchaeology and Taphonomy of Violence at Castle Rock and Sand Canyon Pueblos, Southwestern Colorado. *American Antiquity* 67:486–513.

LeBlanc, S. A., and K. E. Register. 2003. *Constant Battles: The Myth of the Peaceful, Noble Savage*. St. Martin's Press, New York.

McKern, T. W., and T. D. Stewart. 1957. *Skeletal Age Changes in Young American Males: Analyzed from the Standpoint of Age Identification*. Natick, MA: Technical Report EP-45, Headquarters Quartermaster Research and Development Command.

Monastier, A. 1859. *A History of the Vaudois Church from Its Origin, and of the Vaudois of Piedmont to the Present Day*. Translated from French, Religious Tract Society, London.

Pinker, S. 2011. *The Better Angels of Our Nature: Why Violence Has Declined*. Viking, New York.

Roberts, D. 2004. *The Pueblo Revolt: The Secret Rebellion That Drove the Spaniards Out of the Southwest*. Simon and Schuster, New York.

Ross, E. A. 1901. *Social Control: A Survey of the Foundations of Order*. Macmillan, New York.

Rousseau, J.-J. 2008 [1762]. *The Social Contract*. Translated by G. D. H. Cole. Cosimo, New York.

Saul, F. P. 1972. The Human Skeletal Remains of Altar de Sacrificios: An Osteobiographic Analysis. *Papers of the Peabody Museum of American Archaeology and Ethnology, Harvard University* 63(2).

Sémelin, J. 2007. *Purify and Destroy: The Political Uses of Massacre and Genocide*. Translated by Cynthia Schoch. Columbia University Press, New York.

Staub, E. 1989. *The Roots of Evil: The Origins of Genocide and Other Group Violence*. Cambridge University Press, Cambridge.

———. 2011. *Overcoming Evil: Genocide, Violent Conflict, and Terrorism*. Oxford University Press, Oxford.

———. 2016. The Origins and Inhibiting Influences in Genocide, Mass Killing and Other Collective Violence (reprint). In *The Ashgate Research Companion to Political Violence*, edited by M. Breen-Smyth, pp. 205–223. Routledge, Abingdon, UK.

Thieme, F. P. 1957. Sex in Negro Skeletons. *Journal of Forensic Medicine* 4:72–81.

Todd, T. W. 1920. Age Changes in the Pubic Bone: I. The Male White Pubis. *American Journal of Physical Anthropology* 3:285–334.

Turner, C. G., II, and N. T. Morris. 1970. A Massacre at Hopi. *American Antiquity* 35:320–331.

Winter, D. D., and D. C. Leighton. 2001. Section II: Structural Violence. In *Peace, Conflict, and Violence: Peace Psychology for the 21st Century*, edited by D. J. Christie, R. V. Wagner, and D. D. Winter, pp. 99–101. Prentice-Hall, New York.

CONTRIBUTORS

Cheryl P. Anderson is lecturer of biological anthropology at Boise State University. She is the recipient of a Fulbright U.S. Student Award to Turkey and a University of Nevada, Las Vegas, Foundation Board of Trustees Fellowship, which supported her dissertation research. She coedited *Bioarchaeological and Forensic Perspectives on Violence: How Violent Death Is Interpreted from Skeletal Remains.*

Cate E. Bird completed her PhD in anthropology at Michigan State University in 2013. She has received postdoctoral fellowships in forensic anthropology at the Harris County Institute of Forensic Sciences, Pima County Office of the Medical Examiner, and the University of South Florida.

William E. De Vore is a cultural resources specialist and bioarchaeologist working for the University of Alabama Museums Office of Archaeological Research. He is the coauthor of *The Removal of Ear Trophies Associated with Scalpings in Prehistoric North Alabama* and researches trophy taking, its associated evidence, and cultural implications.

David H. Dye is professor of archaeology in the Department of Earth Sciences at the University of Memphis. He is the author of *War Paths, Peace Paths*, editor of three additional volumes, and author of numerous articles and book chapters.

Julie M. Fleischman is postdoctoral forensic anthropology fellow at the Harris County Institute of Forensic Sciences in Houston, Texas. Her research focuses on forensic anthropology methods and skeletal trauma analysis and how these intersect with human rights violence or atrocity.

Julia R. Hanebrink is assistant professor of anthropology and codirector of the National Institutes of Health Minority Health International Research Training (MHIRT) Program at Rhodes College. Her research foci in Uganda include medical syncretism, health beliefs and behaviors, community-based needs assessments, and psychosocial initiatives in the aftermath of violent conflict.

Ryan P. Harrod is associate professor of biological anthropology at the University of Alaska Anchorage. His research is biocultural in nature, focused on bioarchaeology, paleopathology, forensic anthropology, and 3D reconstructions of human skeletal remains. He has studied human skeletal remains from precontact Native American communities in the U.S. Southwest, Great Basin, Plateau, and Alaska.

Keith P. Jacobi is professor of anthropology at the University of Alabama and curator of human osteology at the University of Alabama Museums. He wrote *Last Rites for the Tipu Maya: Genetic Structuring in a Colonial Cemetery* and has authored or coauthored numerous journal articles and book chapters.

Ashley E. Kendell is assistant professor at California State University, Chico. She was the recipient of a Committee on Institutional Cooperation predoctoral fellowship through the Smithsonian Institution and Michigan State University, which helped to fund the research presented in this volume. Her research interests include data standardization methods and trauma analyses in the fields of bioarchaeology and forensic anthropology.

Krista E. Latham is associate professor of biology and anthropology at the University of Indianapolis. She is a Board Certified Forensic Anthropologist (D-ABFA) and director of the University of Indianapolis Human Identification Center. She coedited *New Perspectives in Forensic Human Skeletal Identification*; *Sociopolitics of Migrant Death and Repatriation: Perspectives from Forensic Science*; and *Age Estimation of the Human Skeleton* and has produced numerous scientific publications.

Justin Maiers is an MS candidate in human biology at the University of Indianapolis. He currently serves as forensic anthropologist 1 for the University of Indianapolis Human Identification Center and as adjunct instructor of anatomy.

Debra L. Martin is Distinguished Professor of Anthropology at the University of Nevada, Las Vegas. She has coauthored or coedited ten books, including *Bioarchaeological and Forensic Perspectives on Violence: How Violent Death Is Interpreted from Skeletal Remains* and *Bioarchaeology of Violence*, and published over a hundred journal articles and book chapters. She is the coeditor of the *International Journal of Osteoarchaeology* and editor of *KIVA, Journal of Southwestern Anthropology and History*.

Alyson O'Daniel is assistant professor of anthropology at the University of Indianapolis. Her published works include *Holding On: African American Women Surviving HIV/AIDS* and *Sociopolitics of Migrant Death: Perspectives from Forensic Science* (coeditor). Her work has also been published in journals such as *Medical Anthropology: Cross-Cultural Studies in Health and Illness*; *Human Organization*; and *Transforming Anthropology*.

Anna J. Osterholtz is assistant professor of anthropology at Mississippi State University. She has two edited or coedited volumes, including *Commingled and Disarticulated Human Remains*, coauthored *Bodies and Lives in Ancient America: Health before Columbus*, and published many journal articles and book chapters.

Marin A. Pilloud is assistant professor of anthropology at the University of Nevada, Reno. She is also a Board Certified Forensic Anthropologist (D-ABFA) and registered professional archaeologist. She has active bioarchaeological research programs in Neolithic Anatolia and prehistoric California and is interested in the use of teeth in the estimation of ancestry in forensic anthropology.

His Excellency Sonnara Prak is director general for heritage for the Ministry of Culture and Fine Arts in Phnom Penh, Cambodia.

Tricia Redeker Hepner is associate professor of anthropology at the University of Tennessee, Knoxville, and directs the Disasters, Displacement, and Human Rights Program. She wrote *Soldiers, Martyrs, Traitors and Exiles: Political Conflict in Eritrea and the Diaspora* and has coedited three volumes in addition to her other publications.

Sophearavy Ros is deputy director of the Choeung Ek Genocidal Center in Phnom Penh, Cambodia.

Al W. Schwitalla is a professional archaeologist and artifact reproduction specialist with more than twenty-seven years of experience in the western United States. He earned both a BA and MA in anthropology from California State University, Sacramento. His research interests include Native American health and behavioral trends and artifact analyses in central California.

Dawnie Wolfe Steadman is professor of anthropology and director of the Forensic Anthropology Center at the University of Tennessee, Knoxville. She is a Board Certified Forensic Anthropologist (D-ABFA). She edited *Hard Evidence: Case Studies in Forensic Anthropology* and has authored or coauthored many journal articles and book chapters.

J. Marla Toyne is associate professor of anthropology at the University of Central Florida. She has authored or coauthored numerous journal articles and book chapters, including articles in the *American Journal of Physical Anthropology* and in *Latin American Antiquity*, and coedited (with Haagen D. Klaus) *Ritual Violence in the Ancient Andes: Reconstructing Sacrifice on the North Coast of Peru*.

Vuthy Voeun is director of archaeology and prehistory for the Ministry of Culture and Fine Arts in Phnom Penh, Cambodia. He directed the Choeung Ek Conservation of Victims at the Killing Fields project.

P. Willey is a Board Certified Forensic Anthropologist (D-ABFA) and professor emeritus of anthropology at California State University, Chico. He is the author or coauthor of more than a hundred articles, chapters, monographs, and books and coeditor of *Health of the Seventh Cavalry: A Medical History*.

INDEX

BIOARCHAEOLOGICAL INTERPRETATIONS OF THE HUMAN PAST: LOCAL, REGIONAL, AND GLOBAL PERSPECTIVES

Edited by Clark Spencer Larsen

Ancient Health: Skeletal Indicators of Agricultural and Economic Intensification, edited by Mark Nathan Cohen and Gillian M. M. Crane-Kramer (2007; first paperback edition, 2012)

Bioarchaeology and Identity in the Americas, edited by Kelly J. Knudson and Christopher M. Stojanowski (2009; first paperback edition, 2010)

Island Shores, Distant Pasts: Archaeological and Biological Approaches to the Pre-Columbian Settlement of the Caribbean, edited by Scott M. Fitzpatrick and Ann H. Ross (2010; first paperback edition, 2017)

The Bioarchaeology of the Human Head: Decapitation, Decoration, and Deformation, edited by Michelle Bonogofsky (2011; first paperback edition, 2015)

Bioarchaeology and Climate Change: A View from South Asian Prehistory, by Gwen Robbins Schug (2011; first paperback edition, 2017)

Violence, Ritual, and the Wari Empire: A Social Bioarchaeology of Imperialism in the Ancient Andes, by Tiffiny A. Tung (2012; first paperback edition, 2013)

The Bioarchaeology of Individuals, edited by Ann L. W. Stodder and Ann M. Palkovich (2012; first paperback edition, 2014)

The Bioarchaeology of Violence, edited by Debra L. Martin, Ryan P. Harrod, and Ventura R. Pérez (2012; first paperback edition, 2013)

Bioarchaeology and Behavior: The People of the Ancient Near East, edited by Megan A. Perry (2012; first paperback edition, 2018)

Paleopathology at the Origins of Agriculture, edited by Mark Nathan Cohen and George J. Armelagos (2013)

Bioarchaeology of East Asia: Movement, Contact, Health, edited by Kate Pechenkina and Marc Oxenham (2013)

Mission Cemeteries, Mission Peoples: Historical and Evolutionary Dimensions of Intracemetery Bioarchaeology in Spanish Florida, by Christopher M. Stojanowski (2013)

Tracing Childhood: Bioarchaeological Investigations of Early Lives in Antiquity, edited by Jennifer L. Thompson, Marta P. Alfonso-Durruty, and John J. Crandall (2014)

The Bioarchaeology of Classical Kamarina: Life and Death in Greek Sicily, by Carrie L. Sulosky Weaver (2015)

Victims of Ireland's Great Famine: The Bioarchaeology of Mass Burials at Kilkenny Union Workhouse, by Jonny Geber (2015; first paperback edition, 2018)

Colonized Bodies, Worlds Transformed: Toward a Global Bioarchaeology of Contact and Colonialism, edited by Melissa S. Murphy and Haagen D. Klaus (2017)

Bones of Complexity: Bioarchaeological Case Studies of Social Organization and Skeletal Biology, edited by Haagen D. Klaus, Amanda R. Harvey, and Mark N. Cohen (2017)

A World View of Bioculturally Modified Teeth, edited by Scott E. Burnett and Joel D. Irish (2017)

Children and Childhood in Bioarchaeology, edited by Patrick Beauchesne and Sabrina C. Agarwal (2018)

Bioarchaeology of Pre-Columbian Mesoamerica: An Interdisciplinary Approach, edited by Cathy Willermet and Andrea Cucina (2018)

Massacres: Bioarchaeology and Forensic Anthropology Approaches, edited by Cheryl P. Anderson and Debra L. Martin (2018)

9 781683 400691